Communications and the 'Third World'

Studies in Culture and Communication
General Editor: John Fiske

Communications and the 'Third World'

Geoffrey Reeves

London and New York

First published 1993
by Routledge
11 New Fetter Lane, London EC4P 4EE

Simultaneously published in the USA and Canada
by Routledge
29 West 35th Street, New York, NY 10001

Typeset in 10 on 12 point Times by
Computerset, Harmondsworth, Middlesex
Printed in Great Britain by T.J. Press (Padstow) Ltd, Padstow, Cornwall

British Library Cataloguing in Publication Data
Reeves, Geoffrey W.
  Communications and the Third World
  I. Title
  302.2309172

Library of Congress Cataloging in Publication Data
Reeves, Geoffrey W.
  Communications and the 'third world'/Geoffrey W. Reeves.
    P. cm. -- (Studies in culture and communication)
  Includes bibliographical references.
    1. Mass media--Developing countries. 2. Mass Media—Research—
  Developing countries. I. Title. II. Series.
  P92.2.R4 1993
  302.23'09172'4—dc20   92-13310

ISBN 0–415–04761–7   ISBN 0–415–04762–5 (pbk)

Contents

Tables

Preface

Where possible this study makes use of analyses and research findings produced by writers in the countries which form the principal subject. A frequent criticism of analyses of 'Third World' communications is that they are written from a western or Eurocentric perspective which ignores traditions of critical analysis in 'Third World' countries. Schmidt (1989), for example, criticized Roy Armes' *Third World Film Making and the West* (1987) on the grounds that, when dealing with Africa in particular, it largely ignored non-western critics and reviewers. Although this omission is perhaps a valid criticism, it is also indicative of the difficulty confronting the researcher in trying to locate the disparate writings on various aspects of African communications and culture.

In the case of Latin America, and Asia to some extent, it is difficult to ignore local perspectives. Latin American writing on communications and culture in Portuguese, Spanish, and English, is voluminous (Hinds 1980b; Hinds 1984; Tatum and Hinds 1986). However it is not entirely clear how Latin American and other analyses differ in significant and substantial ways from those written from 'western' perspectives since the dominant theoretical traditions and shifts have been largely shared: functionalism and modernization theory, cultural and media imperialism perspectives, cultural dependency perspectives, and Marxist and structuralist critiques of dependence. Perhaps this sharing could be construed in cultural imperialist terms, with intellectuals from many 'Third World' countries using critical concepts and theoretical perspectives established in advanced capitalist countries such as the United States. However the principal shifts have come about through a combination or dialectic of intellectual responses to changes within Latin American societies and the utilization of theories and research methodologies developed principally, but not exclusively, in the advanced capitalist world.

The gulf between many Latin American writers on mass media and culture on the one hand, and African and Asian on the other, is at times immense. For African writers on the media, still so preoccupied with 'development' and the 'correct' relationship between the state and mass media, and still embroiled in a struggle to overcome cultural dependence and imperialism, the move of many Latin American critics to a post-modernist position would have to be incomprehensible. Regardless of how critical they are of the media, their ownership, use by ruling parties and classes for their own purposes, and role in the stifling of dissent and any critical discourse, they nevertheless predicate their analysis on the media's developmental role which would only be enhanced by democratization of access. Rarely are the mass media, whether in their organizational structures, institutional practices, programming and production of 'messages', and reception and appropriation by audiences subjected to a rigorous, detailed empirical analysis. Clearly researchers are hampered by inadequate research resources, political costs, and by the basic intellectual parameters in which they work.

The gulf can be explained principally by the fact that in Latin American countries such as Brazil and Mexico, analysts are dealing with much older, more substantial, and considerably more differentiated media apparatuses. They are also the products of, and dealing with societies which have undergone a much more profound commodification than most of those of Africa and Asia. While it is clear that in Brazil and Mexico, and other Latin American countries, the further expansion of commodification and consumerism is inhibited by low wages and high unemployment,[1] it is also the case that the penetration of consumer forms of consciousness has probably extended much further than it has in most Asian and African countries. In Brazil, for example, TV Globo, one of the world's largest television networks which relies on and supports a high level of local production, has been at the forefront of this.

In addition, Latin American analysts have witnessed the successive failures of liberal democratic politics and bourgeois parliamentarianism, the revolutionary strategies of the left, and military dictatorships which have in some instances supported surprising mass communications and cultural policies. The rhetoric of the democratization of the media, and pressures for media

reform, run up against the trajectory of capitalist media development. The pessimism promoted by a failure to challenge and reform
a media apparatus which in countries such as Brazil increasingly
occupies a powerful central position, has led to intellectual 'left'
strategies involving alternative media and the rediscovery of popular cultural and political practices which are not contained by the
dominant mass communications institutions and forms of political
organization and representation.

The size, long historical development, and diversity of the Latin
American intelligentsia, and its linkages with intellectual developments in Europe and North America have served to distinguish it
from its counterparts elsewhere.

In the case of Africa, certainly compared with Latin America and
to a lesser extent Asia, there has been very little research done,
whether by local or foreign analysts, on communications and culture. Initially this appears odd, since there has been an almost
overriding preoccupation with issues of imperialism and dependence in the analysis of contemporary African literature and
criticism. The coverage of the growth of modern communications
systems has been limited and essentially restricted, as Sydney
Head's *Broadcasting in Africa* (1974) would attest, to largely descriptive accounts of broadcasting systems in African countries. The
Frank Ugboajah edited collection, *Mass Communication, Culture
and Society in West Africa* (1985), attempts to remedy the lacunae by
providing analysis of the press, radio, television, and popular music,
together with some examination of the different theoretical traditions used in media analysis, together with the professional models
and professional training employed in West African mass media.
Graham Mytton's *Mass Communication in Africa* (1983) is restricted to case studies of Zambia, Tanzania and Nigeria. This
book, however, deals with the press, radio, and television, and
relates their development to basic economic and political factors,
including conflicts within post-independence regimes over the media to be given priority in development planning. Nkwabi
Ng'wanakilala's *Mass Communication and Development of Socialism in Tanzania* (1981) performs a similar task in the case of
Tanzania.

Most media research interest in Africa has been devoted to the
colonial origins of the press and its role in the development of
nationalism. Ainslie's historical study, *The Press in Africa* (1966), is
invaluable in this respect. Ghana's press development has been

covered in Jones-Quartey (1974); Nigeria's in Omu (1978). Barton (1979), Hachten (1971), and Wilcox (1975) have provided surveys of the African media – the press in particular – and have concentrated on the strained relations between media and government and the difficulty of upholding notions of press freedom and the values of journalistic practice which tend to be dominant in the media of the advanced capitalist societies of Western Europe, Britain, and North America. Attention has been given to the problems of the post-independence press, not simply in terms of breaking out of the colonial mould, but also in terms of its economic foundations, readership and distribution, position in ideological production and reproduction, and relations with the state and different class forces.

Once attention shifts from the print media, the dearth of material is striking. There is virtually nothing on the electronic communications media (radio, television, video), the development of state communications policies, especially with regard to the international flow of communications and cultural commodities, and on technological 'dependence' in the communications area. There appears to be very little on the development of information technology-based communications, especially for business users. Although there has been a good deal of intense interest in issues of media imperialism and the control of the international flow of communications by corporations in the advanced capitalist countries, as well as in the creation of a new international information order, this interest, certainly in the African case, has not been developed into a more detailed analysis. The establishment of the Nairobi-based African Council on Communication Education, with its journal *Africa Media Review*, and monograph series, is beginning to remedy this.

The major deficiencies in African mass media and communications analysis are probably attributable in part to the problems local writers face in dealing at all critically, and in a theoretically informed way, with mass media and communications in their own countries. State repression, certainly the threat of it, is frequently a major inhibiting factor. It is also possible that media and communications analysis scarcely constitutes an important area of intellectual concern as it has become in Latin America and throughout the advanced capitalist countries. Certainly in most African media analysis there is little evidence that the substantial, diverse, and theoretically sophisticated Latin American debates and approaches are familiar and influential. Much of the Nigerian and

Ghanaian work on mass media reflects quite conventional North American analytical concerns and derives little from the much more critical European and British mass media research traditions which have their roots in Marxism, the critical theory of the Frankfurt School, and French structuralism.

African communications and cultural analysis is in danger of becoming isolated from that occurring elsewhere in the 'Third World'. This isolation, or increased insularity, is partly the product of worsening terms of trade and balance of payments difficulties, which make the importation of cultural commodities, including books and other printed material, and materials such as newsprint, increasingly costly. The effects of worsening terms of trade and balance of payments difficulties are akin to state censorship since access is restricted to much intellectual-literary material produced elsewhere. The 'free flow of information', which critics from 'Third World' countries have viewed as a doctrine used by advanced capitalist countries, and their media corporations, to justify continuing cultural penetration and subordination, is rendered highly problematic by the very nature of relations within the global capitalist economy.

When added to such basic economic problems of intellectual production, state repression and intellectual suppression serve to cut off media and cultural analysts from relevant literatures being produced elsewhere – in Asia, Latin America, Europe and North America, as well as other African states.[2] The insularity, which often fits into narrow nationalistic concerns, means that the basic a priori assumptions and categories used in communications research are rarely questioned. Models of communications behaviour and influence which have been effectively challenged are accepted without demur (for example, behaviourist and functionalist traditions in communications research), and views of cultural and media imperialism, located in a broader body of theory (for example, Galtung's (1972) dreadfully simplistic structural theory of imperialism) which scarcely stands up to more critical scrutiny and empirical analysis.

Asian communications studies have generally been better served by both local and foreign scholarship (Lent 1971; 1978). Nevertheless there are some significant gaps in research. Indonesia, despite the proliferation of modern electronic and print media, remains largely unstudied. This also appeared to be the case with India until recently. Certainly the history of the colonial press, especially in its

nationalist phase, has been well served, as have the general development and problems facing contemporary mass media. Given the
vigour and diversity of mass communications production and popular forms of expression, the apparent dearth of analysis is a little
surprising. The largest feature film production industry in the
world; a multitude of Indian and English-language newspapers,
magazines – many of them devoted to films and television, comic
books, and book publishers; substantial radio and television production and broadcasting; a substantial popular music industry
linked in major ways to Indian film; and a bewildering array of
popular forms of expression ranging from political street theatre in
West Bengal to increasingly commodified religious festivals, would
suggest a corresponding level of analytical interest. In some magazines such as *India Today* and *Sunday* there are the beginnings of a
serious television and cultural criticism similar to that to be found in
the 'serious' media of the advanced capitalist countries. In the case
of the film industry, while there has been the vigorous growth of
meta-industries – fan and scandal magazines, music, videos, advertising, and memorabilia – there have been until recently surprisingly
few studies. Interest is increasing, but as is so often the case with
other intellectual production in India, the writing is often inaccessible; uneven distribution, geographic dispersal, and poor or
incomplete bibliographies, ensure that a great deal of the material is
largely unknown, or known only to the few who are able almost
accidentally to stumble across it.

The lacunae can perhaps be accounted for by two principal
factors. The first is that the scale of contemporary cultural production in India is such that many of the issues of cultural dependence
and imperialism found elsewhere have not been so considered in
India. And yet Valicha's semiotic analysis of Indian film, *The
Moving Image: A Study of Indian Cinema* (1988), is located within a
largely unquestioned dependency perspective and many of the
short writings on advertising and television adopt such a perspective
and question whether the consumer-oriented models of development they promote are the most appropriate. The second, and just
as unsatisfactory explanatory factor, is that major sections of the
Indian intelligentsia have not considered mass communications and
popular cultural expression worthy of much serious interest and
rigorous analysis. This could well be the product of an academic
orientation developed in the English university tradition and in-

stitutional setting which is often antithetical to such subject matter and forms of analysis.

In recent years in India, studies have appeared of film (Baskaran 1981; Vasudev and Lenglet 1983; Vasudev 1986), radio and television broadcasting (Chatterji 1987) which includes state policy, the press and journalism (but still almost nothing on magazines, despite their abundance), and new information technologies (Singhal and Rogers 1989). Since the late 1980s there has been a proliferation of studies of television and video, which range from analysis of the depiction of women in 'soapies' to the differential impact of television on rural and urban areas. There have also been Doordarshan and other reports into broadcasting which have considered issues of media–state relations and privatization. There still appears to be almost nothing on Indian popular literature including comic books and chapbook-type literature available in Hindi and other languages. Some studies have been concerned with traditional communications models and philosophies, and the ways in which they may be of some relevance to contemporary developmental communications (Kincaid 1987).

Acknowledgements

I am indebted to John Fiske for first suggesting this book. The staff of the Inter-Library Loans section of the Curtin University Library provided invaluable assistance in locating material. Special thanks are also due to my colleagues Roger Woods, Scott MacWilliam and Jan Sinclair-Jones for their support and intellectual encouragement.

Chapter 1

Introduction

One of the most dynamic sectors of the international economy since the early 1970s has been that associated with the production, management, transmission, and dissemination of information in its multiplicity of forms. Especially since the end of World War II, the expansion of capitalism has involved the organization of economically productive activities on a global scale. Fundamental to this reorganization has been the expansion of information activities, whether understood as the production and distribution of communications and information technologies, and in particular those based on the microchip, or production and distribution of cultural commodities ranging from books, records and tapes, and films and television programmes, to data for administrative, commercial and production purposes. This expansion of communications and information activities has been, as many writers have argued, a response to the continuing crises of the accumulation and valorization of capital since the end of the 'long boom' in the early 1970s. Limited opportunities for profitable investment in traditional manufacturing areas, brought about by a combination of overproduction and shifts in production locations, encouraged often large-scale investment in sectors such as leisure, tourism and entertainment, as well as in mass communications and cultural production, telecommunications, and information technology.

The international expansion of information activities may also be seen as part of two highly interrelated processes of transnationalization and informationalization. The former has at its core the activities of transnational corporations, while the latter process involves radical shifts in the means of storing, processing and retrieving information, the rapid development of telecommunications hardware (microwave, fibre optic, satellite technologies) and software, and television.

The combined processes of transnationalization and informationalization raise fundamental questions for all societies, regardless of whether they are advanced capitalist, 'peripheral' capitalist, or socialist ones subject to strong, insistent 'disintegrative' pressures and economic 'liberalization' tendencies. The questions relate to a number of basic issues: cultural domination and subordination; the control of communications, cultural production, and distribution; access to economic, political, and other information; the creation of a 'new world information order' and the regulation and control of transborder data flows; the determination of state policy in economic, cultural and other areas; the development of 'indigenous' technological and production capacity; and the understanding and constant reconstruction of what is 'national' in the cultural, historical, or any other sense. While such issues have a universal applicability and relevance, for many in 'Third World' countries, including key sections of the intelligentsia, they appear as more pressing and poignant, principally because the countries of Africa, Asia, and the Middle East are in a basic sense the product of European colonialism and relatively recent decolonization. For many the further penetration of international capital in the form of the transnational corporation, coupled with the growth of information and cultural industries dominated by them, simply deepens the subordination established under colonialism. Continuing subordination, even if it has come in a new guise, or has assumed different forms, serves further to undermine national forms of cultural expression and to weaken the possibility of some sustained, non-dependent form of economic development. As importers of advanced information and communications technologies, as well as a vast range of cultural commodities, they seem virtually powerless to resist and establish a real measure of control over their own cultural production processes, including development of mass communications.

COLONIAL ORIGINS OF MASS MEDIA IN 'THIRD WORLD' COUNTRIES

There was no real equivalent of the institutions of modern mass communications in pre-colonial African, Asian, and Latin American societies. African writers are quick to assert that prior to the introduction of the press (newspapers, magazines, pamphlets, and books) there were 'oramedia' which were effective in reaching all levels of society. Such 'folk' media, as a type of collectively 'owned' communications network, were grounded in an 'indigenous culture produced and consumed by members of a group' (Ugboajah 1985: 166). As a system of interpersonal communication they usually relied on strict convention, reinforced the values of the group, and contributed to the maintenance of the basic social relationships and world view of the group; in other words, such oral media played a vital role in the social and cultural reproduction of pre-colonial African societies. Folk media, as interpersonal media, used a language accessible to the 'common man', manifested little differentiation of producers and consumers, and as part of the public domain, were essentially anonymous in origin.

Ugboajah's account perhaps tends to romanticize the 'democratic' and 'collective' character of folk media, especially when communications or information 'reaches the traditional authority usually represented by a king or a chief or in some cases a council of elders' (Ugboajah 1985: 167). Clearly in pre-colonial (and colonial) African societies marked by much greater social differentiation, including feudal-type structures, ruling groups were concerned to establish some control over communications processes, if only by employing specialists in communications and the manipulation of the symbolic realm. Marketplaces, together with communal shrines, were an important part of the communications infrastructure, with the basic means of communication ranging from body-language and town-criers, drama and dance performances, to songs which served as 'media of moral instruction'.

With the introduction of formal western schooling and the print media, and changes in economic production, administration, and basic social relations, new connections were established among the old oral and other media, and the new, colonially introduced ones. The 'oramedia', in their changed context, became important bases of mass mobilization for nationalist, development, and in some cases revolutionary purposes. They have also been drawn upon by the mass media – radio and television in particular – in a way that has given expression to indigenous art, even if ultimately the combination of the mass media and basic economic change is destructive of folk cultural practices (Ugboajah 1985: 171–3).

The 'oramedia' identified by Ugboajah were not restricted to Africa; they were the principal means of communication in the pre-colonial, pre-literate societies of Asia, Latin America, and the Middle East. While in India, China, and elsewhere, there were extensively developed literate traditions, they were restricted to the few – to the literati, the priestly castes, and to the courts. There was also the reproduction of books and visual images (through copying, woodblock prints), but this did not occur through the mechanical means which had become dominant in European societies in the eighteenth and nineteenth centuries. Even where, as in Japan, there was an extensive market for prints and books, there was no strict historical counterpart for the modern print media.

The modern means of mass communication were introduced into the 'Third World' by the extension of European colonial rule and through contact with the major industrialized economies. Their technologies, including the social organization of production, were the product of European and North American development. Although introduced in fundamentally different economic and social conditions, they were nevertheless dependent on the emergence, however limited, of new social relations. The new media required capital investment, skilled technical labour, a journalistic pool, and means of distribution which presupposed at least some rudimentary road transportation system. The social relations of the media, integral to distribution and consumption, were predicated on a new literacy, a readership with the financial means to afford newspapers and other print products, and a predisposition to purchase and to read. The requirements of literacy, usually in a foreign language (English, French, Portuguese, Spanish) served both to restrict wider access to the new media and to further their expansion. Unlike older, oral media, and the electronic media of radio and television, the print media required access to a specialized language which helped erect barriers between social strata and classes.

Initially responsibility for print media production fell to colonial governments (publication of government gazettes, for example) and mission societies which quickly established presses and took the initiative in vernacular language publication. The latter were associated with religious pamphlets, books, and newspapers, often in vernacular languages, which were used in primary education and for religious proselytization. Early newspapers in Africa and Asia were usually government gazettes, although once both private newspaper proprietorship was established, and proto-nationalist and nationalist organizations began to make greater use of the press, this changed. The shortage of capital for investment in media, combined with limited circulation, gave the colonial state, certainly in Africa, a greater role in print media production than the state had in any of the metropolitan countries. Private, commercial print media developed in Africa and Asia during the late nineteenth and early twentieth centuries. In some instances they were the result of investment by media organizations based in the metropolitan countries (for example, the Mirror Group, Lonrho), in others the result of association with such interests.

The experience of the Latin American countries which had achieved independence early in the nineteenth century from the Portuguese and Spanish was markedly different from the colonial experience in Africa in particular. In Latin American countries the models and practices of the developed western nations, including private ownership of media, were adopted and adapted. The introduction of broadcasting in countries such as Brazil and Peru by private individuals led to an essentially uncoordinated and fragmented system very much along North American lines (Boyd-Barrett 1977a: 40). The 'free enterprise' model of communications, with a minimum of direct government intervention or regulation, was generally chosen. Many of the radio stations were owned by the local oligarchic interests which were already established in the print media, and which had done a great deal to establish newspaper chains.

Initially the entry of too many radio and television broadcasters into a restricted advertising market posed problems for investment. However the early proliferation of locally owned stations encouraged high levels of local production. By the late 1950s, as a result of a concerted North American export drive and the use of new broadcasting technologies, the proportion of local programming in relation to the total declined dramatically as station proprietors found it cheaper to depend on imports. In Brazil local television production was completely dominant until 1959 when telecine technology was introduced (Boyd-Barrett 1977a: 40).

The early independence of Latin American countries was decisive in giving them a greater degree of choice in the importation of western technologies and media philosophies than existed elsewhere throughout the European colonial world. Certainly the former colonial powers Portugal and Spain were hardly at the cutting edge of industrial transformation, the development of modern communications technologies, and new forms of imperial expansion. United States power in the late nineteenth and twentieth centuries largely ensured that American technological models and philosophies were the most influential, and was undoubtedly a key factor in the relative lack of importance attached to private rather than public broadcasting.

Since the mid-1960s there has been an increase in formal state intervention in Latin American broadcasting. The formal nature of this intervention has perhaps deflected attention from the very high level of informal political intervention which cannot be gleaned from an examination of the formal constitutional and legal frameworks in most Latin American countries (Boyd-Barrett 1977a: 41).

'THIRD WORLD': A PROBLEMATIC CONCEPT

The very concept of the 'Third World' is highly problematic, and rendered even more problematic by the disintegration of the state socialist regimes of the Soviet Union and Eastern Europe. Originally coined to bring out sharply the great differences between the countries of the advanced capitalist or industrial world, the state socialist societies of the Soviet Union and Eastern Europe, and the countries of Africa, Asia, Latin America and the Middle East, it assumed that the similarities of the last were greater than their dissimilarities. The vast majority of these countries were subject to European colonialism in the nineteenth and first half of the twentieth centuries. They witnessed the rise of nationalist and anti-colonial movements which helped bring about an end to formal colonial rule. Latin American countries had 'won' their independence from Portugal and Spain in the early part of the nineteenth century, only to become subordinate, first, to dominant British commercial and banking capital, and second, and progressively throughout the first decades of the twentieth century, to the United States in economic, political, military and cultural terms.

In addition to the 'similarity' of their nineteenth- and twentieth-century historical experiences, the countries were generally characterized by low levels of industrialization, the employment of the vast majority of the labour force in agricultural and rural production, and by a reliance on agricultural commodities and raw materials for export earnings. They were marked by extremely low per capita incomes, extreme inequalities of income distribution and wealth, generally high illiteracy rates, and, by the standards of the advanced capitalist countries, poor nutritional levels, abnormally high infant mortality rates, and low life expectancy. Whatever the indices used, and however imprecise and ambiguous their measurements, the countries of the 'Third World' stood in sharp contrast to those of the 'First' especially. As such they were linked in their underdevelopment.

Many writers, while continuing to use the concept of the 'Third World', nevertheless acknowledge its highly problematic nature (Worsley 1990). Pierre Jalée, for example, recognizes the major difficulties it poses, but adopts an economic definition predicated on 'underdevelopment stemming from the dominance of colonial or neo-colonial powers'. Jalée also notes 'the expression is short, practical and everyone knows pretty well what sort of country it refers to' (Jalée 1968: 3). Certainly the concept 'Third World', like many of the dichotomous schemes associated with modernization theory, tends to set up divisions or barriers which only obfuscate rather than facilitate the analysis of the countries of Africa, Asia, Latin America and the Middle East, their relations with the major capitalist economies, and role in the global accumulation of capital (Harris 1990). Increasingly the criticism is advanced that the concept of the 'Third World' provides no rigorous, even adequate basis for comparative analysis, and merely deflects attention from the different locations of such countries in a world capitalist economy dominated by the advanced capitalist countries and transnational corporations based in them. Other attempts to grasp and encapsulate the common situation of the countries of the 'Third World', and the nature of their differences from those of the advanced capitalist or industrial, are little more satisfactory: the North–South division; information-rich and -poor, and so on. Theories of underdevelopment, dependency, and peripheral capitalism, while often criticized for their conceptual and explanatory shortcomings, at least to some extent eschew the gross simplification of the 'Third World' concept, and start from the premise of the structural relations between the advanced capitalist countries and those of Africa, Asia, Latin America, and the Middle East. Even so, if we take Wallerstein's (1974) 'world systems theory', which has influenced many writers on communications and culture (see, for example, Armes, *Third World Film Making and the West* (1987)) the differences it sets up between the core, semi-periphery and periphery of the world capitalist system do not carry analysis much beyond the functionalist problematic of earlier modernization theory.

Armes in *Third World Film Making and the West* clearly recognizes the problems associated with the term 'Third World'. While adopting its usage, he nevertheless develops an analysis of the relationship between industrialization, state policy, and film production that effectively undermines its usefulness. A brief glimpse at some of the countries which are lumped together as 'Third World' quickly reveals the depth of the problem. Brazil and India, for example, have levels of industrial production and capacity which place them in the top ten in the world; indeed they have much greater production capacity and output than many countries thought of as advanced capitalist or industrialized. Their economies have moved increasingly into areas of high technology production such as microelectronics, computers, and aerospace, with impetus coming from a combination of national capital and large military apparatuses. India publishes 12,543 books (1986), produces 912 feature films (1985), and publishes well over 1,000 daily general-interest newspapers (1,334 in 1984) with a circulation of about 15 million. Brazil publishes 21,184 books, produces 86 feature films, and publishes 314 daily newspapers with a circulation of about 7.5 million. Contrast India and Brazil with two African countries – Angola and Mozambique, two former Portuguese colonies that have experienced long wars of national liberation and which have been plagued by civil war and a destabilization programme which has concentrated on destruction of the basic means of production. In 1986, 14 books were published in Angola; 66 in Mozambique in 1984. In 1984 there were 4 daily general-interest newspapers in Angola with a circulation of about 112,000, while in Mozambique there were 2 with a circulation of about 54,000. There has also been sporadic feature film production in the two countries, although in recent years this only amounts to a handful of films. If we use per capita consumption figures for film, television, and printed material, the differences between India and Brazil in cultural production, and Angola and Mozambique to persist with the example, will be obscured, as will their levels of industrialization and economic diversity.

Clearly there are often immense differences between countries of the 'Third World' in their capacity to engage in advanced and diversified forms of cultural production and utilization of modern mass communications systems. The differences in capacity can be reduced to a number of factors: the level and extent of industrialization, as Armes stresses; the size of domestic audiences or markets for cultural and communications production (in Brazil and Mexico audiences of up to 70 million for *telenovelas*); the availability of capital through private and state sources for investment in mass communications and cultural production; the extent of urbanization and the level of development of distribution networks for cultural commodities and communications systems; state policy which facilitates investment in, and encourages local forms of, cultural and communications production; the formation of a diversified intelligentsia which provides a substantial 'creative' base for cultural production; and skilled personnel who can be employed in communications and cultural production.

It needs stressing that the overall patterns of cultural and communications production and distribution (the international flow of cultural commodities) can easily obfuscate the differences between 'Third World' countries. Film production provides an apt example. The United States, in spite of a declining share of total world feature film production, is still able to exert a disproportionate influence on national film markets and production elsewhere; and certainly as yet has not been penetrated to any great extent by films produced in Europe, Asia, or Latin America. While advanced capitalist countries such as the United States, France, Germany, Britain, Italy and Japan are still of importance in world film production and distribution, a number of 'Third World' countries have moved to a much more important position in feature film production. This rise to prominence is perhaps a reflection of the decline in importance of film as a mass medium in advanced capitalist societies where television has attained a pre-eminent position. The production, however, is generally consumed within national markets, although some producers such as Brazil and Mexico, and India, Hong Kong and Egypt have, principally for language reasons, been able to tap regional markets extensively as well.

Throughout Africa, and some other parts of the 'Third World', feature film production is largely non-existent, or basically sporadic in nature. It is often dependent on a few isolated individuals (for example, Sembene Ousmane) who work under extreme difficulty: inadequate and uncertain funding; a mixture of state indifference, suppression, and censorship; poor distribution and exhibition circuits for their work; and a tiny pool of skilled technical and other personnel to be employed in film production. Problems of production and distribution are often compounded by language differences and, in some notable instances, by the enforced or voluntary exile of directors. In other countries such as India and Brazil the situation is one of sharp contrast.

While in India the film industry does not have the industrial structure, especially the vertical integration, of Hollywood during the heyday of the studio system, it is nevertheless characterized by sustained, high levels of production. A high level of commercial Hindi film production is maintained in Bombay. The volume of Southern regional language production (Tamil, Telegu, Malayalam, Kannada) is as great, and concentrated in Madras to such an extent that this city challenges Bombay's pre-eminent position in film production. In addition there is Bengal cinema associated most notably with Satyajit Ray and Mrinal Sen. Apart from the dominant commercial cinema there has been 'serious' film, initially located in West Bengal in the work of directors such as Ray and Sen, which has been strongly influenced in its development by Italian neo-realist cinema of the immediate post-World War II period. This serious cinema has extended to Hindi, and other regional language production, and has drawn a good deal on state support for funding, as well as state provision of training facilities, film schools, and archives. Clearly the major markets for Indian film are domestic ones – both regional and national – but there have also been markets in areas of Indian migration such as East Africa and Southeast Asia.

This book can be little more than suggestive, raising issues which can be examined more fully in further work with a more specific national or local focus. The immense diversity of countries in the African, Asian, Latin American and Middle Eastern regions, expressed in often markedly different national histories, experiences of European colonialism and extent of incorporation into capitalist production and exchange relations, levels and diversity of industrialization and economic development, size of population and geographic area, and ethnic, racial, linguistic, religious, and class differences, makes comparative analysis exceedingly difficult and more than the vaguest generalizations highly problematic. Nevertheless through concentration on a relatively small number of countries which may loosely be seen as 'representative' of different types of 'Third World' countries, it should be possible to indicate something of the different modes and rates of insertion into increasingly internationalized communications and cultural production, different national responses, and something of the way in which factors associated with the internal development of these countries have fundamentally affected the nature of communications and cultural practices in them.

This study concentrates on newly industrializing societies in Southeast Asia (Thailand, Singapore, Hong Kong, Indonesia) as well as large states such as India and Nigeria which have both a substantial indigenous capacity in communications and major strategic positions in their regions. For Latin America, Brazil and Mexico fit very much into this last category. The socialist countries are represented by China and Cuba, communications reforms and practices in the latter having significant influence on alternative communications thought and pressures for mass media reform throughout Latin America. The poorer countries of sub-Saharan Africa are represented by Mozambique and Tanzania, both of which are socialist and, in view of a limited capacity to engage in substantial conventional communications production, have had recourse to the exploration of alternative communications systems. Kenya is an African country which has undergone considerable capitalist transformation, including substantial private ownership of print media, and where pressures for the privatization of the electronic media have, despite increasingly repressive forms of state control, been developing and partly successful. Egypt, as an Arab African state, developed modern forms of communication and cultural production much earlier than most other African countries and was able, especially through film, to exert a pronounced influence on the Arab countries of the Middle East.

'THIRD WORLD' COUNTRIES AS IMPORTERS OF CULTURAL COMMODITIES

'Third World' countries are essentially importers of cultural commodities (Miège 1989: 103). This applies to electronic equipment used for receiving, recording and replaying images and/or sound – radios, tape recorders, television sets, film stock, musical instruments, and stereo systems. It also applies to commodities which have been reproduced or published, including books and magazines, records, tapes, and films and television programmes.[1] The reliance on imported commodities extends into the technologies of telecommunications, satellites, and business and information systems which are increasingly interlocked with more conventional forms of communications and cultural production and distribution. Most of the countries of the 'Third World' at this stage represent secondary markets where additional profits can be made on products which have already covered their costs in primary markets

(Miège 1989: 97). In some instances such markets have been highly protected. However, as Miège notes, the types of economic changes occurring in many 'Third World' countries, and concomitant changes in class relations, are rapidly producing markets for audio-visual and other commodities which are worth targeting. These markets may still be narrow in that they are composed predominantly of upper-income earners with a predisposition to consume in particular ways, but are of sufficient size to attract the interest of cultural producers in the advanced capitalist countries, as well as in 'Third World' countries with much greater and more diversified cultural production potential.

Many transnational corporations have relocated basic production and assembly to 'Third World' countries in order to take advantage of a mixture of low wage costs, advanced technologies which can easily be decomposed and transplanted, taxation concessions, and often tight state controls over the labour force. Much of this relocated production has been in Southeast Asia and has involved 'the production of image and/or sound recording and playback equipment'. But as Miège notes, this relocation also increasingly applies to 'published products' – to printers and record pressing factories (Miège 1989: 103).

While 'Third World' countries are important as secondary markets for cultural commodities, and are involved to a varying extent in the production of particular cultural commodities and electronic goods, or at least stages of them, they also occupy another position in the international division of labour – that of a type of reserve army of artistic or cultural labour on which producers can draw to 'revitalize artistic forms' (Miège 1989: 103).[2] West Indian music, especially reggae, has been conspicuously successful. Recent interest in West African music in Britain and France, and in Latin American writers such as Gabriel Marquez and Carlos Fuentes, could be seen as part of the same process. It is rare for cultural commodities – books, films, television programmes, music on records and tapes – produced in 'Third World' countries to penetrate advanced capitalist markets, although the flow of Spanish-language television programmes, films, and books from Latin American countries, Mexico in particular, to the United States, represents a significant if only partial exception (Gutierrez and Reina, 1984). In cases where transnationals wish to establish and cater for regional markets they may promote a star, as for example the promotion of an African band whose music is to be broadcast primarily in Africa.

FLOW OF TELEVISION PROGRAMMES

Television programmes have certain key features in common with film: they normally involve a high cost of production and a low cost of reproduction and transportation. In many countries dependence on the import of television series is not as great as in the case of film (Miège 1989: 101). This is partly due to the tendency for imported programmes to supplement locally produced ones rather than compete directly with them. Internationalization, Miège suggests, seems to be less pronounced in the case of television primarily because most industrialized and industrializing countries have national production structures. Dependence on imported programming in many smaller and poorer countries is limited by restricted transmission hours and shortages of foreign exchange required for programme purchase. The major exporters, and the United States in particular, have been able to take advantage of economies of scale and the ability to recoup substantial production costs in large domestic markets, and have been prepared to make programme material available at relatively low cost to small purchasers (Hoskins, Mirus and Rozeboom 1989; Miège 1989: 103). The high cost of local production makes imported programming very attractive for smaller Latin American countries such as Panama, El Salvador, and Costa Rica (Wert and Stevenson 1988).

In television programming there is still essentially a 'one-way flow of traffic from the big exporting countries to the rest of the world' (Varis 1984: 143). Entertainment material dominates this flow. In the decade 1973–83 there nevertheless occurred some notable changes, primarily as a result of increases in local production in countries such as Brazil and Mexico, and increases in regional exchanges similar to those which have affected news flow. The bulk of imported programmes still originate in the United States, and to a lesser extent in Western Europe and Japan (Varis 1984: 150). However the one-way flow thesis requires some revision in view of the substantial growth of regional exchanges. This has been important in Eastern and Western Europe, in the Arab countries 'where approximately one-third of the imported programs come from other countries within the region', and among Latin American countries 'where the figure for interregional imports is around ten per cent' (Varis 1984: 151).

In the case of Latin America entertainment programming accounts for most of the imported materials, which take up half of the total transmission time (Varis 1984: 148). The United States is clearly the major source of Latin American imported programming (about three-quarters). There are, however, significant differences between Latin American countries in levels of local production (Brazil, Mexico, Argentina and Venezuela are the principal programme exporters) and dependence on imported programming from the United States. Locally produced series in Brazil and Mexico – *telenovelas* especially – dominate prime-time slots (Antola and Rogers 1984: 197–8). Export/import flows of programmes throughout Latin America are affected and restricted by state censorship and government regulation, thus reflecting the often considerable differences between national regimes.

In Asia and the Pacific some 36 per cent of all television programmes are imported, but there are enormous differences between countries. China produces virtually all of its own programming while India imports relatively little (Tracey 1985: 22). In the Arab countries some 42 per cent of television is imported, with one-third of that coming from other Arab states and 32 per cent of the non-Arabic programmes coming from the United States (Tracey 1985: 22; Varis 1984: 149). The spread of television is still relatively limited throughout Africa and use is concentrated in urban areas. Data from Kenya, Nigeria and Uganda indicates that about 40 per cent of programmes are imported, with the United States and the United Kingdom the principal suppliers (Varis 1984: 149).

INDICES OF COMMUNICATIONS AND CULTURAL PRODUCTION

Using a number of key indices it is possible to establish major differences in cultural production and consumption, and the extent of mass communications use, between the countries of Africa, Asia, Latin America and the Middle East, and those of the advanced capitalist world. The indices also reveal some significant differences between 'Third World' regions and countries. They do not, however, indicate the extent to which within countries there are profound differences in mass communications usage and cultural consumption based on language and literacy, educational level, income, class, rural and urban location, and the extent of the development and spread of a communications infrastructure.

Although there are obviously major deficiencies in the gathering of basic descriptive statistics, there are, as the *UNESCO Statistical Yearbook* (1988) attests, distinct differences between 'Third World'

Table 1   Television broadcasting: number of receivers, and receivers
per 1,000 inhabitants

Country	Receivers in use and/or issued (000s)		Receivers in use and/or licences issued per 1,000 inhabitants	
	1980	1986	1980	1986
Africa				
Algeria	975	1,610	52	72
Angola	30	40	3.9	4.5
Egypt	1,400	4,000	34	83
Ghana	57	146	4.9	10
Kenya	65	115	3.9	5.4
Mali		1		0.1
Mozambique	2	10	0.1	0.7
Nigeria	450	550	5.6	5.6
Tanzania	7	13	0.4	0.6
N and S America				
Cuba	1,273	2,050	131	202
Mexico	3,820	9,490	55	117
USA	155,800	195,000	684	813
Brazil	15,000	26,000	124	188
Asia and Middle East				
China	4,000	10,500	4	9.8
Hong Kong	1,114	1,312	221	232
India	1,548	5,000	2.2	6.5
Indonesia	3,000	6,600	20	39
Malaysia	1,119	1,800	81	113
Saudi Arabia	2,100	3,210	224	269
Turkey	3,410	8,300	77	165
Europe				
France	19,000	22,000	354	402
FRG	20,762	23,011	337	379
Italy	22,000		385	
UK	22,600	30,000	404	534
Oceania				
Australia	5,600	7,500	381	472
New Zealand	862	1,200	272	358

Source: *UNESCO Statistical Yearbook*, Paris, 1988

countries and the advanced capitalist and industrialized countries in
the ownership of audio-visual equipment – radio and television
receivers especially (see Table 1). In 1985 there were 911 radios per
1,000 inhabitants in the industrialized countries and only 142 in the
'Third World' ones. On a regional or continental basis the disparities are even more pronounced, Africa and Asia having much

lower levels than either Latin America or the Arab states. In the case of television receivers the disparities are even more pronounced: in 1985 there were 447 television sets per 1,000 inhabitants in the advanced capitalist and industrialized countries compared with 36 in the 'Third World' (even if collective forms of ownership and use of radio and television receivers are taken into account major differences in access still obtain). African countries in particular, and Asian, not unexpectedly had much lower ratios of television sets to inhabitants (Table 1). The broad figures tend to obscure both substantial national variations within regions, and markedly different levels of ownership and access within countries.

Figures for the distribution of new audio-visual products such as video recorders are difficult to obtain and incomplete, but would suggest even greater disparities than in the case of radio and television. The distribution of VCRs depends on many factors including price, government restrictions (import duties and tariff barriers to encourage local production as in Brazil), income distribution, and the range of broadcast facilities available in different national societies (Boyd and Straubhaar 1985). The relationship between high levels of disposable income and high VCR penetration is particularly marked in Middle Eastern oil-based economies, and certainly in Saudi Arabia and the Gulf States of Kuwait, Bahrain, Qatar, Oman, and the United Arab Emirates.[3] Available statistics would also suggest an important relationship between the variety of content available through broadcast television and the spread of VCR use. Video provides an opportunity in many countries for local populations to circumvent government restrictions on viewing (Tracey 1985: 24–5). Often material which is banned from normal television broadcasts for political and moral reasons (pornography, for example) is available through pirated and smuggled videos. This is clearly the case in countries such as Saudi Arabia, Taiwan and Thailand (Hamilton 1990).

In poorer countries VCR ownership and use is essentially restricted to the rich urban classes who see it as major status symbol. It was estimated that in 1983 there were only 778,000 VCRs in the whole of Africa. In absolute terms the cost of VCRs in twenty-nine African countries was higher than in the United States, France and Japan, and represented something like twenty-nine times the average wage. The use of mainly imported material by privileged classes, coupled with the lack of social or communal use of VCRs, has the potential for many critics of deepening cultural conflict and alienation. However, low per capita or family ownership of VCRs is not necessarily an accurate indication of the extent of access to the technology since in many countries, including India (Agrawal 1986; Noble 1989), Nepal, and Thailand (Hamilton 1990), a great many video parlours have been opened, in some cases as a means of paying for the purchase of the VCR.

DAILY NEWSPAPER PRODUCTION AND CIRCULATION

Basic figures on the number and circulation of daily newspapers indicate the extent to which there are profound differences between 'developed' and 'developing' countries (Table 2). The difference is at its greatest in estimated circulation per 1,000 inhabitants; in 1984, for example, it was 319 to 33. The basic figures also reveal significant regional differences; Africa has a much smaller number of daily newspapers, estimated circulation, and newspaper circulation per 1,000 inhabitants, than either Asia or Latin America. In Asia the very large number of daily newspapers and total circulation is offset by the huge population served so that the circulation per 1,000 inhabitants remains low.

Closer scrutiny of the number and circulation of daily newspapers in particular countries reveals how misleading or unhelpful the basic statistical description can be. In Africa, for example, there are substantial national variations in numbers of daily newspapers, total circulation, and circulation per 1,000 inhabitants. In Asia, countries such as China, Hong Kong, Indonesia, Malaysia, and India in particular, have a great many daily newspapers and large total circulation, certainly by African standards. Argentina, Brazil and Mexico have large numbers of daily newspapers, large total circulation, and relatively high per capita circulation. Even where, as in India, the estimated per capita circulation is very low, the sheer number of daily newspapers and total circulation suggest there is a substantial, diversified newspaper industry able to support a large, diversified corps of journalists, and to attract advertising support from Indian commerce and industry. The same observation can be made for Argentina, Brazil and Mexico, thus indicating the way in which broad statistical description may provide little guide to the differences in the level and capacity of cultural and media production between countries.

Table 2   Daily general-interest newspapers: number and circulation in selected countries

Country	Number		Estimated circulation(000s)		Circulation per 1,000 inhabitants	
	1979	1984	1979	1984	1979	1984
Africa						
Angola	5	4		112		15
Egypt	9	12	2,475	1,912		43
Ghana	5	4	345	460		35
Kenya	3	4	156	255	10	13
Mozambique	2	2	42	54	4	4
Nigeria	15	14		516		
Uganda	1	1	20	25	2	2
Tanzania	2	2	189	101	10	5
Latin America						
Mexico		312		9,252		120
Argentina	133	188		3,767		
Brazil	328	314	5,094	7,599	44	57
Asia						
China		60		30,000		29
Hong Kong	41	60				
India	1,087	1,334	13,033	14,847	19	21
Indonesia		55		2,878		18
Malaysia	44	40	1,796	1,670		
Thailand	18	25	1,943			
Turkey	1,115	457	3,880			

Source: UNESCO Statistical Yearbook, Paris, 1988

BOOK PRODUCTION

Book production is still very limited in many 'Third World' countries (see Table 3). Since 1960 the overall world distribution of book production (in number of titles) has not changed significantly, although the share of Europe, the USSR, and North America in the total has suffered some decline.

In Africa, despite notable exceptions such as Nigeria and Egypt, book production continues at a low level, with fewer than 400 new titles being published annually in individual countries. In Asia, with the exception of Japan, countries such as China, India, Indonesia, Malaysia and Thailand publish large numbers of titles, as do Mexico, Argentina, Brazil and Colombia in Latin America. When compared with major producers such as the United States, France, the former Federal Republic of Germany, the United Kingdom, and the USSR, most 'Third World' countries are relatively unimportant in total production terms. The main 'Third World' exporters, Mexico and Argentina, have only one-tenth of the sales of the leading exporters, the United States and the United Kingdom. Educational books, as well as scientific and technical books, represent an appreciable proportion of those published, especially in the United States and Britain, and also represent significant parts of total book exports from those two countries (Miège 1989: 101). As in the case of other areas of media and cultural production, there are clearly important continental and regional variations in production.

With the imminence of independence in Africa, British pub-

Table 3   Book production: number of titles by UDA classes

Country	Year	No.	Country	Year	No.
Africa			*Asia*		
Angola	1985	47	Indonesia	1984	5,254
	1986	14		1985	2,480
Egypt	1984	1,277	Japan	1985	45,430
Mozambique	1984	66		1986	44,686
Nigeria	1984	1,836	Malaysia	1984	3,975
	1985	2,213		1985	2,554
				1986	3,397
Tanzania	1984	363	Thailand	1984	8,633
				1985	7,289
Latin America				1986	7,728
Cuba	1984	2,069			
	1985	2,168	Turkey	1985	6,685
	1986	2,174	*Europe*		
Mexico	1984	4,505	France	1984	37,189
	1985	5,482		1985	37,860
	1986	4,897	FRG	1984	48,836
Nicaragua	1984	26		1985	54,442
Argentina	1986	4,818		1986	63,724
Brazil	1984	21,184	UK	1984	51,411
Colombia	1984	15,041		1985	52,861
			USSR	1984	82,790
Asia				1985	83,976
China	1984	34,920		1986	83,472
	1985	40,265	*North America*		
India	1984	9,954	USA and		
	1985	11,660	Canada	1986	106,000
	1986	12,543			

Source: UNESCO Statistical Yearbook, Paris, 1988

lishers embarked on an 'indigenization' programme which generally has fitted comfortably with the continuing importation of books. The expanding educational market, including scientific and technical books, represented a key area of production for transnational publishers, and one they were anxious to protect. In a number of countries, however, the local branches of transnational publishers have increasingly had to contend with shifts in state policy, expanded direct state involvement in book production – often through parastatal organizations – and increased competition from local publishing companies. Publishing in Kenya provides an excellent illustration of this phenomenon.

CINEMA ATTENDANCE AND FEATURE FILMS

There is an absence of comprehensive and reliable statistics on world cinema attendance. While the indicator used by UNESCO – cinema seating capacity – is problematic, it provides an indirect gauge of the extent of cinema use.

Table 4   Cinema seating capacity per 1,000 inhabitants (1985)

Country	No.
Africa	3
North America	49
Latin America	13
Asia (excluding China)	7
Arab States	5
Europe and USSR	62
Oceania	21

Source: *UNESCO Statistical Yearbook*, Paris, 1988

Despite the decline in both feature film production and cinema attendance in the 'developed' countries, they are still important in total markets (Miège 1989: 99). The substantial decline in cinema attendance in Europe and North America between 1950 and 1970 has not been offset by increased attendance in the 'Third World', even when the estimated weekly attendance of some 70 million at Indian cinemas is taken into account.

Table 5   Estimated annual cinema attendance by continent and major areas (in millions)

County	1975	1985
Africa	125	210
North America	1,310	1,100
Latin America	900	800
Asia (excluding China)	3,700	7,000
Arab States	300	220
Europe and USSR	6,600	5,700
Oceania	47	47

Source: UNESCO Statistical Yearbook, Paris, 1988

In terms of feature film production there has been no basic world redistribution since 1960. Since that time Asian countries have accounted for over 50 per cent of total production, with African production remaining largely insignificant. Closer examination of national film importation figures shows that while there are many non-film producing countries which have very high levels of film importation, and especially American film, other countries which are substantial film producers and exporters to regional markets also have high levels of film importation (Miège 1989: 100). The figures for world feature film production provide some indication of the way in which the economic and ideological functions of the dominant industrial cinemas of the advanced capitalist countries in particular, both nationally and internationally, have been shifting to television production (Willemen 1989: 17–18). Indeed, there are indications that this process is also occurring in countries such as Brazil, Mexico, and India to some extent, as a result of much greater investment in television series production and the construction of enormous television markets. The figures, however, do not reveal the way in which there appears to have been a shift in film production and marketing strategy in the major exporting countries – the United States in particular. Increasingly emphasis has been placed on the intensive exploitation of high-budget 'hits' rather than on sheer volume (Miège 1989: 100–1).

Table 6   Number of feature-length films produced (including co-production)

Country	1965	1970	1975	1980	1985
Africa					
Algeria					
Egypt	47 (5)	47 (1)	90		
Ghana		3	1		
Nigeria				20 (20)	
Asia					
Hong Kong	203	137	112 (3)	141	
India	325	396	473	742	912
Indonesia		14	41 (3)	73	63 (1)
Japan					
Pakistan	89	141 (1)	120 (1)		92 (4)
Turkey			160	74 (1)	96
Latin & North America					
Argentina	32 (1)	28	34 (1)	27	
Brazil		72	90 (1)	103	86
Cuba		1	8	6	10 (3)
Mexico	52 (3)	124 (2)	162	109 (48)	88 (5)
USA		191	236	264	
Europe					
France	142 (47)	138 (27)	222 (62)	189 (45)	151 (45)
FRG	72 (47)	129 (27)	81 (26)	49 (12)	71 (18)
Hungary					
Italy	188 (126)	240 (135)	203 (43)	160 (32)	73 (7)
Poland					
Sweden					
UK	69	85 (2)	70 (4)	57	
USSR	167	218 (3)	184 (8)	156 (6)	156 (7)

Source: *UNESCO Statistical Yearbook*, Paris, 1988

Chapter 2

Dominant perspectives

The study of the mass communications and contemporary cultures of 'Third World' societies has essentially gone through the same stages as development and underdevelopment theory. Although it is doubtful whether any of the theories identified with particular stages ever assumed a paradigmatic status in the Kuhnian sense, it is nevertheless possible to distinguish between particular perspectives which have substantially directed analysis: the shift is largely one from modernization theory to cultural imperialist and dependency perspectives, and more recently in the Latin American case in particular, to what may be loosely regarded as a 'post-modernist' position. The shift in perspectives, which corresponds fairly closely to those in economic development theorizing, was produced principally by the failure of theory, and its application to the policy formulation and implementation process, to be validated by the historical processes of change. While modernization theory, including its mass communications version which held that the media would play a crucial role in promoting economic development through attitude change and the encouragement of innovative behaviour, was in tatters by the end of the 1960s, cultural dependence and imperialism views were being advanced which seemed to square much better with the apparent failure of most countries in the 'Third World' to restructure their economies and change their position in the international division of labour. But even while dependency theories were being elaborated to account for the 'underdevelopment' of much of Africa, Asia, and Latin America in terms of the overall development of world capitalism, such theories were already being challenged, especially by Marxist critics, for their theoretical and empirical shortcomings.

The whole field, including the communications and cultural analysis area, is clouded with uncertainty and confusion. Nevertheless it can at least be asserted that there is a growing recognition that the problems of media and cultural analysis, despite the significant differences between national societies and the unequal relationship between advanced capitalist societies and those of Africa, Asia, and Latin America in the volume of cultural production and the flow of information, are not substantially different from those of the advanced capitalist world. Latin American writers in particular, while still predominantly operating within a radical dependency framework, are much more preoccupied with the analysis of internal processes of cultural reproduction, and the role of the mass media in them. This preoccupation has witnessed interest in semiotic analysis of cultural commodities, and more recently a concern with both the 'impossibility' of transforming dominant media structures and differentiated audience responses to centrally transmitted media 'messages'.

MODERNIZATION THEORY AND MASS COMMUNICATIONS

In earlier modernization theory the dominant communications and national development paradigm emphasized the contribution of the mass media to promotion of western-style capitalist development. This approach, dubbed by Boyd-Barrett as the 'missionary', was derived from structural-functionalism, which, with its emphasis on, indeed reification of, 'certain postulated features' as essential for the 'homeostatic equilibrium', survival and reproduction of complex industrial societies, encouraged the view that industrialization in the 'developing' world would be facilitated by the replication of these essential features in them. The transplantation of western media technologies and models would be an important factor in ensuring that poorer economies would ultimately become facsimiles of advanced capitalist ones (Nordenstreng and Schiller 1979; Boyd-Barrett 1982: 175–6).

This model of the relation between communications and development was largely supplanted by a neo-Weberian, pluralist one which sought to overcome the Eurocentricity of the first, and to relate the media to different models of development. The neo-Weberian perspective recognized the inability of functionalism to explain change, its teleological nature, and its reification of society.

It re-established the primacy of conflict as a driving force of change, especially conflict between groups for power, status, and income. It also led to the rediscovery of 'motive, interest, and perception, and "redelivered" society to human groups' (Boyd-Barrett 1982: 176). Writers working from within this perspective recognized that European nation-state formation and capitalist industrialization was not inevitable, and was not a process of uninterrupted rationalization of government, extension of political participation, and pacification of the masses (Lee 1980: 21). The countries of Africa and Asia differed from European ones in critical respects (just as European countries differed in critical respects from each other), with substantial differences in the timing and sequence of events in the modernization process.

The publication of Barrington Moore's *Dictatorship and Democracy* (1966), while not necessarily a part of this developing neo-Weberian perspective, served to emphasize the multiplicity of historical modernization routes by drawing out the differences in the British, American, French, German, Japanese, Chinese and Indian experiences. By the late 1960s mass communications research had shifted to the analysis of the media as a segment of the entire social system. This shift in emphasis entailed the identification of rigid and inequitable social structures as providing the key obstacles to development, and not the empathic or motivational traits of individuals suggested by writers such as Hagen and McLelland.[1] The mass media, rather than being catalysts of change, were seen increasingly as agents of elites anxious to maintain their own privileged positions. This was a significant shift since it was the elites, with their formal western education and adherence to modernizing values, who were contrasted in early modernization literature with the masses sunk in traditional popular cultures which represented massive impediments to development (Pye 1963: 3–26). However the adoption of the neo-Weberian perspective still left untouched the crucial relation between internal structures and externally derived forces: there could be no enhanced understanding of the media unless priority was attached to the 'international socio-political-economic system that decisively determines the course of development within the sphere of each nation' (Boyd-Barrett 1982: 175). This became the concern of what Boyd-Barrett has labelled the 'totalistic' paradigm or approach which is associated with 'neo-Marxism' and dependency theory (Boyd-Barrett 1982: 175).

Paradoxically, the modernization theory position that the media would play an important role in promoting national development through encouragement of attitude change and the dissemination of 'useful' information ran counter to the dominant view in advanced capitalist societies. In the latter the mass media were held to play mainly a reinforcing role with respect to attitudes and values. In a sense this was shared by both conventional media analysts and radical critics. The former, who largely eschewed any concern with questions of media ownership and control, as well as with consideration of the media's role in the reproduction of ideology, produced research findings which pointed to the media's role in reinforcing existing attitudes and values rather than in promoting change. Such findings in effect suggested that questions of media ownership and output, and by extension the role of advertising, were largely unimportant since it could not be demonstrated by statistically oriented empirical research that they had any real impact in changing values or shifting the dominant forms of consciousness. In contrast the radical critics, strongly influenced by Frankfurt School critical theory, emphasized that the mass media, as large-scale commercial-industrial enterprises, were crucial in reproducing the dominant ideological-cultural relations of that society.

The fundamental point which most modernization analyses of the diffusion and developmental role of the media completely overlooked is that the media serve the interests of particular classes and strata more than others, help maintain certain power structures by contributing to their legitimacy, and encourage or hinder penetration by external forces upon which they may be reliant for capital, technology, international news coverage, and programmes. During the colonial period in many African and Asian countries the European-owned press was generally, although not completely, concerned with the maintenance of colonial relationships and the defence of metropolitan capitalist interests (Ainslie 1966; Barton 1979). However in countries such as Kenya, where there was a substantial European settler population, many newspapers served as the voice of settler opinion and were opposed to both colonial government policies on devolution of power and metropolitan capitalist interests which could see the advantages in the political defeat of the settlers and the swift transfer of power to African governments. In Kenya the oppositional nationalist press largely disappeared with independence: the two main newspapers which emerged were the old-established *East African Standard* (owned by

Lonrho), and the *Daily Nation* owned by the Aga Khan but with substantial local shareholding. The fact that the two major newspaper groups were substantially foreign-owned quite obviously conditioned their policies with regard to the role of foreign investment in Kenya's development, as well as defined their relationship with the Kenyatta and Moi regimes. Foreign ownership meant that editors and journalists were often sensitive to notions of the free press and investigative journalism, but they were equally sensitive to the various pressures and forms of censorship the state could bring to bear to restrict their local news coverage in particular.

The historical practice in 'modernizing' countries quickly controverted modernization theory assumptions about the role of the mass media in achieving developmental goals and contributing to social change. Privately owned media groups, although subject to often harsh governmental constraints and threats of nationalization in many countries, had little incentive to 'engage in development-type programming' if this threatened profits, or worked against the interests of the capital associated with the media (Boyd-Barrett 1982: 185). A basic dependence on advertising meant that media groups were invariably promoting a model of consumer-oriented development which in some cases directly contradicted that espoused by governments. In addition, the very nature of advertising in many Asian and African countries ensured that unlike in much of Europe and North America, it could never become a source of independent patronage of indigenous media – thus allowing a relative freedom from government and political patronage and control (Smith 1980: 45). According to writers such as Anthony Smith this was primarily because international advertising was dominated by United States advertising agencies, although this dominance is probably stronger throughout the rest of the advanced capitalist world (Canada and Australia, for example) than it is in many parts of Africa and Asia.

The small size of the advertising market, combined with a substantial government share of total advertising expenditure, poses major problems for press proprietors, editors, and journalists. Apart from the more obvious problems of repression and censorship, including banning and detention, governments are able to sway editorial policy and news coverage, and indeed, put out of existence newspapers which are seen as contradicting or questioning government policy, simply through the withdrawal of essential advertising revenue (Smith 1980: 164–5). This happened in Kenya with Hilary Ng'weno's short-lived *Nairobi Times*, and has been important in the case of the Indian press. For example, while the state of emergency was in force *The Statesman*, one of the most important newspapers in India, was systematically deprived of governmental advertising revenue. In Tanzania the nationalized *Standard*, under the editorship of Frene Ginwalla, was expected to be self-sufficient, but could not be, simply because of the nationalization of much of the economy. The principal source of advertising revenue was the new parastatal organizations. *The Standard (Daily News)* which often pursued a Marxist-Leninist line critical of Tanzania's *ujamaa* socialism, could not sustain this for, amongst other reasons, the lack of an independent, that is, private, advertising base (Barton 1979: 111–24).

Governments in most of the countries of Africa, Asia, and Latin America have been primarily concerned with intervention in media programming rather than with the role of the media in national development. This interventionism to protect their own political security and economic interests is usually couched in terms of national unity, anti-imperialism, and developmental strategies which require a reduction in social conflict. In the case of Kenya, for example, there is a whole post-independence history of government intervention in the press. This has taken many forms, including the detention and deportation of journalists, intimidation, forced changes of editors, the provision of misleading and embarrassing news stories designed to discredit newspapers and their editors, and the withdrawal of vital government advertising (Barton 1979: 73–86).

CULTURAL IMPERIALISM AND CULTURAL DEPENDENCY

Cultural imperialist and dependency analysis is predicated on the interrelatedness of economic (including technological) structural relations, and ideological-cultural relations, between advanced capitalist or industrial societies and those of most of Africa, Asia, and Latin America (Golding 1977: 291). The media analysis that takes place within this rather loose perspective emphasizes that the mass media in 'Third World' regions were not the result of indigenous evolutionary development. Rather, they developed almost invariably as derivatives of those in the major capitalist societies and were transplanted and imposed from their metropolitan centres of origin during the extension of colonial and imperialist power from the nineteenth century onwards. This simple fact of colonial history is held to have enormous implications for the analysis of the structure and role of the media throughout the 'Third World'. Any analysis of the media in any single country will be 'empirically and theoretically barren' unless it takes into account both this historical fact of colonialism and the 'international context of dependence' (Golding 1977: 291).

Theories of cultural imperialism and dependency, with few exceptions, ultimately have their roots in Lenin's 'classic' formulation of imperialism as the highest stage of capitalism. This is the case even with the re-working of the imperialism thesis in the form of development/underdevelopment and dependency theorizing of the late 1960s and 1970s. With the break-up of the old colonial empires after World War II, and the emergence of the United States as the clearly dominant capitalist power, capitalism for many writers entered a neo-colonialist or neo-imperialist phase in which old formal colonial controls were no longer necessary for the maintenance of metropolitan and international capitalist power (Brewer 1980: part III). Indeed the break-up of European colonial empires was seen not simply in terms of the emergence of ultimately successful nationalist movements, but as the result of inter-imperialist rivalries and the need for more dynamic capitals to remove the political and other impediments to their further and more rapid accumulation.

The central feature of Lenin's theory of imperialism, and of subsequent Marxist theories, including those of underdevelopment and dependency, was that economic and other relations between the advanced capitalist and other societies had to be understood in the context of the continuous, recurring valorization, accumulation, and investment crises of capitalism. The underdevelopment or dependence of much of the world is a necessary corollary of the development of the advanced capitalist world. Political and ideological-cultural relations both flow from and ensure that the primary economic relationship is maintained. It is in this 'neo-imperialist' or 'neo-colonial' phase that the media apparatuses of both the metropolitan and dependent capitalist countries assume such great importance.

Cultural imperialist theorizing begins with the nature of media and cultural production in advanced capitalist societies. The understanding of the dynamics of such production, including its ideological nature and role, is held to be essential for providing the framework in which the analysis takes place of the ideological-cultural relations between the advanced capitalist countries and those of the 'Third World'. In some cultural imperialist theorizing the penetration of the 'Third World' by advanced capitalist media and cultural production industries is couched in essentially conspiratorial terms, with an almost symbiotic relationship developing between multinational corporations and the advanced capitalist state to extend and defend international capitalism. In Herbert Schiller's work, for example, and in particular in *Mass Communications and American Empire* (1969), it is the relationship between the multinational corporations and the global market economy which is at the theoretical core of analysis (see also Hamelink 1983). The relationship between nation-states and multinational corporations is in Schiller's formulation largely unproblematic since the governments and ruling classes of the metropolitan countries work to support such enterprises. The United States military-industrial complex (it is significant that Schiller's theoretical position is indebted to that of C. Wright Mills) has its logic and drive in the global expansion of capitalism. Communications imperialism was an organized, conscious effort undertaken by the United States military-communications conglomerates to maintain, above all, United States economic, political, and military domination.

According to Schiller the involvement of the military-industrial complex in communications took two basic forms. In the first, control of the allocation of broadcasting frequencies and the making of national telecommunications policy was placed in the hands of the United States Department of Defence, and not the Federal Communications Commission. In the second, indirectly, major electronic companies such as RCA-NBC are holders of important defence contracts. American media dominance stems from the implementation of United States foreign and defence policy, with the media at the same time being a crucial instrument of that policy. The dominance of American mass media is thus the direct product of the rise to global dominance of the United States after World War II. The cultural imperialism associated with this dominance has been manifested in the exporting of American television programmes to non-socialist countries in particular, and in the role of American communications industries in forcing a commercialization of the international broadcasting system. According to Schiller, even in the most advanced capitalist countries of Western Europe, possibly excluding Belgium, Denmark, Norway and Sweden, the long-standing public administration of postal, telegraph, and broad-casting systems has been eroded under pressure from the expansion of the activities of multinational corporations (Schiller 1979: 25).

In a later formulation transnational media are seen by Schiller as constituting the 'ideologically supportive informational infrastruc-ture for the MNCs'. Such enterprises are engaged in generalized informational activities which include the generation and transmis-sion of business data and the export of management techniques. In addition to these there are 'various categories of transmedia support activities, most important of which are advertising agencies, market survey and opinion polling services, public relations firms, govern-ment information and propaganda services and traditional media' (Schiller 1979: 21).

Also typical of this type of approach is the earlier work of Nordenstreng and Varis (1973) which is predicated on the identifica-tion of the three major functions of mass communications in capitalist societies: first, the concealment of class antagonism and the compensation for the systems of alienation largely through escapism; second, the denial of, or the stressing of, the illegitimacy of social alternatives to the existing order; and third, the making of profit as a branch of commercial industry. Intra-societal class con-flict, which is controlled partly through the mass media, is transposed to the international setting in which the national oligarchies of the underdeveloped countries are allied with interna-tional capitalist corporate interests in opposition to poor 'mass' publics.

The extremely asymmetrical flow of communications materials and cultural commodities between the advanced capitalist countries and those of the 'Third World' is not simply a commercial exchange, but rather a part of the process whereby the latter are dominated by the communications ideologies of the major capitalist countries. Also integral to this process is the incorporation of these countries into the market-oriented, consumer-capitalist economies through apparently neutral or harmless media products. In Nordenstreng and Varis's approach the expansion of the market and control in communications, and cultural production in general, stems from the internal contradiction of the capitalist 'system', including its finan-cial, industrial, military, advertising, and cultural structures. This cultural imperialist position, as with economic dependency models, assumes that there are levels of dominance and dependency amongst nations: there are exploiting metropoles or centres, and exploited satellites or peripheries. While there is conflict between them, the latter are never really in a position to challenge the former successfully, since the cultural-ideological strength of the former is part of, and flows from, their advanced means of production and ownership.

Developments in information and communications technology, in satellite broadcasting, as well as the growth of transborder data flows and the concentration of data banks and bases in the hands of a few transnational corporations and countries, are seen by many dependency theorists as reproducing the old colonial patterns of dependency and domination in the economic, political and cultural senses (Rada 1981; Kaplinsky 1982; Hamelink 1983). Reliance on highly concentrated data banks and information technology hardware means that decisions in crucial areas of economic investment and public policy will be made in accordance with criteria established in the major corporations of the capitalist world – and thus in accordance with their interests. As users of the 'end products of the technology', 'Third World' countries are not in a position either to establish technological control or to engage in competitive research and development (Hamelink 1983: 18).

In the cultural dependency model, ideological-cultural relations of domination and dependence are expressed in the control of the production and distribution of culture and ideology by the metropolitan capitalist countries, and more specifically their transnational corporations. Metropolitan centres such as the United States, Britain, France, and Germany (and increasingly Japan), have 'world' languages, and largely control the flow of news and information to dependent societies in Africa, Asia and Latin America. They also account for the vast bulk of world television, film, record, compact disc, audio cassette, book, magazine, newspaper, video, and educational package production, much of which is exported (Tunstall 1977). They are responsible by and large for the greatest share of world advertising, especially through transnational corporations, including transnational advertising agencies. They exercise a largely unchallenged dominance in scientific and technological research and development, and produce the basic technical means of media and cultural production throughout most of the dependent world.

One of the central postulates of this dependency model is that local cultural identity is subverted and destroyed so that the values of the dominant metropolitan economies and their transnational corporations can be adopted, even imposed (Hamelink 1983: 5–7).[2]

These values are bound up with advertising and the extension of consumerism, principally of products which are initially of greatest interest to the middle classes, and help deepen the penetration of the dependent societies (Sauvant 1979: 15). It is also postulated that the social and economic policies, indeed the responses of politicians, state administrators or managers, and many intellectuals in the dependent societies to the conflicts and problems of their own societies are substantially conditioned and constrained by the intellectual and ideological frameworks set in place and dominated by the metropolitan capitalist centres. It has frequently been asserted that their consciousness is to a significant extent formed by the 'central economic, social, and political philosophies' derived from the European or advanced capitalist historical experience (Seers 1970: 30). The universities, research institutes, foreign aid programmes, transnational corporations, and advertising agencies from the advanced capitalist world, as well as international financial institutions such as the World Bank, facilitate this ideological-cultural domination. In other words, it is claimed that peoples in dependent societies see their societies increasingly through modes of perception and categorization substantially controlled by metropolitan capitalist interests, even to the extent of adopting and internalizing the consumption patterns and values characteristic of advanced capitalist societies. Intellectuals, and the educated strata in general, have developed analyses of their own societies, and engaged in policy formulation, within the intellectual traditions of the advanced capitalist countries. This reached the stage where, according to Edward Shils, the supposedly universal standards of the metropolitan countries have been applied to evaluate intellectual activity in the dependent societies (Shils 1972: 474).

Metropolitan cultural-ideological domination both reinforces and is a part of capitalist economic domination. It helps ensure that subordinate classes remain locked into a capitalist hegemony which they will not, or are unable to, challenge fundamentally since their consciousness is profoundly conditioned by metropolitan-derived ideologies and values. The domination is such that it ensures that dependent or comprador ruling classes stay within and help maintain this hegemony.

In his early work Armand Mattelart, one of the most influential cultural dependency or imperialism writers, referred to 'the superstructure of dependency' which has to be understood in relation to the 'expansion of the international capitalist system' and the place of the dependent societies in it. The role of the mass media in this is essentially the diffusion or transmission of 'collective representations' (the major values, ideologies, myths, images) developed in the advanced capitalist countries to dependent ones (Mattelart 1978: 13–33; Mattelart 1980: chapter 1). The development of international cultural production and mass media means that 'consciousness' can progress greatly beyond the real bases of social life, well beyond the state of productive forces in any one national society. The mass media, with their typical programming, are the product of, and are shaped by, the highly developed productive forces and cultural practices of advanced capitalist societies. The culture produced and disseminated by the mass media has to be grasped in relation to the state of the development of technology and economy in advanced capitalist societies, and the United States in particular.

According to Mattelart's early approach, in the dependent society the advanced capitalist mass media may penetrate all social levels despite the low level of economic and technological development. For example, Mattelart suggests that the Indians in the Andes, who live in a 'pre-capitalist world', have access to certain elements of the superstructure of highly technological societies even if the prizes of consumption dangled before them by the media are beyond their reach – the phenomenon referred to in conventional modernization theory as 'the revolution of rising expectations' (Mattelart 1978: 25). In effect Mattelart is suggesting that there is a major disjunction between the dependent society's economic structure and its ideological superstructure since the latter is largely the product of imperialist or capitalist power rather than of internal development.

Mattelart argues that the mass media 'demonstrate' the imperialist system's concept of change, a conception which in fact ends up being a denial of change. The media produce and reproduce the 'rhetoric of change' in order to prevent 'any real alteration in that mode of producing life which characterizes the system' (Mattelart 1978: 23–4). The mass media are programmed in such a way that the nature of the relationship between the economic base and the ideological superstructure is lost; that is, the media extend the aspirations, collective representations, images, myths and values developed in the advanced capitalist countries and which circulate in dependent ones. Thus, according to Mattelart, the forms of developed societies, including consumption patterns, are imported devoid of content. Cultural and media dependence both perpetuates and deepens economic dependence and underdevelopment, and permits the absorption or integration of peoples in dependent societies into an imperialist-dominated universal order which creates the illusion of change while simultaneously denying its possibility.

The nature of this capitalist domination is such that people in dependent societies are led to live the 'history of other people'. This ensures, first, that they do not have time to get involved with their own history, and second, that they live by proxy (Mattelart 1978: 24). Historical time is converted into a consumer good like any other product, an argument somewhat akin to John Berger's in *Ways of Seeing* (1972), where it is suggested that consumerism becomes a substitute for political democracy and history is robbed of class struggle and becomes both a commodity and a key legitimating principle of consumption. For Mattelart the role of dependent ruling classes is crucial to the understanding of cultural dependence and the impact of the mass media. Dependent ruling classes 'manage' the myths and ideologies that emanate from the advanced capitalist world. They may indeed own and control the mass media organizations as they do throughout Latin America, but they mechanically reproduce the externally derived dominant ideologies in order to preserve their own restricted hegemony.[3] This assures the hegemony of the imperialist world as well as the subordination of dependent ruling classes. It promotes models of development which keep leading to underdevelopment and dependence, and contributes to the intensification of dependence under the appearance of universalization. Thus, for Mattelart, ruling classes in dependent societies are ideologically and economically subordinate to international capitalism. As dependent classes they are neither able to challenge international capitalist interests ideologically nor capable of mounting an economic challenge to them by becoming fully-fledged national bourgeoisies or capitalist classes.[4]

THE LIMITATIONS OF THE CULTURAL DEPENDENCY PERSPECTIVE

The cultural dependency perspective, like that of economic dependency, assumed a widespread orthodoxy during the 1970s in accounting for the nature of ideological-cultural relations between advanced capitalist and 'Third World' countries. The perspective was also used to account for the position of countries such as Canada and Australia which were often seen as economically, politically and culturally dominated by the United States. Although still widely accepted by many intellectuals in Africa, Asia and Latin America, the position has been subjected to wide-ranging critical attack. As with economic dependency, the criticism has concentrated on the inadequacy of the conceptualization of capitalism, the problems of dealing with the 'residue' of the pre-dependence or pre-colonial period, internal class relations and their intersection with external factors, the nature of the state with its communications apparatus and cultural practices, and the various processes of cultural mediation (Garnham 1979: 123–46).

Dependency writers often verge closely on the economic and cultural autarky view in which a necessary connection is established between an independent cultural and economic development. Hamelink, for example, with his notion of cultural synchronization, makes independent development dependent on a cultural autonomy which can only be secured through the pursuit of policies of international dissociation. Whereas historically there has existed a great diversity of historical cultures characterized by internal division and reciprocal interactions, since the 1950s a particular global cultural pattern has developed which has helped shatter 'the validity of the autonomous national state or national culture' (Hamelink 1983: 6). Continuing integration into the American-based trans-national corporation-dominated global economy, with its communications apparatus and global culture, only serves to perpetuate metropolitan capitalist interests. Indeed, following the early André Gunder Frank, Hamelink suggests that the mechanism of cultural synchronization is basic to the maintenance of the metropolitan-satellite structure (Hamelink 1983: 5). His understanding of cultural systems as 'the totality of instrumental, symbolic, and social adaptive relations' (Hamelink 1983: 22) is essentially functionalist, and is largely devoid of any examination of class and other contradictions. The examples he chooses of attempts to resist cultural synchronization, including Mozambique and Tanzania, are perhaps unfortunate given such countries' generally crippling economic problems.

In much of the dependency writing on ideology it was assumed that the dominant ideologies in the dependent social formations are either imposed by the metropolitan capitalist powers (or their agents, the transnational corporations) in accordance with their interests, or else adopted by the ruling classes in the dependent countries as a way of defending and extending both their interests and those of international capital (Hamelink 1983: 7). This transfer of the dominant ideology of capitalism from the advanced centres takes place through a great many agencies, including the mass media. While this approach increasingly understood dependence as part of the dynamic interaction between international and national forces, it nevertheless largely placed the production of the dominant ideology, and even its reproduction, outside the internal dynamics or dialectic of the dependent society. There was even the suggestion in Mattelart's early writings that there was a transfer of the ideological superstructure of the advanced capitalist societies – with its specific collective representations and myths – to the dependent societies. This transplanted and imposed superstructure was quite out of step with the relatively undeveloped state of the productive forces, although it was able to penetrate effectively the consciousness of the masses, including the peasantry in remote areas, through advertising and the mass media.

As Mattelart himself and other critics realized, the principal problem with this formulation was that it assumed an ideological superstructure could be created and reproduced elsewhere and somehow imposed on or implanted in a society without being, or becoming, a part of the internal dialectic or processes of change and social and cultural reproduction. There can be little argument that in terms of the sheer volume of capital investment in and output of mass media and cultural production, as well as in the size and complexity of the whole ideological-cultural apparatus, there is substantial inequality between advanced capitalist societies on the one hand and most of those of the 'Third World' on the other. There is also a substantial inequality between countries in their ability to develop and utilize sophisticated electronic communications technology – the means of mass communications and cultural production. In addition the flow of world communications messages and cultural commodities is very much uni-directional between the advanced capitalist and 'Third World' countries, although the flows between advanced capitalist countries (including intra-corporate communications) are in volume of much greater importance. However, the existence of these often massive inequalities, while perhaps indicating that certain economies and their corporations exercise, or are capable of exercising, a preponderating cultural-ideological influence which could be referred to as 'imperialist', provides us with little understanding of the nature of the internal reproduction of culture and ideology, and the way in which metropolitan or international capitalist ideologies and cultural commodities enter that process and affect its development.

Within a few years Mattelart's position had, in order to grasp the complexity of ideological-cultural relationships in different social formations, shifted considerably. The internationalization of cultural production and communications could not simply be reduced to the 'growing penetration of American companies in the marketplace', especially as the dominant classes in 'dependent social formations' have gradually realized 'the efficiency of the models and representations produced by the metropolis' and adapted them to concrete reality (Mattelart 1980: 69). As a result, cultural imperialism has to be understood as a 'correlation, a combination of national and international forces'. Mattelart also pointed out that it is necessary to reject simple 'manipulation' or 'conspiracy' models of the communications apparatus since they reduce its role to one of propagandizing rather than cultural reproduction. The reduction in the importation of North American cultural products by many Latin American military states, and their replacement with local cultural production, indicated the extent to which 'cultural messages must necessarily be coherent with the state apparatus found in the particular country' (Mattelart 1980: 74). In other words, the types of cultural commodities and messages furnished by North American communications and culture industries often fail to be consonant with the types of developmental models adopted by ruling classes in dependent societies. This, Mattelart suggests, clearly indicates the need to link the cultural product in each and every case with the class structure to which it is directed.

There are substantial differences in communications practices and the role of the communications apparatus between civilian, populist states, and the military states in Latin America – and by extension, in Africa and Asia. For example, in Chile under the Frei regime, where the leadership of the political parties was drawn from the middle classes, the communications media 'expressed the mediating function of the liberal state' (Mattelart 1980: 77). The communications, which had the civic function of integrating 'the oppressed majority into the values and aspirations of consumption' were based on a class alliance that favoured the middle class. According to Mattelart, this bourgeois communications model, which is essentially premised on 'social peace' and bound up with the concept of public opinion and the legitimacy of the representative apparatus, is inappropriate in the case of the military state. The military state, Mattelart suggests, 'cannot actualize an alliance with the middle class', and is not able to integrate peasants and workers into the values of consumption since this is of no use to its objectives. The notion of public opinion which is so central to the communications practices of populist states does not exist since the distinction between civil and military society has been elided (Mattelart 1980: 78).

Sarti notes that the 'considerable merit' of the cultural dependency approach was its demonstration that domination did not simply depend on repressive methods but also on a 'sophisticated ideological component' (Sarti 1981: 319). While the cultural dependency approach provided a denunciation of the process of ideological domination, and helped reveal its mechanisms, it did little to establish the effect of this ideological domination of the peoples of Latin America. It was deficient in references to class and class fractions, and tended to treat Latin American countries as a 'homogeneous block suffering the ideological aggression of the transnational corporations' (Sarti 1981: 319).

Critics such as Sarti have argued that any theoretical elaboration of the cultural dependency position suffers from internal contradictions which stem from a 'mechanistic approach to society' and from an essentially dichotomous view of social reality that 'fails to apprehend the complexity and variety of the so-called Latin American culture' (Sarti 1981: 324). The cultural dependency position is in danger of being little more than a theoretically elaborated radical version of nationalist ideologies, and in many instances, is predicated on the authenticity, whatever that may be, of indigenous cultural expression. This is certainly the case with much of the African writing on communications and culture where the often strong emphasis on the persistence of traditional forms of oral communication and cultural practice has not led to a major revision of the understanding of media audiences and 'effects'.

Perhaps the principal problem with the elaboration of cultural dependency as theory is that it has elevated to a position of primacy a notion of dependency which was really a complement to the Marxist-Leninist theory of imperialism (Sarti 1981: 324). Dependency theory suffers from an 'economism' in the sense that there is held to be a correspondence between the dependent economic infrastructure and the ideological superstructure. If the economy is dependent, the superstructure must be too. The dependence of the superstructure reinforces and helps reproduce the dependent at the economic level.

As with so many critics of the cultural dependency position, Sarti notes the way in which dependent countries or peoples are seen as 'mere recipients of the ideological process' and largely incapable of evincing some response (Sarti 1981: 326). Local elites or ruling classes are simply agents who adopt and disseminate capitalist ideology produced in the centre and are not seen as having their own internal contradictions. While in many instances there would be a compatibility of the interests of the local bourgeoisie and the hegemonic capitalist centre, 'local ruling classes are capable of dominating their own societies without the aid of instruction from abroad' (Sarti 1981: 327). Sarti could have added that at times there is an incompatibility of interests, with fractions of local ruling classes prepared to challenge international capitalist interests, often through state action, where their own accumulation activities are threatened or not enhanced.

Part of the problem with the cultural dependency formulation of ideological relationships is the influence of the Althusserian concept of ideology and ideological state apparatuses. In Althusser's formulation state ideological apparatuses function to guarantee the domination process. They participate directly in the reproduction and disciplining of labour power, as well as of the basic social relations of capitalism. Althusser's critics have objected that ideology is determined by the production process itself, and thus by the basic contradictions of the capitalist mode of production (Sarti 1981: 327). When applied on a global scale Althusser's concepts encourage the view that the reproduction of capitalism globally requires ideological state apparatuses at the periphery which contribute mechanically and directly to that. The way in which quite different historical forces, combined with the complexities of class relations and conflicts, condition the production and reproduction of ideology at the 'periphery' is not countenanced.

Some African writers have attempted to move beyond simplistic cultural or media imperialism approaches to theorize the role of mass media in the reproduction of social and ideological relations in the national social formation, as well as internationally. Dauda Abubakar, for example, utilizes a radical dependency framework, but locates within it elements of semiotic and Althusserian structural Marxist and Marxist perspectives. His analysis proceeds from the commodity character of information, and more specifically television and cultural production, and the need for different regimes to secure legitimacy in a context of class, class fractions, cultural difference, and continuing imperialist domination. In addition to their legitimating role, the mass media are fundamental to 'cementing socio-economic, political and technological linkages between the core states on the one hand and the dependent peripheral formation of the Third World on the other' (Abubakar 1987: 53). At the basis of such linkages is the uneven flow of information from the advanced capitalist countries, and a technological dependence which is more than that since communications technologies are 'always socially and materially reproduced'. The production and dissemination of information in its widest sense, which assumes a commodity character and involves a multitude of selection and editing processes, is dominated by the class which owns and controls the means of material production.

Abubakar adopts Althusser's concept of the ideological state apparatus to explain the relationship between dominant classes and the control of the mass media – television in particular – in African 'market-oriented' economies such as Nigeria, Kenya, Zaïre, and Côte d'Ivoire (Abubakar 1987: 55–6). His use of ideology relies on the Althusserian distinction between real and imaginary relations, the ideological being concerned with the 'representation of the imaginary relationship between individuals, classes and groups on the one hand and their real conditions of existence on the other' (Abubakar 1987: 57). Abubakar recognizes that the ideological state apparatus is not only a means of class domination but also a site of class conflict. He does not, however, consider that the principal reason why there is such direct repressive intervention in mass communications is that the ideological state apparatuses are brittle and unable to establish and maintain ideological domination easily. The African mass media, especially newspapers, radio, and television, may construct a carefully selected view of the world in which the political leaders are always engaged in developmental tasks which benefit the nation.[5] The capacity to disseminate this particular construction throughout the national social formation, and even more problematically have it accepted as the true representation of the 'lived' reality, is restricted: first, by the limited and uneven reach of the media; second, by the 'lived' reality of those from the subordinated classes who are being acted upon in the name of development; and third, by the particular construction of the world of those from classes and strata still strongly affected by elements, including the ideological, drawn from pre-capitalist social relations.

The first restriction is basic. The distribution of television, for example, is overwhelmingly in urban areas and restricted to those with the financial means to afford them – essentially petty bourgeois strata. Those with greater financial means own video recorders and largely ignore national television broadcasts. Access to newspapers, and the print media generally, is limited by level of literacy, cost,[6] and heavily urban-based distribution. There are substantial differences in African countries, and indeed elsewhere, between newspaper and print media consumption in urban and rural areas, which possibly cannot be reduced to differences in access.[7] Access to radio is obviously greater in urban than rural areas, although the penetration of radio in the latter is considerable and extends well beyond per capita radio ownership. It is possible that the impact in rural areas is greater given that most people do not have access, as their urban counterparts do, to a diversity of media.

Many African writers on the mass media subscribe essentially to a relatively simple cause-and-effect model of communications influence in which messages which have clear-cut, intended meanings are transmitted and received by audiences which interpret them unambiguously. In this respect there is a convergence of functionalist, behaviourist, and Frankfurt School critical theory positions, with the last emphasizing the way in which particular forms of consciousness are constrained and determined by the very nature of the communications technologies, policies, and ideologies embodied in social relations of domination and subordination. This view of the communications process fits comfortably with, indeed, is a concomitant of, the cultural dependency perspective in which local, comprador ruling classes, by securing their own legitimacy, at the same time secure their continuing subordination to international capitalism: 'their legitimacy is also reinforced at the international level by the core capitalist states through their monopoly of the global technology of communication and exchange' (Abubakar 1987: 60). The oppressed in the dependent social formation 'learn' of their oppression through the 'ideological apparatuses' of their oppressors.

Abubakar's analysis, like that of other radical dependency writers, runs into difficulty when contradictions emerge between the national and international. 'Western' newspapers and radio and television programmes may often provide unflattering accounts of

African countries – war, violence, 'tribalism', corruption, crime, famine, the sensational and the aberrational rather than the normal – which are determined by particular news values. On occasion the reporting is offensive to specific regimes because it exposes the nature of state repression of any critical or oppositional expression. Given the usually tight control of the mass media, such forms of repression and suppression are either not reported, or treated in such a way that they appear as natural, legitimate ways of dealing with threats to development and national unity. The mass media, despite internal division, themselves become key actors in the repression and suppression.

LATIN AMERICA: FROM FUNCTIONALISM TO DEPENDENCY AND BEYOND

Communications research in Latin America in the 1950s and early 1960s was essentially dominated, as it was elsewhere, by functionalism. Schools of communications at Latin American universities were set up under various forms of United States sponsorship, with foundations such as the Ford and Rockefeller providing scholarships and grants for Latin American students at places of higher learning in the United States. The penetration of communications studies by the dominant American functionalist approach was also facilitated by the 'intervention of international organizations [in which] the United States played the leading role' (Mattelart 1979b: 31).

According to Mattelart the sharp increase in functionalist communications studies throughout Latin America (and in Africa and Asia as well, it should be noted) was provoked by three principal and interconnected factors. The first was the introduction of television and the resulting adaptation of communications networks to the reinforced penetration of transnational corporations (advertising and public relations agencies, firms specializing in public opinion, and commercial and marketing research). The second factor was the establishment of the link between communication and modernization. The implementation of the mild social reform policies of the late 1950s and 1960s was dependent on a particular model of communication in which modernization was to be promoted through the 'widespread diffusion of new knowledge and techniques'. The modest programme of agrarian reform involved the stimulation of modern attitudes in peasants 'in order to reconcile them to the increasingly urgent need to instil a veritable capitalist economy in agriculture' (Mattelart 1979b: 31). Birth control policies were predicated on a particular model of communications, while educational reforms were initiated as part of the modernization process. The expansion of the educational system allowed United States universities and foundations, supported by the Peace Corps, to intensify penetration by promoting in many countries radio and television pilot projects. The third factor which was essentially restricted to Latin America was the Alliance for Progress, forged out of the challenge posed by the Cuban Revolution and the need to encourage at least moderate reform.

By the mid-1960s the material circumstances of Latin American countries challenged the dominant functionalist perspective. The critical response and rejection was to a considerable extent part of the emergence of the dependency theory perspective which stressed the unequal nature of the structural relations between the metropolitan and peripheral capitalist countries. This, for Mattelart, 'acted as a backdrop for the discussion and the search for alternative policies which marked the decade of the sixties' (Mattelart 1979b: 32). Significantly it was at this time that the import-substitution policies, upon which so much of Latin America's economic development had been predicated, were showing increased signs of exhaustion.

The apparent failure of the older economic strategies to produce sustained growth and break metropolitan capitalist dominance raised fundamental questions about alternative economic models, the possibilities of national development, and whether the Latin American bourgeoisie was simply a comprador or dependent class, or a genuine national one capable of carrying through a historic mission of relatively autonomous national development. It quickened the search for alternatives and spurred those on the political and intellectual left to forge new popular class alliances capable of breaking the shackles of dependence and producing development along non-capitalist and non-dependent lines.

The analysis of the original Latin American dependency theorists, while limited by its undue concentration on centre–periphery relations to the neglect of 'each nation's specific reality', including its class configurations, nevertheless resulted in the first attempt to elaborate a theory of communications. This theory was couched in cultural and ideological domination terms. By the end of the 1960s in countries such as Argentina, Chile, Uruguay and Venezuela, critical mass communications studies were being produced that 'denounced the national and international power structures under-lying the messages of the press, radio and advertising'. Under the influence of the semiotic approach, which had achieved prominence in Europe by this time, the detailed analysis began of cultural products such as television programmes, comic strips, and women's magazines (Mattelart 1979b: 32).

Undoubtedly the Cuban Revolution, and the cultural develop-ments associated with it in the 1960s – the new Cuban cinema in particular – provided a substantial backdrop for the basic changes which occurred in much Latin American cultural and communica-tions analysis. Additionally, ferment in many universities in the late 1960s (for example, the Catholic University of Santiago in 1967), attempts to radicalize and mobilize the peasantry, and the develop-ment of 'popular' struggles in Bolivia and Uruguay, forced a further reconsideration of the major themes of mass communications stud-ies. Mattelart notes:

> The importance of communications in determining the outcome of the revolutionary process revealed that it was essential to approach all the means of mass communication as an integral part of the state apparatus, especially in a period when the principal question was knowing what to do with a state inherited from another class.

> (Mattelart 1979b: 33)

This concern with communications as part of the state apparatus was undoubtedly influenced by Althusser's structural Marxism, and concept of 'ideological state apparatus', which had widespread currency at the time among the left.

A good deal of Latin American writing on communications and culture retains significant elements of the dependency perspective. However, although this continues to be important, some analysis has shifted into what can almost be regarded as a post-modernist phase in which there is an emphasis on 'the popular' (Canclini 1988). The popular is not understood in the commercial, mass media sense which it is throughout the advanced capitalist world; nor as part of the process of nationalization and homogenization of the masses which the state, through the media apparatus, education, and other means, is concerned with producing. Rather it is grasped at the level of the particular forms of cultural practice and expression in which those who are not part of the hegemonic culture are engaged. This conceptualization stands in contrast to 'deductivist' approaches which, while demonstrating the importance of imperialist domination throughout Latin America, have contributed to the overestimation of the 'impact of the dominant on popular consciousness' (Canclini 1988: 471–2). Popular practices and expression may involve the reconstruction of cultural commodities and messages produced in the dominant media institutions, but used in oppositional ways. The widespread development of alternative, grass roots media, including popular radio, community theatre, and the use of sound-slide and video for group-level conscientization, demonstrated the independent capacity of 'the popular classes' for cultural creativity and resistance to transnationalizing and homogenizing culture. Some of the movements have had a clear economic base, as for example in the case of labour and peasant organizations, while others have been forms of political organization including urban neighbourhood -*barrio* or *favelado* organizations (Boran 1989), women's movements, basic Christian communities with their liberation theology, youth and human rights groups, and progressive journalists. Martín-Barbero (1987) notes that these movements have opened a new arena of political action which is largely cultural. They have provided 'communication strategies for the redefinition of the *meaning* of social development and the meaning of Latin American identity in terms of everyday life, and lived experience of oppression'.

In important respects this approach is not far removed from subcultural analysis in British sociology and cultural studies, and the post-modernist emphasis on the collapse of mass structures. The 'rediscovery of the popular', to use Martín-Barbero's phrase, represents a response by many Latin American intellectuals to the recognition of the failure of both bourgeois parliamentarianism, and the left strategy of the 'united front' dependent on the primacy of the role of the proletariat. In Brazil, for example, many intellectuals in the *nova republica* have resorted to a type of cultural pluralism which has largely negated the earlier left emphasis on the promotion of class struggle, if only through cultural means (Dassín 1989).

Martín-Barbero distinguishes between two phases in the 'formation-consolidation of the hegemonic paradigm in Latin America': the 'ideologistic' and the 'scientistic'. The first, the 'ideologistic', derived from an essentially functionalist conception of the media, and resulted in an instrumentalist view of them 'that deprived them of cultural substance and institutional materiality, converting them into mere tools of ideological action' (Martín-Barbero 1988: 448). The linking of mass media with ruling-class domination led to the neglect of the dominated in analysis, as well as any study of conflict. Faced with omnipotent and omnipresent power, audiences were simply passive consumers, very much in the Frankfurt School mould. The textual messages they received did not embrace conflict or contradiction, and were not in any way expressive of struggle, whether in the actual media or cultural production process, or more generally.

The second phase, the 'scientistic', emerged during the 1970s. To a considerable extent it was an expression of the crisis and failure of the Latin American left in the face of a succession of military coups. Brutally repressive military and industrial coalitions crushed any hopes for media reform through progressive governments. Often media researchers and policy experts were driven closer to movements of popular resistance. It was also a recognition of the increasing importance of communications in the sphere of production, and not simply in circulation (Martín-Barbero 1988: 449). In order to overcome the 'disciplinary and methodological fragmentation' problems associated with the analysis of the strategic place of communications processes in contemporary society, analysts had recourse to a supposedly unifying information theory derived from cybernetic and mathematical models. This 'scientistic' approach effectively removed the 'conflict of interests at play in the struggle to inform, produce, accumulate or transmit information' from its purview. Its obliteration of analysis of the social conditions of production of meaning obliterated analysis of struggles for hegemony. Significantly Martín-Barbero identifies a 'complicity between the dominant semiotic model and the informational' in the sense that both the transmitter and the receiver are assumed to be 'situated on the same plane and the message to circulate between homologous instances'. Apart from a real deficiency in being able to account for the social production and transformation of meaning, these models do not cope at all well with the existence of an 'asymmetry between the codes of the transmitter and of the receiver' (Martín-Barbero 1988: 452).

According to Martín-Barbero the forcing of a paradigm shift, and with it the changed 'object' of study for communications researchers, was produced through a combination of the recognition of the 'limits of the hegemonic model (and) real social processes in

Latin America'. Fundamental to these real processes is 'transnationalization', which is distinct from the old imperialism; it is
associated with the rapid extension of communications technologies
– satellites, telematics, and data banks. This development, as
García Canclini notes, largely renders obsolete older conceptions of
struggle against 'dependence'.

> To struggle to make oneself independent of a colonial power in a
> head-on combat with a geographically defined power is very
> different from struggling for one's own identity inside a transna-
> tional system which is diffuse, completely interrelated and
> interpenetrated.
>
> (Canclini, quoted in Martín-Barbero 1988: 452)

This type of transnationalization has brought into renewed and
sharp focus the 'national question'. The problem of identity becomes more acute as there is a convergence of transnationalization
and a homogenization at the national level. Here the pressure is to
'negate, deform, and de-activate the cultural pluralism that constitutes these countries' (Martín-Barbero 1988: 453).

Martín-Barbero's emphasis on the 'rediscovery of the popular'
stems from a recognition of the failure of the political if that is
understood as the 'denunciation of the trap of bourgeois parliamentarianism' and a political strategy predicated on the exclusivist role
of the proletariat. In his reformulation the political is understood
essentially as oppositional and alternative forms of cultural expression and practice which cannot be contained within conventional
political arrangements (parties, parliaments) and practices. This is
to be seen against the backdrop of the 'nationalization of the masses'
which, as we have already seen, converges in its later stages with
transnationalization. There is recognition on Martín-Barbero's
part, as in Armand Mattelart's work, that the specific nature of
national social formations, with their particular class configurations, requires, or leads to, different idioms of rationalization, and
the construction of national history, imagery, and mythology. Nationalization does not constitute a simple subordination of the
national to the transnational. Rather, it involves a homogenization,
a construction of national categories, markets and audiences which
effectively blurs and obliterates cultural diversity and contradiction.
This nationalization of the masses, which may involve the selective
re-working of elements of national mythology and history, is inte-

gral to state-formation as well as private capital accumulation processes.

The 'constitutive process of massness' in Latin America, Martín-Barbero suggests, had its material basis in industrialization, urbanization, and the development of state and media institutions. From the 1930s until the end of the 1950s the mass media in Latin America were a crucial factor in mediating the conflict between the state and the masses and in ultimately incorporating them as a 'people' into a 'nation' (Martín-Barbero 1988: 455). In many Latin American countries nationalist populism and populist nationalism, facilitated by the mass media, amounted to resolution of the conflict to the extent that they met some of the basic demands of the masses and contained some of their modes of expression.

The media which were prominent in recodifying and channelling these demands and expressions, and in marking the birth of nationality and the advent of modernity, differed from country to country. While in some the cinema was important (Argentina, Brazil, and Mexico), in practically all it was radio which provided people from the 'regions and provinces with [their] first daily experience of the nation' (Martín-Barbero 1988: 455). From the 1970s onwards the constitution of the masses entered a new phase in which television was to play the crucial role. This was a period of crisis in which the import substitution industrialization model reached the 'limits of its coexistence with the archaic sectors of the society' and populism could not sustain itself without radical social reform. Although the state, particularly in its military form, still utilized a 'social service' rhetoric for broadcasting, the management of education and culture was handed over to private interests whose task was to make the 'poor dream the same dreams as the rich' (Martín-Barbero 1988: 456). As part of the new developmentalism the 'masses' had to be reconstituted as a consuming mass, even if only, as Martín-Barbero wryly notes, of newspapers, and television and radio receivers. Their numbers, as a sign of communication, are the 'touchstone of development'.

> The experts from the Organization of American States thus proclaim: without communication there is no development. And the radio frequencies will be saturated by stations in towns without running water and the teeming *barrios* will be populated by television aerials.
>
> (Martín-Barbero 1988: 457)

Whether privatized, or run by the state, television operates in essentially the same way as a homogenizing force. By tending to constitute only one public in which differences have been elided, it is possible to 'confuse the greatest measure of communicability with the greatest measure of economic profitability'. Its power as a homogenizing force in reconstituting the masses is much greater than the press, which, for all its catering for a mass market, is still governed by a liberal model and still 'attempts to express the plurality of civil society'. Its power is also much greater than radio, which, from its beginnings, has been responsive to and expressive of social and cultural diversity (Martín-Barbero 1988: 457–8).

Martín-Barbero's work represents a key part of that shift in Latin American media and contemporary cultural research into the way in which the 'popular' classes, rather than being in a passive state of subjection to a hegemonic cultural order, appropriate particular cultural forms and meaning for their own purposes. Canclini, while lambasting 'inductivist' approaches to popular culture analysis for their failure to locate the popular in basic capitalist social relations and the conflicts between classes and other social groups, nevertheless emphasizes 'the persistence of forms of communal and domestic organization in the economy and culture' in the understanding of both the variations in formations and their connection with the 'hegemonic system', as well as their responses to mass communications. Studies in Argentina and Brazil have shown the way in which media messages have been filtered through particular social relations, including those of the family, friends, domestic tasks, and poorly paid wage labour, in ways which render them far from all-powerful (Canclini 1988: 492). Differential consumption, whether of mass communications, urban space, dressing or eating, and of being amused and informed, provides the major key to different forms of media response and to cultural expression: 'Consumption is the locus in which conflicts between classes, caused by unequal participation in the structure of production, continue by way of the distribution of goods and the satisfaction of needs' (Canclini 1988: 493).

Several recent studies have been concerned with family and class-based differences in television use and reactions to the same programmes, *telenovelas* in particular (Penacchioni 1984; Leal and Oliven 1988; Lull 1988; Kottak 1990; Leal 1990); in other words the way in which quite different meanings are constructed on the basis of the same text. Increasingly media production and reception is grasped in terms of different layers of mediation and appropriation which offset the massification and homogenizing tendencies of the mass media. For Martín-Barbero these mediations are the product of a long historical development. They include the primacy of the extended family and the importance of the neighbourhood as the place of annual religio-civic festivals, as well as the incorporation of elements of folk drama and popular sentiment in film, *radionovelas*, and ultimately *telenovelas*. The appropriation of media dramatization of such meanings leads to their reintegration into the popular narrative memory.

CONCLUSION

Changes in the theorization and analysis of communications and culture in 'Third World' societies, including their relations with those of the advanced capitalist world, have fairly closely followed those of economic development. In addition, such theoretical and analytical changes have been part of certain basic changes in the dominant methods and assumptions of media and cultural analysis in advanced capitalist societies.

While dependency perspectives still provide the framework for much of the theorization and analysis of international flows of communications and cultural commodities, as well as for the analysis of mass media and communications institutions and practices in the countries of Africa, Asia, and Latin America, they have been increasingly challenged and modified. As part of a more general shift of emphasis to questions of internal social structure and social reproduction, emphasis has shifted to internal processes of media production and reproduction. The importance of international inequalities in the capacity to produce and distribute media commodities and technologies is not denied; however, it is what happens to those commodities and technologies in the specific context of different national societies which has become the major focus of analysis. As we shall see in the following chapter, greater attention has been given both to the detailed analysis of media texts, where semiotic and structuralist forms of analysis have been influential, and to their reception. Although this remains an area of comparatively little research – effects are assumed rather than investigated and analysed – there is recognition that the use of local and imported media products by highly differentiated national audiences, and the types of meanings and responses which they construct from them, are the product of complex sets of social and cultural relations and mediations. They cannot be understood in terms of simple cultural domination models, whether of international or national focus.

Chapter 3

'Media imperialism' thesis

The enormous problem of defining and analysing cultural imperialism and dependence has encouraged many writers, prominent among them Oliver Boyd-Barrett and Chin-Chuan Lee, to narrow the problem by dealing with the concept of media imperialism. Cultural imperialism, as distinct from more specific media imperialism, embraces a much more holistic view of the media by focusing on the 'relationship between ownership and control of the media and the power structure in society, the ideological signification of meaning in media messages and its effects in reproducing the class system' (Curran *et al.* 1977: 9). For many neo-Marxists the concept 'media imperialism' is too constricting in the sense that it isolates individual media from an overall set of economic and ideological-cultural relations (Lee 1980: 41). Schiller, for example, suggests that it is pointless to pursue the media imperialism line of inquiry since the consequences of the heavy impact of the cultural-ideological outputs of the transnational corporations are not open to any meaningful measurement. In his own vague definition cultural imperialism is viewed as 'the sum of the processes by which a society is brought into the modern world system and how its dominating stratum is attracted, pressured, forced, and sometimes bribed into shaping social institutions to correspond to, or even promote, the values and structures of the dominating center of the system' (Schiller 1976:9).

Boyd-Barrett prefers the use of 'media imperialism' as a distinct analytical tool because it restricts the range of phenomena to be dealt with and allows for a more rigorous examination of the specific institutional arrangements and mechanisms of imperialism. As a result Boyd-Barrett's approach is constrained by a positivistic, empirical perspective which, as Schiller amongst others has recognized, is of limited value in exploring the complexities of ideological-cultural relations. This highlights what appears to be a basic anomaly, indeed contradiction, in cultural and media imperialist analysis. While Tracey (1985) attacks much of the writing on cultural dependence and media imperialism for its failure to provide empirical support for its basic propositions, Fejes (1981) criticizes such writing for its narrow empiricism and theoretical deficiencies. The criticisms, however, are not necessarily diametrically opposed. Tracey, who rejects some of the highly problematic assumptions of national culture and economic autarky upon which media imperialism theory is based,[1] shows, for example, the way in which substantial data on international news flow, and especially coverage of the 'Third World' in the media of the advanced capitalist societies, does not support certain basic assumptions made by radical media analysts which are shared more-or-less universally throughout 'Third World' societies.[2] The theory is deficient because it lacks historical, empirical foundations. For Fejes, in contrast, many empirical studies, as a result of the narrowness of their scope, are of limited explanatory power because they are not located in an elaborated theoretical framework. Fejes suggests that while the media imperialism approach has produced a wealth of empirical data about the operation of communications media 'on a global scale', as well as detailed description of 'concrete examples of media imperialism', its theoretical weakness is a crucial deficiency since

> Without theory delineating the bounds of explanation, there is the danger of media imperialism becoming a pseudo-concept, something which can be used to explain everything in general about the media in developing countries and hence nothing in particular.
>
> (Fejes 1981: 282)

If the media imperialism approach has theoretical underpinnings they reside in a Marxist critique of capitalism and the effort to situate the global expansion of western communications media as part of an overall capitalist expansion. However, Fejes notes, there is little of sufficient precision and detail in the theoretical underpinnings to make them Marxist. Rather, they are better seen in the general context of the rejection during the 1970s of modernization theory and the communications model associated with it – the decade when the dependency approach became dominant (Fejes 1981: 283).

The focus on television culture, as for instance in Lee's *Media Imperialism Reconsidered* (1980), may indicate the highly problematic nature of a cultural dependency or imperialism thesis, without providing much insight into the complex totality of relations between advanced capitalist countries and those of the 'Third World'. A concentration on television, which in the case of a country such as Brazil may cast considerable doubt on the validity of the media imperialism thesis, can lead to a thoroughly misleading impression of the total set of ideological-cultural relations. In many 'dependent' countries, and throughout Africa in particular, television may not be the dominant media institution, even though it is substantially dependent on the technology, organizational arrangements and professional values and practices, and programmes, of countries such as the United States and Britain. Radio is in many societies the dominant mass medium, and the one most open to local programming. Receivers are relatively cheap and widely distributed, and more-or-less continuous programming can be maintained at a fraction of the cost of television programming and production.

Boyd-Barrett defined media imperialism as the

> process whereby the ownership, structure, distribution or content of the media in any one country are singly or together subject to substantial pressure from the media interests of any other country or countries without proportionate reciprocation of influence by the country so affected.
>
> (Boyd-Barrett 1977b: 117)

All the major forms of media imperialism are considered to be a highly probable, perhaps even inevitable, outcome of the imbalance of power between respective countries. Media imperialism, according to Boyd-Barrett, is either the product of the expanding of influence as part of a deliberate commercial or political strategy, or else disseminated unintentionally and without clear direction in a much more general process of political, social or economic influence, such as during the European colonial period in Africa and Asia. This influence is absorbed by countries either through contact, such as under colonialism, or is adopted by them as part of a deliberate commercial or political strategy.

The first dimension of media imperialism identified by Boyd-Barrett, the shape of the communications vehicle, refers to the way in which countries such as Britain, France, Germany and the United States, through early advances in industrialization and the development of sophisticated modes of communication, were in a position to shape the nature of the vehicles of mass communications. These vehicles, whether newspapers and magazines, films, radio and television, or records and tapes, were established not just simply as a result of a series of technological developments, but in relation to specific national markets and processes of capital accumulation and centralization.

The communications vehicles established in the industrialized capitalist world were exported first, as part of colonial relations, and second, as part of the expansion of international capitalism, although different interests, including capitalist ones in the non-industrialized world, were anxious to invest in and adopt them. Dependent societies have generally been forced to adopt the vehicles established in the advanced capitalist world. Often their levels of economic development effectively prevent indigenous development, the usually prohibitive cost of local production of communications technology and programmes encouraging their importation. In this sense there has been a technological dependence; the United States, principally for reasons of an ability to use economies of scale, has been the major provider of technical equipment for other countries, although this role has increasingly been assumed by Japan.

The second dimension of media imperialism is the set of industrial arrangements. Behind the shape of a communications vehicle lies a structure of organization and finance. After World War II in particular, there occurred the growth of transnational media corporations which exported their industrial-organization arrangements as well as finance. Britain and France, as the major colonial powers in Africa and Asia, helped determine the set of industrial arrangements, although shortly after independence in many countries these were overturned or modified very much in accordance with dominant or ruling interests, even if justified in terms of adapting the media to the national development effort, including promotion of national unity. The provision of capital aid and advice in the establishment of new communications systems also represented, according to Boyd-Barrett, part of the process whereby the industrial arrangements of the advanced capitalist countries were transferred to others. The main broadcasting organizations in Britain, France, and the United States (BBC, ORTF, NBC, CBS) provided models of operation, or were directly responsible for setting up transmission and supplying equipment and personnel, to many 'dependent' countries. Advertising, which derives from the Anglo-American capitalist industrialization experience and its movement into a consumer phase, is a key part of the industrial arrangements. As a major source of media revenue it supposedly reduced the need of transnational corporations to own the media (that is, where there are no legislative barriers to foreign ownership and control) by allowing a structural control to be exercised.

The third and fourth dimensions of media imperialism identified by Boyd-Barrett are the values of practice, which refer to notions of professionalism, objectivity and detachment, and appropriate forms of technology developed in advanced capitalist countries, and media content and market penetration. The latter are the most conspicuous form of media imperialism, consisting of television programmes, films, books, magazines, records and tapes, and other cultural commodities, as well as advertisements. The significance of media contents lies in the ideological positions they express, positions which are frequently held to be at variance either with those of the host society or with the aspirations of those groups and classes in the host society which are committed to an alternative course of development and disengagement from imperialism.

Other writers such as Tunstall (1977) and Katz and Wedell (1978) have adopted a similar approach to Boyd-Barrett. Lee, in *Media Imperialism Reconsidered*, does not explicitly acknowledge his indebtedness to Boyd-Barrett in his own less satisfactory formulation. His formulation follows Boyd-Barrett's in its identification of the four basic components or features of media imperialism, but weakens them by largely removing Boyd-Barrett's clear grasp of, and emphasis on, the interrelatedness of technological, organizational, and economic factors. For Lee, media, or more specifically television imperialism, is characterized by: first, television programme exportation to foreign countries; second, foreign ownership and control of media outlets; third, the transfer of the metropolitan broadcasting norms and institutionalization of media commercialism at the expense of 'public interest'; and fourth, the invasion of capitalistic world views and infringement upon the indigenous way of life in the recipient nations.

Significantly, in this definition there is no reference to the crucial production of the means of communication (that is, the production of the technology necessary for modern mass communications) which remains predominantly a preserve of the advanced capitalist world – even in those countries where substantial indigenous capacity in cultural and communications production has developed.

Lee's definition, and Boyd-Barrett's to a lesser extent, robs the concept of 'imperialism' of much of its substance and precision. Basically any inequality in international economic and ideological-cultural relations is construed as imperialistic in nature. This stands in sharp contrast to Lenin's 'classic' formulation, from which post-World War II theories of imperialism, including cultural, are both derived and critically responsive. Imperialism, for Lenin, is the highest stage of capitalism in which monopolists seek profitable investment abroad as a way of overcoming stagnation at home. His basic thesis was that with the development of industrial capitalism, competition led inevitably to concentration of capital in the form of monopoly, cartels, and trade combines. Their control of domestic markets in the advanced economies was so firm that the competition which had fostered innovation had largely vanished, the living standards of the masses could no longer rise, and the expanded profits of the monopolists would eventually find all profitable spheres of domestic investment exhausted. The exhaustion of domestic investment opportunities led to rivalry for profitable investment outlets abroad, which led to the division and re-division of the world by the leading imperialist states. The international wave of imperialist expansion in the late nineteenth and early twentieth centuries was thus the result of the reaching of the stage of monopoly capitalism in the major industrial countries, which forced them into territorial rivalry for investment outlets, especially in the colonial or semi-colonial countries where land, labour, and raw materials were cheap and capital scarce. With the break-up of the old colonial empires following World War II, capitalism entered a neo-colonial or neo-imperialist phase in which the old formal colonial controls were no longer necessary for the maintenance of metropolitan capitalist power.

The central feature of Lenin's theory of imperialism, and subsequent Marxist revisions such as theories of underdevelopment, is that economic and other relations between the advanced capitalist countries and the rest of the world have to be understood in terms of the continuous, recurring crises of investment and accumulation. For some theorists the underdevelopment and dependence of much of the African, Asian, and Latin American world is a necessary corollary of the development of the advanced capitalist world, while for others such as Kay (1975), it is essentially the product of a failure of capital under European colonialism to transform the basic production and social relations in them. The underdevelopment and stagnation is deepened in the post-independence period in so many countries simply because a transforming investment capital is not forthcoming. The low level of current capital investment flows to Africa is illustrative of this.

In the neo-imperialist, as distinct from Lenin's 'classic' formulation, political and ideological-cultural relations are to be grasped principally as a means of ensuring that the primary economic relationship of exploitation is maintained. This is why the media apparatuses of both the 'metropolitan' capitalist countries and the 'peripheral' capitalist ones are considered so important. Ideological-cultural power exerted by the transnational corporations of the advanced capitalist economies is indispensable for continuing control, the ideological subversion or incorporation of indigenous ruling classes, and the encouragement of consumption preferences and internalization of values conducive to the interests of international capitalism.

Whatever the limitations of this neo-imperialist position – and there are many – it at least attempts to locate ideological-cultural relations, and mass media, in a dynamic international political-economic setting. In most definitions of 'media imperialism', and Lee's in particular, this is precisely what is missing: the idea that mass media production and practice in the advanced capitalist world, and its penetration of the 'Third World', is bound up with the contradictory development of capitalism, including factors which are apparently peculiar to the mass media and cultural production industries themselves. It comes as a surprise when Lee, after justifiably lambasting 'neo-Marxist' and dependency theorists for their failure to take sufficiently into account the internal dynamics of 'dependent' societies, including the complexity of their class relations, completely overlooks his criticism when providing some policy prescriptions. His position quickly emerges as idealist, and set firmly in the functionalist modernization theory mould. In his policy prescriptions, Lee suggests first, that 'the media should be harnessed to such development objectives as political integration, socio-economic modernization and cultural expression (Lee 1980: 183). The terminology provides a clear indication of the way cultural dependency has been smuggled into the modernization model. Conveniently there is no reference to the possibility that 'national development objectives' may be those of a ruling class, or the product of the class conflict which Lee suggests dependency theorists have usually ignored. This is made clearer in his second policy proposal, which is that 'a sound communication policy should not only be beneficial to a country's own goals but also fair to other nations'. Clearly we are back in the realm of reification (countries have goals!) and national interest concepts. Further, Lee provides an undialectical and undynamic view of mass media production, and ideological-cultural relations, which removes them from the whole complex set of international and national forces affecting their development.

Boyd-Barrett's formulation has been criticized by Salinas and Paldan (1979) for a formalism which locates the 'circuits of influence' between the media systems of basically unequally ranked countries. At the empirical level this type of formulation gives rise to the problem of separating 'media interests' from those of the interests of large corporations or transnationals engaged in a host of financial, productive, and distributive activities. Mattelart's *Multinational Corporations and the Control of Culture* (1979b), with its attention to considerable empirical detail, clearly shows how difficult this separation has become when transnational corporations in the electronics and aerospace industries have progressively extended their interests in the 'transnationalization' of book publishing and the supply of educational materials, and when there has been a transnational concentration and diversification in the press and the film/television industry. Transnationalization, combined with conglomerate forms of organization and control, in some instances ensures that 'media interests' are subordinate, perhaps even incidental, to conglomerate expansion. For instance, the major record companies are owned by conglomerates whose principal activities lie elsewhere; records, film and video account for only 6 per cent of the turnover of RCA.

Fejes, along similar lines, observes that there is a need to broaden media imperialism analysis so that it embraces other communications and information media (Fejes 1981: 287). An unduly narrow concentration on the flow of media products such as television programmes, films, and news stories between the advanced capitalist countries and the 'Third World' both ignores and obscures 'many important dimensions of the process' and misinterprets the basic concern (Fejes 1981: 287). More thorough and adequate analysis would require examination of the transference of communication technologies, including basic information technologies used in state administration and private business, professional models (Golding 1977; O'Brien 1979), and transnational data flows (Schiller 1979). Such communications technologies, as Boyd-Barrett (1977b), Hamelink (1983), and Mattelart (1979b) amongst others clearly recognize, involve much more than hardware. They usually embrace quite specific models of organization of the labour process, authority relationships, and professional practices. The professional and organizational models are developed through the structures of transnational corporations and their subsidiaries, as well as in schools of business management and administration. This does not mean that the owners and controllers of private enterprises, and senior state managers, are not concerned with the adoption of information technologies and organizational models which secure their position of dominance and at least maintain rates of capital accumulation.[3] It does mean, however, that they are constrained by the dominant and increasingly standardized systems produced by major corporations elsewhere.

Lee reveals his functionalist location by developing a critique of the cultural imperialist view predicated on a separation of culture, as an autonomous order, from the 'political and economic function of the media'. Similarly Haynes (1984), in identifying some of the empirical inadequacies of structural theories of imperialism, especially when applied to communications and culture, insists on separating the cultural and the 'societal'.[4] The separation rests on an essentially false dichotomy of the economic and the cultural, with information an important part of the latter. Haynes notes:

> Structural theories of the international system that are directed towards the societal task of production and allocation of goals and services, both in political and economic terms, have little to say about the flows of information that are influenced by specific cultures.

(Haynes 1984: 214–15)

Significantly 'cultural' and 'media' imperialism positions are often conflated with the result that Boyd-Barrett's detailed framework for the analysis of the latter is completely ignored. Laing's examination of the music industry in terms of the cultural imperialism thesis is an example of this conflation (Laing 1986: 331). It shows without difficulty that while the major record companies, as part of transnational conglomerates, dominate world musical or record production, it is much more difficult to establish what this means for countries in Africa, Asia, Latin America, and elsewhere. In some countries the extensive piracy of recorded music, for instance, serves to discourage the principal record companies, and fledgling local ones, from investing in further recordings (Laing 1986: 336). This undoubtedly affects the incomes of the transnational corporations and their recording artists (although many countries in the 'Third World' would represent an insignificant part of their total market), but is most damaging to local productive capital and the supply of local music in recorded form. One of the peculiarities of the record industry is that by not being able to control the market and consumer taste effectively, it is forced to provide a full 'cultural repertoire' from which only a limited number of recordings are profitable. The 'pirates', who in many countries may account for as much as 75 per cent of total recorded music sales, do not bear any risks at the production level, just simply recording that which is already market-successful. Similar consequences have been noted for both film and television production in countries where video, and both legitimate and pirated video tapes, have become important.

In revealing some of the limitations of the 'cultural imperialism' thesis, Laing refers to the 'liberating' role which the music of the dominant music producers may perform when located in the complex class and other mediations of different 'national' societies. Use of rock 'n' roll, for example, may enable a generation to 'distance themselves from a parental "national"culture' (Laing 1986: 338). The often dominant presence of innovative Anglo-American music in many countries forces local musicians to adopt a stance; they can imitate the music, rediscover and reassert indigenous musical traditions and forms, or produce a domestication of it through fusion, as in the case of Nigerian Afro-Beat and *juju*.

Somewhat paradoxically the fundamental concern in the media imperialism approach with the cultural consequences of the transnational media has surprisingly not led to detailed analysis of their cultural impact on 'Third World' societies. Analysis has generally concentrated on the ways in which the relations of domination and dependence are reproduced within the content of popular media. Theories of media imperialism and cultural dependence have generally relied on a manipulative model of the mass media. The mass media are essentially agents which act in a direct, largely unmediated way on audience behaviour and 'world view' (Fejes 1981: 287).

An audience 'effect' is assumed without a corresponding develop-ment of the means of adequately theorizing and empirically examining that effect. Much of the research, including that influ-enced by literary and semiotic-structuralist forms of analysis, has been concerned with the 'content' of both imported and locally produced material to ascertain the extent to which it may be seen as transferring or imposing imperialistic values. For example, analyses of *telenovelas* and *fotonovelas* reveal the ways in which values central to the dominant capitalist societies are reproduced in forms of popular expression supposedly indigenous to the societies such as Brazil and Mexico which produce them. The forms themselves are usually seen as derivative from or imitative of those from the media of the dominant capitalist societies.

If media imperialism or cultural dependence analysis is to mean more than a dependence on programming produced elsewhere, then it has to provide an explanation of how the particular values and practices associated with that programming are reproduced in the consciousness of 'dependent' peoples as well as within the very structures of the dependent societies. Although obviously useful, empirical, descriptive, statistically-based study of the flow of the production of the mass media, and television programming in particular, is not necessarily the study of media imperialism or cultural dependency. As Fejes wryly observes:

> For some communications researchers, media imperialism is largely a question of how many episodes of Kojak are shown on Bolivian television.
>
> (Fejes 1981: 288)

Descriptive studies may be able to indicate clearly the extent to which there is, first, a 'western capitalist' dominance of mass media (including the technology of production and distribution) and cultural production; second, an unequal flow of products from these societies to the rest of the world – especially 'Third World'; and third, the way in which programmes in many countries rely on dominant models from the United States in particular. More refined descriptive study indicates, first, that some 'dependent' societies such as Brazil, Mexico, India, and Egypt have considerable capacity for media and cultural production, have become significant export-ers of programmes, and have wrought often major transformations of imported cultural and media forms in accordance with the peculiarities of their audiences and 'national' cultural traditions.

Second, many of the advanced western capitalist societies are substantial importers of programmes, especially from the United States, and are 'dependent' on media and cultural technologies produced in the United States and increasingly Japan. Third, crude figures of the flow of programming into particular countries tell us little about their specific locations and patterns of use; whether, for example, imported television programmes are slotted into prime time, or increasingly serve as filler material while locally produced material dominates the prime-time slots.

MEDIA IMPERIALISM AND BRAZILIAN TELEVISION

The development of Brazilian television in the 1950s poses problems for both the cultural dependence and media imperialism theses. While, as Mattos notes, Brazilian mass communications have been influenced by foreign systems, and the United States in particular, internal conditions, including protectionist policies and the political interests of the military regime since 1964, 'have had a stronger influence on mass media development than external factors' (Mattos 1984: 205). The size of the Brazilian audience and advertising market, which are linked to the levels and scale of industrial and commercial development, have provided a revenue base which is generally absent in smaller countries. This, certainly in the case of TV Globo, provided a strong base for local production (Straubhaar 1984: 237).

The initiative for the introduction of television in Brazil came from local capitalist entrepreneurs, not from commercial pressures emanating from the United States as some writers have suggested (Straubhaar 1984: 222). The initially small size of the audience, limited advertising revenue, and expensive television technology, aroused little foreign interest. Foreign, that is United States, technology was used, and there was some foreign impact on advertising revenues, but overall the size and peculiarities of the Brazilian market would not support American-style commercial television broadcasting (Straubhaar 1984: 223). Certainly, often in indirect ways, American influences on programme format were important.

By the end of the 1950s and the early 1960s television in Brazil had shifted from a medium geared to a small, 'elite' audience, to one which was increasingly directed at the working and middle classes. This expansion of the commercial possibilities of television was the result of the industrial and commercial developmental boom of the

1950s and 1960s and the much greater extension of credit for the purchase of consumer goods (Straubhaar 1984: 224). Television's emergence as a truly mass medium attracted the interest of advertisers, especially transnational corporations: 'American multinational corporations participated heavily in the growth of consumer-oriented manufacturing industries and commercial advertising media' (Straubhaar 1984: 224). Brazilian programmers sought a television format likely to have the greatest appeal to the vastly expanded audience and turned to that which was dominant in the United States. The United States became the principal source of imported programming which was considerably cheaper at the time than locally produced material – films, series, and cartoons. The adoption of relatively cheap technology for dubbing English-language material in Portuguese greatly facilitated this.

The shift of television from a medium of limited appeal to a mass one was also reflected in changed local programming: classic, dance, and theatre programmes gave way to *telenovelas*, humour programmes, music shows, and *shows de auditorio*. However, the adoption of the dominant North American programming format did not mean that locally produced programmes were simply replications of American comedy and music programmes. Straubhaar notes that they were 'completely different' and retained distinctive features of Brazilian culture (Straubhaar 1984: 225).

Undoubtedly the influx of television programmes and the initial reliance on an imported television format were vital to the development of Brazilian television. Perhaps more decisive, however, were the conflicts between the Brazilian entrepreneurs who founded the television channels and networks (Straubhaar 1984: 227). The television network which had won out in this competition by 1968 was TV Globo. In the first decade of its existence (1962–71) it entered a special relationship with Time-Life Corporation which brought greater financial backing and technical expertise in return for Time-Life's share of future profits (Mattos 1984: 208). This arrangement had little impact on TV Globo's programming which was geared to mass audiences using *telenovelas, shows de auditorio*, and other popular programmes (Straubhaar 1984: 229). TV Globo's market domination enabled it to establish a substantial industrial base for programme production (Straubhaar 1984: 233) – *telenovelas*, comedy programmes and music shows 'that drew on and supported its film, theatre, and recording industries' (Straubhaar 1984: 234). In contrast to the United States, where the networks relied on programming supply from 'independent' production companies and film studios, TV Globo was able to establish a vertically integrated structure in which nearly all production was its own. By the end of the 1960s foreign production technology was being used in such a way, and local formats such as the *telenovela* refined to such an extent that the domestically produced programmes were in a position to challenge the imported. Sophisticated audience research and ratings surveys established that prime-time audiences responded enthusiastically to the locally produced material, *telenovelas* especially, which acted as a further spur to local production (Straubhaar 1984: 230). In the 1970s imported American programmes were increasingly used as filler material, although the smaller independent stations in Sao Paulo and Rio de Janeiro continued to rely on imported programmes catering for an 'upper-class market'.

The example of Brazilian television, and the TV Globo network in particular, raises many critical questions about the dimensions of media imperialism identified by Boyd-Barrett, Lee, and others. The industrial-organizational patterns, although clearly influenced by those of the United States media industries, have been conditioned by the economic and other conditions prevailing in Brazil. Foreign ownership is negligible, even if transnational advertisers are the major source of television revenue. While Brazil is an important importer of programmes, Brazilian programme exports exceed imports (Straubhaar 1984: 234), even though not as great in volume as Mexico's. The infringement of American commercial broadcasting patterns and professional values is more difficult to establish. Brazilian television programming formats – *telenovelas* in particular – certainly show that even where they are derived from forms from elsewhere (the 'soap opera' from the United States, for example), they have gone through considerable mediation and transformation. If the dominant programming is expressive of capitalist values – and there can be doubt about that in the Brazilian context – it can be asked whether this is merely the result of foreign media domination or influence, or simply that television programming reflects the capitalist nature of Brazilian television and the Brazilian economy.

Clearly it would be unwise to extrapolate too recklessly from the Brazilian example since the conditions affecting television production and programming, or other media production, are not replicated elsewhere. If anything, the Brazilian instance provides a warning that media imperialism analysis, if undertaken, should proceed very much on a nation by nation basis, that is, so long as it is tempered by location within the overall global expansion of capitalist cultural and media production.

MEDIA IMPERIALISM AND VIDEO CASSETTE RECORDERS

The advent of new 'delivery systems', and in particular the video cassette recorder (VCR), calls for further reconsideration of the media imperialism thesis. As Ogan (1988: 93) notes, the VCR has simultaneously expanded the range of choice available to media users while weakening the selective power of broadcast administrators and theatre owners. Frequent use of VCRs by the wealthiest segments of urban populations clearly poses severe problems for state-owned television broadcasting systems which rely to a considerable extent on revenue from private advertisers. The response in countries such as Kenya and Malaysia is often to try to make television more appealing to audiences through a greater importation of programmes. This, however, tends to contradict the explicit national development objectives of media programming. Indeed, some Asian governments have expressed concern that VCR use undermines national development goals (Tracey 1985: 24). In Malaysia, for example, the Chinese population have been by far the major users of VCR tapes. They have a strong preference for Chinese language video tapes from Hong Kong rather than the Bahasa Malaysia-dominated television service. Such usage runs directly counter to government emphasis on the creation of a national culture through the use of a national language – Bahasa Malaysia. The loss of a television audience to video poses a problem for regimes which are anxious to use television for development education purposes and to provide constant legitimation for government policy and actions. Where there is little choice or variety of programmes, or where state censorship severely restricts programming, those with the means increasingly have recourse to smuggled and pirated videos.

The widespread availability of pirated film and television programmes in countries such as Turkey, India, and Thailand, clearly reduces financial returns to foreign, and in particular American, film and television distributors and producers (Lent 1984; Hamilton 1990). It also adversely affects local film production. This is certainly the case in Turkey where there has been a sharp decline in the number of cinemas as well as in feature film production (Ogan 1988: 100–1). Whether the piracy of films and television programmes reduces any foreign imperialist media impact is difficult to assess. Ogan suggests that the increasingly widespread availability of, and access to, video cassette recorders in Turkey, combined with a high volume of both imported and indigenously produced pirated material, at least raises the possibility that use of foreign material will be reduced, and with it the impact of media imperialism. However, the effects of video piracy on different population segments is likely to be different. Ogan's comparison of two districts in Ankara with contrasting class composition found clear differences between video consumption use patterns: in contrast to the working classes, the upper middle classes preferred imported material rather than the locally produced. Ogan attributes the upper middle-class predilection for the foreign to their advanced formal education, income, foreign-language proficiency, and number of trips and length of stay abroad.

If there is a conclusion to be drawn from this for dependency theory, it is that the upper middle classes are 'closer to the values of the core or the Western country producing the programs and are thus more dependent than those people who prefer domestic cultural products' (Ogan 1988: 103). Ogan notes that the advent of the VCR provides opportunities for small-scale production 'of more culturally aesthetic materials and their distribution outside the centralized mass media system' (Ogan 1988: 104). This, of course, is what Latin American alternative video makers have attempted for many years (Sarti 1988). In Nigeria there has also emerged a form of decentralized television programming in which local artists are able to package indigenous material for the home video market (Boyd and Straubhaar 1985).

If there is a conclusion to be drawn from Ogan's work on Turkey, it is that cultural and media imperialism perspectives have been conflated. Media imperialism, as Fejes notes, has been reduced to little more than the unequal flow of media and cultural commodities between countries. Boyd-Barrett's effort to identify with some precision the specific mechanisms and organizational arrangements of media imperialism have been lost in a welter of generalities, and assumptions of economic and cultural autarky. The concern of Latin American writers such as Martín-Barbero with different processes of mediation and appropriation of media products is largely lost.

Beryl

Date: Sunday, October 10, 2004
Time: 3:20 PM

Item   5016745202
Title   ...dia in a globalized society / edited b
Due date: **10-24-04**

Item ID: 415016352013
Title   Mass media and cultural identity : ethni
Due date: 10 24 04

Item ID: ...09142619
Title   ...f television : an introduction : Ch
Due date: 10 24 04

Item ...05 ...200...
Title ...cultural ... it... identity ...ea
due ...e: 10 24 04

...
le... ...ass media / Niklas L
...

...
... ...g obal society / edite
...

...
...American ...g... American
date: 10 2...

...
terms
--------------- Thank y... ---------------

CONCLUSION

When first formulated by Oliver Boyd-Barrett, the media imperialism thesis represented an attempt to overcome some of the
problems of imprecision and generality associated with earlier
cultural imperialist and dependency perspectives. It did this by
examining in greater detail the specific mechanisms whereby the
media of the advanced capitalist countries were able to influence
substantially, if not determine, the nature of communications and
media production in 'Third World' societies. In later formulations,
the specific mechanisms identified by Boyd-Barrett were largely
lost, as media imperialist analysis became little more than a concern
with the uneven flow of international communications. With the
impact of such uneven flow assumed rather than subjected to
rigorous, theoretically informed analysis, little attention was given
to the importance of internal factors in both the reception and use of
imported media products and in local media and cultural production. While under colonial rule in Asia and Africa in particular the
British and French were able initially to establish basic models for
broadcasting, and to a lesser extent print media and journalistic
practice. Such models underwent transformation after independence when conflicts between international and national forces, and
internal social structural factors such as class relations, became
decisive in the determination of state media and communications
policies, and in media organizational change.

Chapter 4

State and communications

This chapter is concerned with a number of fundamental issues relating to the state and communications. To some extent the issues relate to the problems new technologies pose for the determination and formulation of state policy in countries which generally lack the capacity to produce such technologies themselves. This is especially the case in areas of telecommunications, satellites, transborder data flows and business information systems resting on a microelectronic base (dealt with more extensively in chapters 5 and 6). State policies, where they have been formulated in detail, are concerned with both the technologies and the content or the messages of information flow.

A number of major theoretical and other problems stem from the conceptualization and theorization of the state. In the case of most 'Third World' countries theorization of the state has usually taken place within Fanonist and dependency perspectives. The former has generally been stronger in the African context, although as we shall see, it has been influential elsewhere – particularly in Latin America – in the articulation of Third Cinema theory. Such views have essentially been instrumentalist, with local, dependent ruling classes serving the interests of metropolitan or international capitalism. In some Latin American, and to a lesser extent African thought, the simple instrumentalist view has been overlaid by Althusserian concepts of ideology and repressive and ideological state apparatuses which, while perhaps directing attention to basic problems of ideological-cultural reproduction and institutional arrangements, nevertheless reinforces the view that the 'Third World' state exists primarily to enable capitalism on a global scale to reproduce itself continuously. For many writers decolonization throughout much of Africa and Asia represented an attempt by colonial powers such as Britain and France to secure institutional arrangements, and a pattern of class rule, that would protect and serve metropolitan investment and capitalist interests.

Such conceptualizations of the 'Third World' state, which postulated the absence of a true national bourgeoisie (comprador ruling class, lumpenbourgeoisie), were deficient, as critics increasingly pointed out, in denying the importance and role of local class configurations in the determination of the state and state policy. A number of critics in the African context drew attention to the emergence of an indigenous class of capital which was often blocked in its accumulation trajectory by the colonial state apparatus and which since independence has been involved in both co-operative and contradictory relations with metropolitan and international capitalist interests. This class had hardly been deliberately created and groomed by the colonial power to assume state power on its formal departure. Others observed that often the post-colonial state was so weak and fragmented, and in some instances had so degenerated into an apparatus of pillage and erratic, violent repression, that it could not even secure conditions for international investment.

The development of more sophisticated theory of the state and state apparatuses, which was partly the outcome of the so-called Miliband-Poulantzas debate about the nature of the capitalist state (often misleadingly caricatured as the opposition of instrumentalist and structuralist positions), helped shift the theorization of the 'Third World' state. It led to a much greater emphasis on the role of the state in the mediation of relations between national and international forces (capitals), as well as the basic problems of the internal reproduction of ideology and culture. This shift, as we previously noted, was reflected in Mattelart's greater recognition of the 'relative autonomy' of the Latin American state from international capitalist forces, the different theoretical problems posed by civilian and military regimes, and the problem the existence of different class relations presented for the theorization of the state.

State policy and intervention with regard to communications and cultural production may take a multiplicity of forms. Initially they will be dependent on whether the state in question is capitalist or socialist, and/or assumes a military form. In most, if not all the countries covered in this study, issues of state censorship, repression (arrests, detention, intimidation, banning, and exile), and the free press and press freedom are central to analysis. State policy may also be pursued through direct ownership, with media organizations becoming departments of state, and legislative controls, licensing, regulation and registration, and the selective allocation of state or parastatal advertising in both private and state-owned media. In some countries where cultural and communications policies have become a major national priority, state policy may take the form of import quotas to allow local production to be established (as for example in film making), direct investment in production and distribution, tariffs and subsidies, and the provision of infrastructure, including training facilities, for communications and cultural production. The type of media and cultural production to be supported is always subject to political economic conflict, especially class conflict, and in many instances, to the perception of which media are most likely to enable rulers to realize their ends and implement supposedly national development objectives.

The pre-eminent position of the state in communications and cultural production in so many 'Third World' countries does not necessarily mean that state involvement is conducive to the expansion of local production. In the case of film making, for example, state provision of infrastructure and financial assistance may not prove at all supportive of local production unless import quotas on foreign film are introduced, or so many hours of exhibition time a week allocated to locally produced films. State policies may be formulated which, while designed to encourage national cultural reassertion and communications production, do not provide levels of investment in communications infrastructure, or adoption of other measures, likely to produce success. Some African governments have adopted national cinema policies, and even attempted unsuccessfully to nationalize local film distribution (Armes 1987: 217). Ghana has a state organization – the Ghana Film Industry Corporation – as well as a National Film and Television Institute for training young film makers. This has not facilitated feature film production which remains sporadic at best and privately organized (Armes 1987: 217). State repression may amount to the virtual destruction of local production, especially where that is construed as critical and oppositional in nature. Private capital, especially when the attractiveness of investment may be reduced by greater state involvement, may flee to take up production elsewhere. This happened to some extent in Egypt where the state began to assume a much greater role in film making towards the end of the 1950s. The state involvement did little to improve the commercial viability of Egyptian film making at a time when television was making substantial inroads into the film market. The tide of imports was not stemmed and the state's direct role in production ceased in the early 1970s. By this time some Egyptian producers had shifted their operations to Lebanon to avoid greater state control and interference (Armes 1987: 203).

The problem confronting Latin American film makers has not simply been one of overcoming the dominance of foreign cultural models, but of their relationship to the state as well. In Mexico, the state support for film making, which was first established in the 1930s, had become state control by the 1970s. In Brazil early film production expanded rapidly with state-imposed quotas which assured a domestic market. The harsh military repression following the 1964 coup, and the institutionalized torture of the early 1970s, did not bring about an end to film making. Rather, there was a much greater state involvement, especially through the massive state production and distribution company, Embrafilme. The military regime, through Embrafilme, was anxious to maintain Brazilian international film prestige. While the volume of production was maintained, a complex system of legislative controls and incentives meant that film makers were clearly circumscribed in creative and political-ideological terms (Armes 1987: 181–2). Under such increased state repression, where real, explicit commitment was impossible (many committed film makers went into exile), the characteristic Brazilian film of the early 1980s tended to rely on 'sex as a metaphor to raise certain issues too controversial for the authoritarian regime' (Armes 1987: 182). In Cuba after the revolution, in quite different ideological circumstances, cinema was structured much more 'to serve the wider needs of the state' (Armes 1987: 183). The Cuban Film Institute was set up in 1959 and expressed the industrial and cultural aims of Cuban film making. Despite state control, Cuban cinema has been characterized by a relative lack of heavy bureaucratic control, an eclectic range of approaches, and critical documentary and fictional treatments which tend to avoid conventional left-wing didacticism which provides 'solutions', and dull socialist realism (Armes 1987: 185).

AFRICA

Throughout Africa there is an overwhelming preponderance of state ownership of the mass media. This applies almost completely to radio and television, as well as to a considerable extent to the print media – daily newspapers in particular, although book and magazine publishing remain important areas for private capital investment, especially of a limited scale. Radio broadcasting in most African countries began under European colonialism and was a government responsibility. In the African colonies early broadcasting consisted of programmes that were relayed from the metropolitan capitals of the imperial powers – Britain and France. After World War II, following recommendations of the 1936 Plymouth Committee, a more decentralized model was introduced in the British colonies. Stations were established in the separate colonies and although controlled by colonial governments, they were not necessarily run by them, private broadcasting interests in some instances having that responsibility (Boyd-Barrett 1977a: 38). Television has also been predominantly government owned, in the Nigerian case a dual system of government-owned stations reflecting the federal nature of the Nigerian state. Some private production of programmes occurs, but this usually represents only a small part of total local production. Although state owned and controlled, radio and television stations derive some of their income from private advertisers. However, the often tiny size of the advertising base, combined with basic costs of production and distribution, has virtually ensured that radio and television remain under state ownership and control.

In the case of the print media, where formal and informal state controls are generally strong, there is a much greater mixture of private, party and state ownership. Private ownership includes companies (for example Lonrho, the Aga Khan group) concerned with commercial mass media, as well as religious and other organizations involved in publishing newspapers and magazines. While private companies are dependent to a considerable extent on advertising revenue drawn from the commercial and industrial enterprises in the private sector, they also draw much of their revenue from state and parastatal advertising. This applies almost as much to the media in countries such as Kenya and Nigeria where there is substantial private ownership of the media as to countries such as Tanzania where there is complete state and/or party ownership.

During the decolonization and post-colonial phases, British and French broadcasting models had a considerable influence on broadcasting in Africa.

During the period of transfer of power in the British colonies . . .
expatriate staff were seconded from the BBC for two-year tours
of duty to fill all senior, technical and production positions.
(Boyd-Barrett 1977a: 38–9)

Metropolitan broadcasting organizations such as the BBC assisted
with staff training. They often provided advanced forms of technical
training to people with little aptitude for broadcasting and which
was unsuited to indigenous production and the broadcasting technologies employed.

In broadcasting, as with the press, the post-colonial period
witnessed an often dramatic increase in state intervention. This
served to move African broadcasting and print media systems
further away from the old imperial models, procedures, and values
of practice associated with the media in countries such as Britain.
Generally the heavy concentration of broadcasting facilities established under colonialism persisted into and was sustained in the
post-colonial period. Nigeria represented a major exception with a
decentralized structure emerging, although the NBC based in the
capital Lagos still retained a dominant position. The decentralization of Nigerian broadcasting was undoubtedly facilitated by a
federal structure, with powerful concentrations of different language groups and major urban centres in some of the regional
states.

KENYA: REPRESSION AND PRIVATIZATION

In Kenya, after some initial experimentation with private participation in the running of the electronic media (a consortium of foreign
and local interests, mainly with an eye to the introduction of
television, obtained the operating contract of the Kenya Broadcasting Corporation in 1961), state ownership was established for both
radio and television. The inadequacy of advertising revenue, combined in the case of television with very limited television receiver
ownership, meant that broadcasting became the responsibility of the
Ministry of Information and Broadcasting in July 1964. The government service became the Voice of Kenya (Roberts 1974: 55–6).

The fact that the electronic media have directly served the
functions of government has severely restricted their activities –
certainly in giving expression to any dissenting voices. The press,
which is privately and substantially foreign owned, has been subject
to state intervention throughout the post-independence period.

This intervention has posed real difficulties for the Nation and Standard (Lonrho) groups whose commitment to values of editorial independence and professional journalistic values, in part the product of their representation of international capitalist interests, threatens both those interests and local investors. The intervention has taken many forms, including the detention and deportation of journalists, intimidation, forced resignations of editors, the provision of misleading and embarrassing news stories designed to discredit newspapers and their editors, and the withdrawal of vital government advertising (Hachten 1971 and 1981; Barton 1979). This intervention in the press, and the media more generally, was part of the increasing resort to state repression by the ruling KANU faction as a way of dealing with growing inequalities, tensions and conflicts, including class and regional ones, exacerbated by a slowing down in the rate of economic growth and the restricted use of the state apparatus by the ruling faction for their own accumulation activities.

By the late 1980s the funding of Voice of Kenya television had reached 'crisis' point. While advertising revenue for radio was sufficient to meet recurrent costs, television advertising revenues fell well below the level required to meet annual recurrent expenditure (Heath 1988: 101). Increases in revenue from radio and television permits, as well as more efficient collection, posed problems for the government in terms of unacceptable political costs. The problems were compounded by the preference of the Kenyan bourgeoisie and petty bourgeoisie, with their taste for overseas programming, for VCRs which enabled them to by-pass television. For advertisers this was a major problem since they were not reaching the most important market segments through television. Transnational corporation advertisers, as has been shown in Brazil and other countries, are prepared to associate themselves, whether through advertising or sponsorship, either with successful locally produced vehicles or with imported ones. In Kenya there is some evidence to suggest advertisers have been reluctant to sponsor VOK productions, 'ostensibly because they do not wish to be associated with the staff's technically sloppy work' (Heath 1988: 101).

The basic dilemma facing the Kenyan government was whether to import more programmes, which would be costly given declining exchange rates and a worsening balance of payments problem; or to increase local production, which would require a substantial increase in investment, including new production facilities and equipment, which would not necessarily be offset by increases in audience size and advertising revenue. A change in television programming was obviously a prerequisite for the attraction of larger audiences and greater advertising revenue. Such a shift, however, would necessitate less emphasis on local news pro-grammes (really presidential image-building), church services (especially those attended by the President and his entourage and not associated with strident criticism of his regime), and other cheap, locally produced material such as schools quizzes and other competitions.

The privatization of Kenyan television has occurred in essentially a double-pronged way: on the one hand, through the creation of a new television channel, Kenya Television Network; and on the other hand, through the restructuring of the Voice of Kenya as the Kenya Broadcasting Corporation and giving it increased respon-sibility for its own financial affairs. This represents somewhat of a paradox since the Kenya Television Network is owned by the Kenya Times Media Trust whose majority shareholder is KANU, Kenya's ruling party. This channel is in competition with the state-run Kenya Broadcasting Corporation which, as part of its restructuring in 1989, has been given all responsibility for licensing radio and television sets and is expected to run on a commercial footing. The restructuring has also involved allocation of land on the outskirts of Nairobi for the construction of new studios, and the purchasing of broadcasting equipment from a Japanese company.

After initial programming difficulties KTV has sought to boost its popularity by entering into an agreement with MTV Europe, a company partly owned by the late Robert Maxwell whose Maxwell Communications Corporation, at the time of writing, owns a 45 per cent share in the Kenya Times Media Trust, publishers of *The Kenya Times*. Alternative television in Kenya is thus basically a mixture of United States-derived news, locally produced Nairobi news, classic films, and the music programmes from MTV Europe (Lycett 1990: 52). Such programming, as well as that of KBC, hardly conforms to the various recommendations of the MacBride Com-mission, including the establishment of 'national cultural policies, which should foster cultural identity and creativity, and involve the media in such tasks' (MacBride 1980: 259; Heath 1988: 105). It also runs counter to recommendations for the development of non-commercial forms of communication, as well as the emphasis the

President has placed on democratized, decentralized, and diversified communications in a 1983 speech (Heath 1988: 105).

TANZANIA: CONFLICT OVER POLICY PRIORITIES

While communications are usually seen as an area of state investment and control they are nevertheless subject to two further constraints: first, the establishment of priorities in which certain media are given precedence; and second, the competitive allocation of resources to other, non-communications areas which have national priority such as education, health, housing, and the provision of infrastructure for industrial development. In relation to this Osakue (1988: 129) notes that state policy in African countries has often dictated that the resources for communications development should be derived from the consumers of the different services – the application of the user pays principle. The price of such services should ostensibly be determined by market forces. Basically this means that 'the organization of communications development . . . provides largely for urban and commercial demands as well as administrative needs of government institutions'. This gives rise to an inelasticity of demand which justifies pricing policies which place the market value of communications services 'far in excess of the utility valuation by a sizeable majority of the people' (Osakue 1988: 129).

The two constraints overlap to a considerable extent. The first may be illustrated by reference to the debates over communications policy and practice which occurred in Tanzania. Shortly after independence, and with the determination of a socialist strategy, it was decided that the national press should be given greater priority than radio, despite what should have been the obvious greater reach of the latter. It was also decided that the operation of capitalist newspaper production, with its particular news and entertainment values and dependence on advertising revenue, could not be reconciled with socialist transformation (Mytton 1983: 109). In 1972 the English-language party newspaper *The Nationalist*, which had been heavily subsidized by government, was merged with the nationalized *Standard* to form the *Daily Nation*. Originally both *The Nationalist* and *Uhuru* had been established to 'give TANU and its government a mouthpiece both within Tanzania and in the outside world' (Mytton 1983: 94).

The preference of the press over radio rested largely on the belief that it was a more effective means of communication for educational and development purposes. This preference probably reflected the fact that many key TANU personnel were wedded to the printed word, partly as a result of their formal education, and partly because they had been involved in print journalism and the production of political pamphlets and nationalist tracts in the years leading up to independence. Certainly the national functional literacy campaign and adult education programmes were based on the written and printed word and linked to the publication of cheap, utilitarian literature, and the Swahili press. The commitment to the party press in the 1960s – *The Nationalist* and *Uhuru* – with its limited readership, restricted advertising base and need for substantial state subsidy, meant that other communications options could not be explored fully. The Five Year Plan in operation at the time had provided for the building of satellite radio stations and community listening points, but these projects had to be 'shelved for lack of funds' (Mytton 1983: 95).

In the early years of Tanzanian independence state and party policy towards the mass media began to crystallize. Calls for greater state control of the inadequately funded Tanganyika Broadcasting Corporation (TBC) preceded independence, and became more strident as critics within TANU argued that broadcasting had to become a vital information arm of government. Effective government required the ability to address the dispersed peasant masses directly without the intervention of rival, ambiguous, and alternative voices and interpretations of policy. The 1965 dissolution of the TBC, and the incorporation of its successor into the Ministry of Information, Broadcasting and Tourism, meant that it was also effectively absorbed into the TANU ruling party structure, being placed 'under the control and direction of a sub-committee of the Party' which determines the country's broadcasting policy (Ng'wanakilala 1981: 32).

The Tanzanian government, Mytton (1983: 102) suggests, has been marked by a 'mixture of elitism and anti-elitism' in its mass media policies. Whereas in the case of the print media an 'elitist' attitude has generally prevailed, this has not been so in the case of both radio and television. The introduction of television on the Tanzanian mainland has been rejected on a variety of grounds, including its prohibitive cost, the inequity of allowing it to be introduced on economic and technical grounds in Dar es Salaam initially and then subsequently in the regions, and an inability to engage in substantial local production that would overcome a reliance on imported and inappropriate programming such as *Rawhide*, *Bonanza*, and *The Lucy Show* (Mytton 1983: 103).

In Tanzania radio broadcasting, rather than the print media, has been seen as playing a key role in the promotion of a national culture and offsetting colonial cultural influences. The establishment of the Ministry of National Culture and Youth was seen by President Nyerere as a vital instrument in the recovery and construction of a national cultural heritage. A National Dancing Troupe was established which made a study of dance and dance mime throughout the country and performed regularly both at home and abroad. It was radio, however, which played the greatest role in drawing attention to and recording the regional musical heritage, and which provided an important outlet for the commercially recorded, new urban music. Radio facilitated the use of Swahili as the principal language of communication.

STATE AND COMMUNICATIONS IN ASIA

Socialist-communist countries in the Asian region obviously provide different models of relations between state and communications to those which are committed to capitalist development. In China it has been the Communist Party rather than the state which has been the major factor in the control of mass media and cultural production. In India print media, which are predominantly the sphere of private capital, have been subject to legislative and informal means of control, while the electronic media as part of the state apparatus have increasingly become subject to commercial and privatization pressures. In countries such as Hong Kong, Indonesia, Malaysia, Singapore, and Thailand, which are undergoing extensive capitalist industrialization, the print media are essentially privately owned, while the electronic media, even where state or publicly owned, are increasingly important as spheres of private cultural or media production and accumulation.

Usually the media in these countries have a mixture of official legislative controls, as well as unofficial but very real pressures such as the summary arrest of dissident editors and journalists in Malaysia and Singapore, 'non-rejectable' advice from the ministry as in Singapore, and banning of publications such as in Indonesia. These controls are typically justified in national security and unity terms, although clearly they are about the protection of ruling interests and the reproduction of the dominant social relations in them. Underlying the more explicit elements of media policy – the restriction of negative foreign influences and the development of the media for national integration purposes – is a hidden agenda which is simply the maintenance of conditions conducive to the stability of national leaderships (Lent 1982: 187) and the extension of the interests of local ruling classes.

In Thailand modern mass communications are extensively developed. The press – over seventy daily newspapers – is in private hands, although subject to strict censorship and control. All television channels are ultimately owned by the state. However, they are leased to private companies which manage them, purchase their own programmes, and arrange advertising (Scandlen 1978; Hamilton 1990: 5). Television programming is tightly controlled by legislation, and strict censorship codes are applied to all broadcast material. Censorship is concerned with threats to national unity and peace, material which is likely to lead to a deterioration of relations with neighbouring states, pornography and obscene language, and media content likely to encourage criminal behaviour (Hamilton 1990: 9). Tight state control over the mass media is regularly justified in terms of threats to national security, especially from internal dissident elements.

During the 1970s nearly all of the ASEAN countries – Thailand, Malaysia, Singapore, and Indonesia – 'made moves to bar foreign ownership from mass media' (Lent 1982: 171). This was partly a response designed to make available investment outlets for local capital, as well as to establish national control over mass communications. Although some measures were partly successful, they did not address the issues of growing media concentration, or the formation of powerful regional media groups such as the Singapore *Straits Times* which were exporting their media products, buying media properties abroad, and engaging in 'big business journalism' (Lent 1982: 187). Various measures were adopted to initiate binational and regional news and feature exchanges, and to increase and upgrade indigenous media content.

Throughout this period efforts were made to restrict and censor imported films and television programmes, ostensibly for reasons of violence and promiscuity, as in Thailand. While such efforts, along with taxing of imported films, and provision of support for local

production through subsidies, film festivals, and training contributed to local production, they ran up against, first, established
cultural consumption practices conditioned by imported material,
and second, the relative lack of local production. The latter was
inhibited by shortages of investment capital, programming and
production skills, and high costs for relatively small domestic markets. The ever-increasing daily television schedules, which are
driven by advertising and the basic economics of television, put
pressure on local production capacity, and necessitate reliance on
the importation of relatively cheap entertainment programming
from the United States, Britain, and more recently from Japan,
Hong Kong, Taiwan, and India.

INDIA

India represents an example of immense complexity and diversity in
cultural production and communications. Broadcasting, film, newspaper, magazine, and musical production have been characterized
by regional and linguistic diversity, with non-Hindi and non-English
media in the private sphere especially showing signs of remarkable
growth over the last decade or more. While the basic role of the state
and state regulatory framework was established under British colonial rule, it has undergone substantial modification in the post-
colonial period. In contrast to many countries in the 'Third World',
private rather than state cultural and media production has become
increasingly dominant to the extent that it challenges – strong
central interventionist powers notwithstanding – both state production and regulatory frameworks.

Shortly after independence, as part of the effort to bring about a
national reconstruction and expunge many colonial and western
cultural influences, there was concern for the recovery and reassertion of forms of cultural expression which could be regarded as
genuinely Indian and largely free from western influence. This
concern was expressed in the music and literature policies of All
India Radio, where an initial and unsuccessful emphasis was placed
on classical Indian music and poetry. It was also expressed in the
tightening of film censorship and a great deal of hostility to film as a
medium which was popular, corrupting of Indian tradition, and
essentially frivolous since it contributed nothing directly to national
development.

With the development of national broadcasting, and television especially, through Doordarshan, and its increasing commercialization as a result in particular of the success of 'soapies' such as *Hum Log*, and the *Mahabharata* and the *Ramayana*, a concerted questioning of the relationship between the state and Doordarshan has begun. Pressures for privatization have grown, while others have expressed concern over the amount of control the state is able to exercise over production and editorial content. Similar concerns have been expressed in relation to the print media.

Since the 1960s the Indian national government has played an active role in the cinema. This involvement, Vasudev (1986: 2) suggests, reflected the growing concern in the 1950s that without state involvement in the patronage and preservation of classical music dance, as well as other arts, their existence would be threatened by the growth of new commercial entertainments such as film and film music, and the destruction of the older forms of patronage associated with the 'feudal princes and wealthy *zamindars*'. Prior to the early 1950s film was treated by government with indifference and distaste, and the imposition of crippling regulation. Independence, rather than ushering in a new era of improved relations between film producers and the state, only exacerbated and intensified conflicts between the state and censors on the one hand, and film producers and distributors on the other. The introduction of new levies and taxes, including increased taxes for censorship, and greater state regulation, proved a heavy burden. The exclusion of private producers from the documentary field added to the tension, not so much because it removed an area of lucrative return, but because it indicated the way in which state production was given precedence. This partly reflected the Indian government's preference for public rather than private enterprise, as well as the view that film could only be an important vehicle of information and national reform when under state control. Barnouw and Krishnaswamy (1980: 142) comment that it was clear the government was 'not growing in admiration for the film industry, which seemed by now to consist of hundreds of ephemeral enterprises that felt accountable to no one and were engaged in wild and irrational gambles contributing little to the great task of nation-building'.

In the changed cultural environment of the late 1950s film was considered as a possible art form worthy of greater encouragement and support. During the 1960s a National Film Archive was established, and a Film Institute (now the Film and Television Institute) set up in Pune. A more direct government involvement in the industry was initiated through the establishment of the Film Finance Corporation and the Indian Motion Picture Export Association which was merged in 1980 under the umbrella of the National Film Development Corporation.

The most conspicuous form of state intervention in film production and distribution is censorship. The new centralized Board of Censors which was instituted in 1950 was caught up in a nationalist reformist programme which had seen Bombay and other states introduce prohibition and ban drinking scenes in films. There was condemnation of the corrupting western influence on Indian film song. This led to the introduction of a music programming policy on All India Radio (AIR), which concentrated on classical Indian music. In film censorship there was determination to enforce stricter decorum in manners and dress; kissing became strictly taboo after independence, even for some time in the case of foreign film as well (Barnouw and Krishnaswamy 1980: 214).

The complexity of the federal state structure in India provides the Board of Censors with a 'relative autonomy'. The state apparatus, including the judiciary, provides many access points for those who have particular interests in film production and distribution, and thus censorship: film producers and distributors; women's and other groups, including religious organizations which feel affronted by films or scenes in them; the various state governments; and the central Indian government.

The Indian press was well established in the pre-independence period. Largely Indian-owned, it had played a key role in the articulation of nationalist demands and in giving expression to party and intra-party conflict. For some time a growing concentration appeared to threaten diversity, with the *Times of India*, *Indian Express*, and *Hindustan Times* groups the most powerful (Sarkar 1984: 210). The freedom of the Indian press has been circumscribed by a legislative framework which has been added to and modified since the early 1950s. The 'Objectionable Matter' law of 1951 'forbade newspapers to publish anything which might be indecent, scurrilous or intended to blackmail' (Boyd-Barrett 1977a: 35; Sarkar 1984: 30). The substantial dependence of the private media on state advertising has been a considerable source of state power and one which was exercised during Indira Gandhi's State of Emergency (Sarkar 1984: 113–20). The 1962 Defence of India rules granted government complete powers of control over the press in times of crisis, and as such prepared the ground well for Emergency Rule in 1985. In 1976, during the Emergency, a bill was introduced to give the central government even wider powers to 'prevent publication of material it considered objectionable once the state of emergency and censorship are lifted' (Boyd-Barrett 1977a: 35–6). Under the legislation the government could close offending journals, ban reporting on specific subjects for up to two months, and demand security bonds. This act, however, was repealed in 1977 (Sarkar 1984: 30).

All India Radio was originally developed along the lines of the Reithian tradition of public broadcasting. The adaptation and continuation of this, combined with the concern of 'some Hindi-speaking politicians [who] saw the radio as a key means of introducing classical Hindi and traditional Indian music to the Indian masses' meant that AIR had little market orientation (Tunstall 1977: 121). Few were interested in this music or literary Hindi; many were much more interested in the Indian film music broadcast by Radio Ceylon to audiences in South India. The Indian government response was to reply in kind. A popular music service, *Vividh Bharati*, was introduced in 1957. Film music, humorous skits, short plays and features were presented in their programmes. Leading Indian film personalities introduced their favourite songs and recounted their experiences (Ramachandran 1978: 27). In 1967 there was an acceptance of advertising, partly as a result of pressure from Indian advertisers who felt aggrieved that their competitors were able to advertise to Southern India through radio in Ceylon.

Indian television, which was introduced as a limited service in 1959 as part of a UNESCO project, developed very slowly (Awasthy 1978: 208). It was given a low priority by the Indian government as it did not fit in well with national industrial and economic strategies and social objectives. The Indian electronics industry was in its incipient stage of development, there was an absence of broadband telecommunications links, and there was the concern on the part of AIR that its 'own corps of trained personnel should produce indigenous programming' (Awasthy 1978: 207; Bhatia *et al.* 1984: 36). However, by the early 1970s the situation had changed considerably as a result of the expansion of local production of television transmission and reception equipment, the setting-up of a television training institute, and the proposed introduction of nationwide broadband microwave linkages. After protracted debate, by 1972 the Indian government was committed to the expansion of television services based on the co-existence of a substantial earth-bound network and a satellite system – INSAT (Singhal and Rogers 1989: 64–6).

The expansion of television services occurred against a backdrop of debate about whether it was to be used for information, educational, or entertainment purposes, and whether it would drain scarce resources away from sound broadcasting which, despite its crucial role in communicating development programmes, still did not have a complete national coverage (Awasthy 1978: 208; Singhal and Rogers 1989: 71–4).

In the late 1960s, when Indira Gandhi was in charge of the Ministry of Information and Broadcasting, expansion of television broadcasting was given much more serious consideration by the government (Bhatia *et al.* 1984: 37). Thought was given to finding a way of creating an industrial infrastructure, possibly with foreign collaboration, able to engage in the indigenous manufacture of television broadcasting equipment. In 1971 collaborative arrangements were worked out between state-owned Bharat Electronics Limited and Fernseh (FRG) and NEC (Japan) for local production of studio and transmission equipment.

The commercialization of Doordarshan basically began in 1976 when television services were separated from AIR and commercial spots were introduced. Advertising sponsorship followed in 1980. The pace of commercialization has been encouraged by the sharp increase in the number of television viewers since the mid-1970s, and since the mid-1980s by the success of locally produced soap operas – initially *Hum Log*, subsequently the *Ramayana* and the *Mahabharata*. As a result of commercialization and the success of soap operas, there has been a sharp increase in annual revenues from advertising spots (a leap from US $0.6 million in 1976 to $130 million in 1988), increases in advertising rates, and increases in Doordarshan's operating costs (Singhal and Rogers 1989: 79).[1]

Undoubtedly the drive for the increased rate of commercialization – indeed privatization – of Doordarshan has come from a government anxious to reduce its funding commitment from transnational corporations, their Indian subsidiaries, and local companies interested in expanding their markets, and from programme producers. For Bombay film producers adversely affected by the expansion of television audiences and intense competition in the industry, there are definite advantages in producing programmes for Doordarshan: 'there is relatively less financial risk in producing television serials, as eager commercial sponsors are plentiful, and problems with box office sales, film distribution, and piracy do not exist' (Singhal and Rogers 1989: 83).

In the late 1980s the commercialization of Doordarshan and AIR had reached the stage where proposals for greater autonomy were being advanced and a bill introduced in the Lok Sabha. Many critics were somewhat sceptical of the meaning of the proposed autonomy. Under the Rajiv Gandhi administration the electronic media were used for party propaganda purposes (Singh 1990); the distinction between party and government at times was a blurred one. Shortly before the end of his administration a number of news programmes tested the limits of new-found freedom. In the bill a two-tier structure for Doordarshan was introduced which consisted of a board of governors and a watchdog broadcasting council. Financial control remains vested in government which retains the right to issue directives to make or prevent any broadcast 'in the interests of security of the state or preservation of public order' or 'on any matter of public importance'. The government resisted pressures to go further along the privatization route by invoking familiar arguments about problems of development, unity and national order, as well as the dangerous promotion of a consumer ethos which cannot be sustained by current production levels and uneven distribution. According to Singh (1990: 129), however, the major obstacle to greater autonomy for the electronic media, and privatization, is that 'whatever the party in power, control of the electronic media is too valuable a weapon to give away'.

CHINA: STATE, PARTY, AND MEDIA

In India the electronic media, as part of the apparatus of state, have been strongly subject to ruling-party intervention in their operation. In China perhaps the most significant feature of the post-revolutionary period has been the dominance of the Communist Party in the operation of the mass media. Indeed, party control of the media has been an important weapon in factional fights, and used against what has often been seen as the inertia and reactionary character of the state apparatus.

For Mao the function of the mass media was to publicize party decisions, educate the masses, and forge a link between the party and the masses (J. Chu 1978: 22). Maoist conceptions exercised a decisive influence on the mass media in three basic ways: first, through an emphasis on anti-intellectualism and mass mobilization which stressed the basic importance of face-to-face contact with the masses (Liu 1971: 44); second, through an anti-professional ideology which stressed the importance of the journalist as an agent in the Communist Party's struggle to achieve revolutionary transformation; and third, through an early stress on a 'united front' doctrine which 'legitimized the formal existence of a nonparty press' (Liu 1971: 44). The party's role in the translation of policies into the action of masses required that the mass media be run by the whole party, and not just a cadre of professional journalists whose values of practice might clash with this basic role (J. Chu 1978: 23).

Within the actual structure of the Chinese press there was a functional division between newspapers published by political organizations (the Communist Party), mass organizations, and public institutions such as schools and factories. The most authoritative and highest official newspaper, the *People's Daily*, is an organ of the Central Committee of the Communist Party. This paper, which represents political authority, provides the general ideological parameters within which the rest of the press and mass media operate.

The rationale for the separation of the party, with its crucial role in mass media, and the state, resided in the revolutionary role of the party and the concern to establish its hegemony. State institutions would ultimately become ossified, even counter-revolutionary, and would have to be subject to constant pressure by party forces. The Cultural Revolution could be seen as part of a campaign by the party, or at least factions within it, to purge the state apparatus, as well as the party, of counter-revolutionary forces. As such it hit the press, and more generally media and cultural production, very hard. Mao placed much of the responsibility for the failure of the press basically to change the psychology of the Chinese people on the shoulders of professional party propagandists and journalists (Liu 1971: 54).

One of the very distinctive features of post-revolutionary Chinese communications is the way, and extent to which, a good many traditional folk forms have been utilized, along with modern mass media, to contribute to political mobilization and the development of appropriate socialist forms of consciousness. The traditional folk forms were used principally because they were so firmly rooted in the life and cultural experiences of the vast majority of Chinese and lent themselves to incorporation in modern communications media (traditional and revolutionary opera, and revolutionary songs, for example). Traditional folk tales, popular drama and folk songs have been adapted and replaced by media created and controlled by the Communist Party – revolutionary opera, children's songs, picture books and short stories, and *tatzepao* (Poon 1978). These forms are not alternative simply because they are part of the overall apparatus of party and state communications. They certainly reflect and express some of the deeper cultural and political struggles marking the post-revolutionary period, including the fall from grace of particular party leaders. Such media are popular, rather than folk, since they are actively propagated by the party. Their content reflects the party's ideological orientation, although there is considerable input from the grass roots level in the actual production process (G. Chu 1978: 5).

The Cultural Revolution had a profound impact on the content of such forms, as well as to some extent on the forms themselves. Much of the debate surrounding them, and their condemnation, centred first on the extent to which the forms were products of previous historical eras – feudalism, and the bourgeois order – and somehow expressed their social relations, and second, on the extent to which by taking traditional themes and characters they were merely promoting reactionary and anti-socialist tendencies.[2]

The Chinese broadcasting system has been organized under the control of the Department of Propaganda of the Communist Party Central Committee (J. Chu 1978: 23). The Department operates through divisions in every regional, provincial, and local branch of the Communist Party and governmental agencies in charge of cultural and educational affairs. There was an early recognition of the importance of radio as an instrument of mass education and mobilization. It could bypass major problems of shortages of newspapers, illiteracy, and distribution (J. Chu 1978: 27). Radio-receiver networks were organized in the early 1950s, and used in conjunction with *tatzepao* (big-character posters or wall newspapers) and mimeographed sheets for public meetings. Also, as part of the monitoring system, the Chinese developed 'wired broadcasting networks' along the lines of the Soviet Union's radio-diffusion exchange system. These networks involved the installation everywhere of loudspeakers and collective listening (J. Chu 1978: 27–8). However, after the failure of the Great Leap Forward movement in 1959 the development of the wired broadcast systems came to a standstill and the emphasis shifted to 'expert-operated broadcasting' policy (J. Chu 1978: 29).

During the Cultural Revolution, radio, along with other media, was initially an important arena of struggle between the Maoist and anti-Maoist factions. Maoists expressed concern that the media were becoming influenced by professional ideologues who were helping to sever the special relationship between the party and the masses (J. Chu 1978: 31). The appearance after 1961 of political criticism in short stories and plays in the party-controlled newspapers and journals was particularly disturbing. In the early stages of the Cultural Revolution, when many newspapers and journals were in the hands of the pro-Liu Shao-chi faction, the Maoists had recourse to radio and to *tatzepao* to rally support amongst the masses (J. Chu 1978: 31).

After Vice-Premier Den Xiaping's rise to power, and the establishment of new economic and political priorities, the functions of the mass media expanded beyond the original mobilization role to include advertising, entertainment, and a coverage of news which was 'decidedly more Western in approach' (Robinson 1981: 58). While the media remained concerned with socialist transformation, the creation of a classless society, and general improvements in the economy, they became more geared to producing higher standards of living through increases in productivity.

For some analysts the media have been used to facilitate the rapid move of China towards a consumer society. Central to this has been television which was inaugurated in May 1958 in Beijing and gradually spread to other urban areas and to the provinces. Its programming was limited in terms of hours of transmission and content which was almost exclusively news, revolutionary ballet, and film. The concern of government was that people should buy not only sets (sales increased dramatically) but also the products advertised on them. Certainly Chinese leaders have not been unmindful of the relationship between production, marketing, and consumption (Robinson 1981: 65). There has been recognition of the relationship between media content and the attraction of audiences, with the result that the media which carry advertising are those providing popular entertainment (Robinson 1981: 67–8). This is the case with radio, the press, and especially television whose programming has increasingly taken on the structure characteristic of media in advanced capitalist society, even to the extent of some shift in the nature of news construction and presentation (Robinson 1981: 71).

THE STATE AND COMMUNICATIONS IN
LATIN AMERICA: BRAZIL AND MEXICO

In the early years after the introduction of radio broadcasting, throughout Latin America there was a good deal of experimentation with its organizational forms: Fox (1988b: 173) notes that 'there appears to have been . . . a wide variety of different models and experiments with policies and structures of broadcasting and cultural institutions, many of which were short-lived or rapidly absorbed into a commercial system'. Some of this experimentation produced the limited adoption of national public broadcasting structures, although the public service model of broadcasting never really took hold anywhere. In Mexico there were efforts after the Mexican revolution, when the Revolutionary Party dominated the government, to provide radio with a major role in the promotion of social change and the implementation of national development goals. Where experimentation with public broadcasting occurred outside the increasingly dominant commercial media interests, it generally came under a direct state control (Fox 1988: 174). This control was vested in the executive branch and not in a 'relatively autonomous' form of public control, as for example in the case of the BBC or an independent broadcasting authority. Without media institutions which stood outside direct executive state control, governments, whatever their political complexion (democratic, dictatorial, military) felt no compunction in directly intervening in the media.[3] The 'liberal' free-press tradition established in the early twentieth century was used by commercial media interests, including foreign ones predominantly from the United States, to oppose the development and introduction of public service broadcasting, and the development of different types of broadcasting structures.

Latin American countries are obviously to be distinguished from the vast majority, if not all, of the rest of the countries designated as 'Third World' by a number of salient factors which profoundly affected their cultural and mass media development. First, they had substantial, urban-based populations, which were highly literate and predominantly of European origin. Second, the literate 'middle class' and professional strata were able to sustain high levels of literary production and contribute to modern intellectual and artistic movements which, while often nationalistic, were nevertheless strongly linked to contemporary intellectual developments in Europe in particular. Fox (1988b: 172) notes that in Peru by 1928 there were 'eighty-eight literary and artistic newspapers registered'.

Third, there were strongly entrenched European high cultural practices which helped condition the attitudes of the intelligentsia and the bourgeoisie and middle-class strata to the role of the mass media; as in Europe, many saw the new broadcasting media not as mere vehicles for popular entertainment, but as providing opportunities for the extension of the cultural practices and critical traditions with which they were so closely identified. Fourth, the urban, literate strata provided the readership (they were also the source of advertising revenue) for a vigorous press which was influenced by the liberal 'free'-press tradition of the early twentieth century (Fox 1988b: 172). Newspapers, certainly in countries such as Peru, were often aligned with, or were the mouthpieces of, different political factions, and usually in a more subtle way, lent support for the 'traditional oligarchy' or ruling classes (Fox 1988b: 172). Fifth, by the beginning of the twentieth century most Latin American countries had experienced at least some industrialization and manifested much more differentiated economic structures than those in Africa (Egypt and South Africa being possible exceptions), most of Asia, and the Middle East. This economic development was skewed in favour of a small minority in the urban-industrial areas, and wealthy landed interests, leaving the vast majority of people in comparative poverty. For some economists this represented the continuation of a dual economy consisting of an advanced, modern capitalist sector and a backward, essentially subsistence sector largely outside capitalist social relations – often misleadingly referred to as the cash–subsistence economy dichotomy. It was clearly not that since there had been a 'progressive' incorporation of the vast majority of people into some paid wage labour and capitalist social relations of production. The pursuit of import substitution and consumer goods production gained momentum in the late 1920s as the depression set in, and increased during World War II when Latin American countries could no longer depend on the supply of manufactured goods from Europe and the United States (Fox 1988b: 174).

Dependency writers such as Frank saw this type of industrialization as only possible at a time of weakened metropolitan dominance, as for example during global depression or war. The growth of national industry and advertising, combined with the expansion of urban markets in particular, produced a changed environment for Latin American magazines, films, and radio – one which differed in significant ways from that which had supported early twentieth-century experimentation in film and radio, and supported the literary and intellectual culture. The expanding industrial labour force, which in countries such as Argentina, Brazil and Mexico was often organized by populist movements and ruling parties, provided a new, larger market for the consumer goods and mass media industries. It seldom, as Fox (1988b: 174) notes, 'pushed for structural changes in ownership or content'.

During this period of industrialization and expansion of the mass media there was little pressure from any significant political quarter for the formulation and implementation of a media policy concerned with wider goals of social and cultural development. State policy towards the private media was supportive in the sense that there was provision of communication infrastructure and electrification, as well as credits, which subsidized the national expansion of private media monopolies.

After some limited and sporadic flirtation with public sector model broadcasting, Latin American media, with few exceptions, became privately owned and controlled. The private ownership of the newspaper press was carried over into both radio and television. In this respect the history and nature of Latin American mass communications stand in sharp contrast to elsewhere in the 'Third World' where public ownership has been a key feature. Throughout much of Africa – Egypt, South Africa, Nigeria, and perhaps Kenya represent exceptions – conditions were not suitable for private capital investment in, and development of, the media. In such circumstances the state had to assume increasing responsibility for the funding and provision of the mass media, whether the newspaper press or electronic media, although in many instances state-owned media are partly dependent on advertising revenue from state departments, parastatal organizations, and private companies. The almost complete dominance of state ownership and control does not mean that public service models of broadcasting have been accepted, if we are thinking of media institutions with a 'relative autonomy' to pursue and operate with charters, which are not immediately subject to direct state or government ownership and control. Media institutions are expected, of course, to contribute to the realization of cultural, economic and social goals which are part of national development or nation-building. Such goals, however, are rarely open to question, and in actual practice usually mean little more than lack of opposition to, or criticism of, the policies of the particular regimes in power.

LATIN AMERICAN STATE INTERVENTION: CENSORSHIP

Until the 1970s, and indeed since then, state intervention in the mass media in Latin America took an essentially erratic course. It consisted of a somewhat unpredictable censorship which reflected the insecurity of those holding state power, and the constant struggle between different fractions of capital, and the different factions within the military.

A favourable context for the 'commercial and frequently transnational expansion of the mass media' was created by the alliance of centralist states and private media owners who had no reason to challenge government policy or the aims of United States investors (Fox 1988b: 174–5). Indeed, private media owners were unfettered in their expansion by government regulation and the constraints and commitments imposed by public service obligations. In a number of Latin American countries, in a climate of all-pervasive undemocratic and corrupt politics, the growing media monopolies were able to become increasingly important 'autonomous' entrepreneurial and political actors (Fox 1988b: 175; Guimarães and Amaral 1988). While Latin American states provided support for the expansion of private media monopolies, they did little, if anything, to protect local production and support particular forms of national cultural expression. Local markets were not protected from imported films, recordings, television series, and magazines and comics which came mainly from the United States. In order to survive local radio stations, magazines and films were forced to respond by engaging in increasingly bland, standardized forms of production designed to tap a mass audience. The economics of media production and distribution were such that it was cheaper and more profitable for Latin American media proprietors to attract large audiences with 'bland, standardized and frequently imported content' (Fox 1988b: 175). The types of television programmes imported – United States action adventures and light-comedy programmes – attracted large audiences and, largely devoid of social criticism, 'seldom caused problems with the government' (Fox 1988b: 175).

During the 1940s and 1950s the Latin American liberal democratic and reactionary civilian and military regimes rarely included mass media production in their programmes of support and protection for national culture and the arts. Where state subsidy and protection of national cultural production occurred it was invariably bound up with rank political opportunism couched in nationalistic terms.

The development of private media monopolies in Latin America occurred in a context of increasing United States influence which had been growing since World War I. In the inter-war period the consolidation of American economic and security interests in the region occurred through the 'good neighbour' policy and the Inter-American system. After World War II this influence was greatly extended and linked with opposition to communism. A strong network of military, commercial, and development ties was established between the United States and Latin American countries. While there had been United States investment in Latin America prior to the war, after World War II the scale increased enormously, and there was a significant upsurge in the distribution of American magazines, comics, and news services (Fox 1988: 176). This increased American investment included investments by United States television networks in the commercial television systems of almost every Latin American country, as well as a considerable increase in the number of American films, television series, magazines and records (Fox 1988: 176).

By the end of the 1950s the extension of United States influence into private mass communications was accompanied by the promotion of development communications. As we have already seen, modernization theory embraced as a key component a diffusion model of communication in which the penetration of the 'traditional' hinterlands was to be achieved using modern communications technologies. In Latin America, and elsewhere throughout the 'Third World', development programmes of agricultural extension, health and education were predicated on particular communications technologies and models of diffusion. Under the influence of this essentially American-derived model, and mindful of the growing economic and social disparities in the region, Latin American governments embarked on the setting up of formal organizations designed to spread developmental, educational messages to urban and rural audiences. Significantly, this state involvement in the extension of development communications did not in any way involve the commercial mass media which were largely absolved from responsibility for the meeting of public service obligations (Fox 1988b: 176).

Many of the initiatives associated with the development of the concept of a New World or International Information Order – the development of national media and communications policies, and the restructuring or reorganization of the press and broadcasting

during the 1970s – emanated from Latin America. Not unexpectedly, vigorous, uncompromising, almost unanimous opposition to
mass media reform and debate on national communications policies
came from private radio and television proprietors, and newspaper
owners and advertisers. They were anxious to prevent changes such
as had occurred in Cuba after the revolution, in Chile under the
Allende government, and in Peru after the military coup, and
concerned that changes such as those proposed in Mexico and
Venezuela should not be implemented (Fox 1988a: 24).

A multiplicity of forces contributed to the pressures for the
reform of Latin American mass media. The industrialization and
economic change of the post-World War II period brought basic
changes in social relations, including class, increased and exacerbated cultural and social inequalities, and contributed to growing
political unrest. The new urban populations, so important in providing an audience for the expanding mass media monopolies, were
more volatile than in the past and represented a new type of political
constituency. Throughout Latin America dissident groups committed to revolutionary struggle and change were formed. In many
countries (Bolivia and Uruguay, for example) urban and rural
guerrilla movements developed, a host of revolutionary theorists
appeared (Regis Debray, Che Guevara), and political movements
based on alliances between urban dissidents and sections of the
urban and rural labouring classes emerged to challenge the previously politically dominant fractions. The Cuban revolution
provided the new forms of popular movement with an ideal of
radical structural change, although the adoption of a strategy of
revolutionary change based on the Cuban experience was to prove
disastrous in many instances (Bolivia, for example).

Important shifts in American policy occurred in the wake of the
Cuban revolution and the rise of new, popularly based movements.
Anti-communism remained fundamental to United States policy,
but there was a shift in emphasis which was expressed, for example,
in the Alliance for Progress, and in political and financial support
for educational and agrarian reform and other programmes (introduction of progressive income tax) designed to reduce social
inequalities and reduce the pressure for more radical social
transformation. Pressures for change also came from other direc-
tions. The Catholic Church, strongly anti-communist in orientation
and usually closely identified with ruling oligarchies, also underwent transformation as the influence of new philosophies and

Christian social movements took hold. Divisions within the church were deep and became exacerbated as some sections became much more closely identified with popular movements committed to far-reaching changes and were anxious to participate in the determination of national development policy. The Church's radio and other communications networks in many instances provided the basis of alternative media for the rural and urban labouring classes, the peasantry, and the lumpenproletariat.

The convergence of these forces helped to provoke a basic reconsideration of the role of the mass media in structural reform. The importance attached to communications was undoubtedly partly due to an enormous expansion of the private, commercial media monopolies, as well as increased investment in telecommunications and other information technologies. Many Latin American intellectuals and analysts of the mass media – some of them closely identified with radical social movements, and most operating within a radical dependency perspective – were vigorous in their call for a structural transformation of the media (Fox 1988b: 177). Media reform proposals were incorporated in the programmes of structural change of some social movements, political parties, and church-led organizations.

The reforms which were instituted by a number of Latin American governments hardly met the demands of the more vigorous reformers. As Fox (1988b: 178) observes, such reforms as were carried out were 'top heavy' and 'government-oriented' and could not meet the calls for a greater decentralization and democratization, simply because they would have placed the control of the mass media in the hands of grass roots and radical social movements. The public sector was viewed by most of the reformers as the principal author of cultural policies, which meant that the basic problem of the structure and role of the private mass media was not directly addressed. Where it was, it usually led to authoritarian interventions such as occurred in Peru between 1968 and 1975. Gargúrevich and Fox's (1988) analysis suggests that the Peruvian media reformers lacked the political, financial and technical means to put into effect fully the proposed measures of social ownership.

In Mexico the focus of media reforms in the 1970s was on the recovery of the social and political accountability of the mass media and making them more accessible to ruling-party pressures (Fox 1988b: 179). The political and social reforms proposed by the Mexican government, which were aimed at accommodating 'new

social and political groups in the system', required some severing of
the traditional ties with the private media as well as the establishment of new state channels of communication. In order to meet the
challenge posed by the expanding private mass media and telecommunications industries (Mahan 1985), the Mexican government
emphasized the expansion of government-owned media and the
constitutional right to information. The government effort, however, foundered on the mobilized opposition of entrenched private
media interests and groups within government (Fox 1988b: 179).
While Mexico's

> more haphazard planning process resulted in enormous publicly
> supported media operations that provided coverage to areas
> otherwise ignored by the media (and alternatives in populous
> areas), its single comprehensive communication development
> plan was destroyed by its radical political character. The plan was
> designed to harness private media in support of the state's social
> objectives and, not surprisingly, it was bitterly opposed by the
> private, commercial media.
>
> (Gardner and Stevenson 1988: 2)

As with so many instances of proposals for media restructuring, the
reformers were pushing for greater public participation when such
participation and accountability were not present in either government or the capitalist economy. In Kaplan's (1988) assessment, the
ruling party was hardly in a condition to absorb the greater popular
participation envisaged in its media policies.

LATIN AMERICAN MILITARY REGIMES AND
THE MASS MEDIA

The new military regimes which came to power in the 1960s and
1970s used an increasingly autocratic state apparatus to carry out
their programmes of 'economic development'. Technocrats worked
in close collaboration with transnational corporations. As many
commentators have noted, these regimes, often through the mass
media, sought to exploit national and modernizing symbols, and
manipulated education for such purposes. The military dictatorships established firm controls over the mass media while providing
conditions for their expansion. The mass media were used to
'control public and private information and communication' (Fox
1988a: 26). Private television and radio stations were placed under

tight political control. Newspapers and magazines were censored, and journalists were intimidated, arrested, and even killed.

For the military rulers the mass media, with their sophisticated new techniques and large-scale organization, fitted in very well with their technocratic vision, and were well suited to their propaganda and information-control goals. Although the state controls over the mass media were tight, the economic policies pursued by the military dictatorships were conducive to the rapid development and further transnationalization of the media. Military rulers grasped that new communications/telecommunications technologies were fundamental to economic development, the furtherance of military power, and state surveillance and control of the civilian population. Their substantial investments in such technologies, combined with an often dramatic increase in advertising expenditure (after the military coups in Chile and Argentina, government expenditure on advertising increased by as much as 60 per cent), gave private broadcasting companies, and some newspapers, an enormous boost (Fox 1988a: 26).

At one level the mass media were major beneficiaries of military dictatorships and the economic policies pursued by them. The mass media, however, were caught in a major contradiction: on the one hand they were of fundamental importance in the maintenance of military dictatorship through their role in the manipulation of symbols of nationalism and economic development; on the other, they were a site for conflict. The latter, understood by some in Althusserian terms of conflict within an ideological state apparatus, embraced competing capitals as well as labour and other forces pushing for redemocratization. In Brazil the major private media corporations such as TV Globo were ultimately identified with the forces pushing for redemocratization, strongly supporting moves for full presidential elections against the direct wishes of the military rulers. The TV Globo media empire, which was put together during the period of military rule in Brazil, had emerged by the mid-1980s as a major 'independent' political force able to exert considerable pressure on the military regime through its support for civilian political forces (Guimarães and Amaral 1988).

CONCLUSION

The analysis of the state and communications has to move beyond a simple instrumentalist, radical dependency position, in which the state is seen as a major instrument of metropolitan capitalist interests involved in the reproduction of dominant social and cultural relations, to the recognition of the complexity of indigenous class and other forces in the determination of the nature of the state and state policy. State policy in the case of media and communications normally takes a multiplicity of forms, including direct ownership, which are more expressive of internal relations and contradictions than of the relations between advanced capitalist economies, their transnational communications, advertising, and other corporations, and 'Third World' societies. State broadcasting policies and organizational arrangements are always subject to, or provide an arena for, competing interests. For example, the strong pressures for the commercialization and privatization of Doordarshan in India are expressions of the extent to which manufacturing production has moved into a substantial consumer phase, as well as the effective creation of a vast television-consuming public with disposable income and a propensity to spend. As the Brazilian television example attests, the major role in the determination of state media policy can be captured by concentrated capitalist interests in both opposition to, and alliance with, international media and other interests; a reliance on advertising revenue from overseas-based transnational corporations does not alter this, even if it does have a strong bearing on programming policy.

Whereas in Latin American countries the operation of mass media has generally been the sphere of private capital, in African and Asian countries state intervention has taken the predominant form of government ownership of broadcast media in particular; where, as in the case of newspapers, there has been some private ownership, often very strict controls in the form of licensing, prohibition, censorship, and selective withholding of advertising have operated. Throughout Africa, media and advertising markets have with only a few exceptions been able to sustain private ownership of media. However, in countries such as Kenya and Nigeria, private ownership of tightly state-controlled print media has been characteristic, and state-owned television has come under considerable privatization pressure from an alliance of local and international capitalist interests.

Chapter 5

The new international information order

Until the mid-1960s the emphasis in the United Nations, and in UNESCO in particular, was on both the 'free flow of information' and the use of mass media in building 'modern' societies in the 'Third World'. By the mid-1960s, however, widespread, increasingly shrill criticism had developed of what appeared to be the overwhelming dominance of western mass media and news agencies over the 'Third World'. The shift was a reflection of both the changing composition of the membership of the United Nations, with the almost dramatic influx of new member countries from independent Africa, and the call for the creation of a 'New World Economic Order' (NWEO) in which many of the obstacles to 'Third World' economic development would be removed. The call for a New World Information Order, issued almost simultaneously with that for the new economic order, amounted to a demand for the more equitable distribution of resources between the advanced countries and those of the 'Third World' very much along the lines of NWEO proposals.

Several key issues have dominated the debate about the New International Information Order (NIIO). One has been the flow of information between western capitalist societies and the former socialist societies of Eastern Europe and the Soviet Union. A second has been the imbalance in flow between North, understood as the industrialized, predominantly capitalist, information-rich, and South, understood as 'Third World' countries. Within these two major areas of contention there have been three principal areas of complaint: first, the imbalance of flow between East and West, and North and South; second, the content of the flow in each direction; and third, the control of the flow of information. The complaints have invariably been couched in cultural and media imperialist terms, with the United States domination of media and communications production under attack. Anglo-American news agencies – AAP, UPI, Reuters – along with the largest suppliers of news film – Visnews, UPITN, and CBS – which are also Anglo-American, have been identified as of fundamental importance to the imbalance, content, and control of international information flow (Masmoudi 1979: 172–3) and thus central to cultural imperialism.

Critics of the old international information order have condemned the dominant role western media have played in news definition, which has been seen by them as distorting and excluding authentic cultural values and expression in 'Third World' countries. The cultures of such countries have been presented to the rest of the world through western filters which have effectively excluded much of the world not of immediate interest to them (Stevenson and Cole 1984: 7–8). The information from 'Third World' countries which does get into the world news system emphasizes their fragility, instability and corruption, and serves to provide the erroneous view that their economic backwardness is due to internal failure rather than their subjection to European colonialism and neo-colonial forces. The distorted, negative treatment of 'Third World' countries which appears in western media is ultimately transferred to them through their dependence on the major western news agencies; in other words, for images of their own societies, people in 'Third World' countries are dependent on the news agencies and mass media of the advanced capitalist countries especially. The distorted, negative treatment fosters the neglect of 'development news' which may provide a more accurate indication of the various programmes designed to produce economic and social change. Whereas in advanced capitalist societies such as the United States it is possible to have media institutions which are frequently, if only mildly, critical of government, and which are so enmeshed in the basic institutions of economy and society that they contribute in major ways to their reproduction, in 'Third World' countries governments have to control the media for basic development purposes, including the definition of what that development is.

By the mid-1970s the governments and major media interests of most of the advanced capitalist countries were actively opposed to the gathering momentum of the call for a new information order.

Both the 1974 and 1976 UNESCO General Conferences avoided a definitive declaration on the role of the mass media because

most of the western nations . . . would not accept language that incorporated the idea of state responsibility for the mass media.
(Stevenson and Cole 1984: 5)

This partly expressed the continuing influence of the United States, which had previously been dominant in the determination of UNESCO policy, as well as the deeply ingrained, historically founded opposition to greater state intervention in the mass media.

The MacBride Commission report (International Commission for the Study of Communication Problems; MacBride 1980) recognized the need for improving the balance of international communications while at the same time endorsing traditional principles such as a 'free flow of information'.

According to Pendakur,

the energy, the vitality, and the confrontational character of the NIIO debates have been redefined by the US and its supporters into IPDC (International Program for the Development of Communication) as 'a mechanism', selling 'practical solutions to information and communications imbalance'.
(Pendakur 1983: 398)

Unable to win support for an autonomous body independent of UNESCO, the United States, working through its western allies and some moderates of the non-aligned group, was able to restrict emphasis to communications infrastructural development, involving technical assistance, while preserving the 'free-flow' principle (Pendakur 1983: 399). United States policy towards IPDC was designed to weaken the position of the 'Third World' countries which formed the majority of its Intergovernmental Council and to ensure that United States corporations had access to communications development and markets in 'Third World' countries. In addition, there was concern that IPDC funds should be made available to capitalist interests in 'Third World' countries who wanted to build private and not state monopoly media in them. The United States push for the funding of bilateral 'aid' projects was designed to keep them under direct control, in sharp contrast to IPDC projects which were multilateral.

Under the Reagan administration the United States pushed for 'a bigger role for the private sector at the financing end as well as at the receiving end'. This policy, Pendakur notes, was consistent with both the increased provision of opportunities for American transnational corporation exploitation of 'Third World' markets, and the weakening of the power of 'Third World' countries in multilateral agencies such as UNESCO and the IPDC by reducing financial participation – indeed the United States ultimately withdrawing from UNESCO (Pendakur 1983: 401). The former could be seen in the context of strong pressures for the deregulation of both domestic and international communications markets, as well as part of a much longer-term pressure on public broadcasting and telecom- munications authorities to privatize (Greenberg 1985; Roach 1987).

The international information trade is characterized by its dual economic and cultural impact (Collins *et al.* 1988: 50). Frequently this duality is blurred, with the cultural impact seen as having major implications for the economic: particular types of information flows carry with them models of economic development, including con- sumption preferences, which critics contend help produce further subordination of the weaker or 'dependent' economies. Local or national cultural and information production is often facilitated by state intervention on a combination of cultural and economic grounds (Brazil, for example). The development of a local film or television production industry is necessary to preserve, or to con- struct, national cultural identity and to represent it internationally; the state assistance which facilitates this – import quotas, tariffs, taxation concessions, subsidies, direct state intervention in produc- tion – is often justified on economic rather than cultural grounds, that is, a fledgling industry will be allowed to mature under pro- tected conditions so that it will be able to compete nationally with imports and 'compete internationally unprotected by subsidy or quota and make a return to investors' (Collins *et al.* 1988: 52). The intervention of cultural and linguistic factors, for example the concern of the non-Anglophones for the survival of their languages, as well as state support for the development of local programme production which may serve indigenous capitalist interests, poses problems for the application of absolute and comparative advantage concepts to cultural production. On strict economic criteria it would be advantageous for most countries to rely on imported television programmes and not engage in domestic production where costs could not be amortised in the domestic market.

While much of the 'Third World' preoccupation has been with the cultural ramifications of the international information trade, more recently it has shifted to the economic implications of trans- border data flows in particular. This shift reflects not only implications for employment in the information/data processing

industries (information production, storage, retrieval, distribution), but also the recognition of the centrality of information to
production, distribution, marketing, accounting, administration,
financing, research and development.

The growth of the international information economy for many
represents a challenge to, and places limits on, national sovereignty.

> The threat to communications sovereignty latent since the begin-
> ning of the twentieth century has, with the triple impact of new
> distribution technologies, new ideologies of deregulation and the
> accelerating demand for high-budget but low-cost software be-
> come a matter for general concern.
>
> (Collins *et al.* 1988: 56)

The expansion of capital accumulation on a global scale has increasingly challenged the ability of national governments to control
economies which are subject to constant shifts in the flow of capital,
fluctuations in exchange rates, and alterations in demand and price
for commodities on international markets. Legislation defining
national ownership and control in the economic sphere is constantly
challenged when corporations legally defined as 'national' accumulate capital through international circuits and often raise their funds
for 'national investment' through international financial institutions. Certainly the shift towards an international information
economy has made national boundaries largely irrelevant, with
nation-states generally unable to control information movements
and the types of information being disseminated effectively (Langdale 1987: 140). In relation to this Collins *et al* (1988: 81–2) note
that 'culture and cultural production are international phenomena,
and the political institutions of the nation-state are highly imperfect
tools through which these practices and activities can be controlled
and regulated'.

National sovereignty is usually understood in two broad senses.
In the legal sense it refers to the legal powers which a state has to
exercise legal jurisdiction over a specific tract of territory and to
control national policies. In the second, and broader sense, it refers
to a country's ability to influence the direction of its political,
economic, social and cultural change (Langdale 1987: 140). This
involves attempts to restrict citizens from undesirable, negative
external influence, as well as more positively allowing national
economic, cultural and social policies to be formulated and implemented. For many 'Third World' countries the issue of national

sovereignty tends to be much more pressing than it is for the older states of the advanced capitalist world. Some critics concede that 'the impact of western culture on other societies is often disturbing' but view much of the opposition to it on religious, moral, and cultural grounds as essentially conservative. They suggest that underlying the critique of the loss of national sovereignty through the internationalization of communications is a qualitative assumption that somehow 'the new order and its products are inferior to the old' (Collins *et al.* 1988: 58). It may be the case that internationalization represents a progressive and liberating force: 'At the micro level there are many cases in which the freedom, welfare and contentment of individuals are sustained and extended by the contestation of the authority and hegemony of the nation-state and the national culture' (Collins *et al.* 1988: 58).

In Africa in particular, many countries represent a somewhat fragile association of peoples with quite distinct histories, ethnic origins, and languages, brought together under a single administration by European colonial powers. The post-colonial period has often been marked by fragmentary tendencies and secessionist movements exacerbated by the uneven nature of change throughout the colonial and post-colonial periods, state policies which have been seen as disadvantaging, even disenfranchising particular ethnic, religious, and language groups, and the often desperate struggle for control of the state apparatus. In some countries, secessionist movements, or movements for national self-determination, have been fostered and encouraged by external powers (for example Angola and Mozambique), or civil insurrection aimed at producing regimes more amenable to foreign powers. Such problems are exacerbated by the fact that independence from European colonial powers has been quite recent and yet has done little to reduce the vulnerability to external economic, political, military and cultural forces which seem to undermine the very basis of the claims for independence and national sovereignty. Development is 'dependent' on incorporation into economic relations with, and the flow of information from, advanced capitalist economies which only seems to deepen their subordination to them.

EUROPEAN COLONIALISM AND INTERNATIONAL COMMUNICATIONS

European colonialism during the nineteenth century and the first decades of the twentieth century was crucial in the establishment of the international lines of communication: these lines included trans-oceanic cables and the European wire service cartels, and subsequently radio broadcasts. More generally the basic international and national communications routes established throughout this period (sea and air routes, as well as roads and railways in colonial countries) served to facilitate the flow of manufactured goods to colonies and markets in Africa, Asia, and Latin America, and raw materials and agricultural commodities from them to the metropolitan powers in Europe and North America. Although their development was often quite haphazard, the communications systems were designed to link metropolitan centres such as Britain and France with their colonies (useful for political, administrative, trade and military purposes) and those areas which were important for trade and capital investment purposes (various parts of Latin America, for example). At a much later stage, certainly after formal decolonization, satellite communications were added to the international lines of communication, reflecting in part the desire of the United States to break some of the dominance established by the European colonial powers, and Britain in particular, in terrestrial and oceanic communications.

The evolution of the major international news agencies (AP, UPI, Reuters, AFP – formerly Havas, and Tass) is inextricably linked with imperial and post-imperial competition in the nineteenth century (Smith 1980: 73). The great powers – Britain, France, Germany, the United States, Russia – sought to 'spread their news networks throughout the areas of their economic and political suzerainty'. The expansion of agencies such as Reuters was clearly driven by the need to spread networks of information into as many politically and economically important regions as possible, even when this involved the supervision of the construction of cable systems. While driven by commercial competition, the agencies were also constrained by government control and pressure and generally acted in accordance with imperial interests.

The development of the international news agencies, as well as the overall network of international information flows, was not simply the outcome of capital expansion; it was also an important part of that expansion. As a mode of production with particular financial and productive arrangements, capitalism's development required internationalization and the integration of previously un-exploited regions into a single market in which companies, financial institutions, transportation methods, social classes, and stock markets were locked into complicated, contradictory, and inter-dependent relationships. At the heart of capitalism

> there had to be information, for the central concept of capitalism is the market and, in a global system, physical markets have to be replaced by national or vicarious markets in which prices and values are assessed through the distribution of regular reliable information. The communications network which grew up in the nineteenth century was one outcome of the imperial system, by which competing capitalist powers fought for more of the world in which to operate a privileged trading system; at the same time, the information network was a fundamental support for the development of international capitalism itself – it was, that is, both the cause and result of capitalism.
>
> (Smith 1980: 74)

Tunstall (1977: 44) notes that 'international arrangements for con-tracting the trade in news had been established long before 1920'. The international news agency was the principal instrument of international news trading. By 1870 the British agency Reuters and the French agency Havas were the dominant exporters, with all other countries essentially being their customers. The newspapers of South America were completely dependent on Havas until the 1920s for 'the whole flow of news from the outside world' (Smith 1980: 70). Importers were of course most likely to be national agencies which could be controlled by governments through a variety of indirect means so that the news which reached the domestic press was highly selective. It was hardly surprising that great financial, diplomatic, and imperial nations such as Britain and France 'should dominate the world wholesaling of news'. Germany, as a rapidly rising industrial and political power, was able to break into the cartel with 'its own special area in Scandinavia and Russia' (Tunstall 1977: 44).

Early British and French domination of the international dis-semination of news meant that it acquired 'a strong flavour of free trade' (Tunstall 1977: 44). The rise of American agencies in the early twentieth century introduced greater competition and helped break down the basic imperialist pattern which had predominated.

The Havas monopoly in South America was broken in 1920 by the American United Press Association (which became UPI in 1939 after merging with another agency), which started to provide news about the United States direct to *La Prensa* of Buenos Aires and soon to other Latin American newspapers. Gradually United Press, together with its major American competitor AP (owned by the principal clients among American metropolitan dailies), established control over the Latin American news market, although Reuters remained important and the French linkage has persisted.

The Latin American press continues to draw an enormous amount of its news content from the two United States agencies (about 50 per cent), and about 10 per cent from Reuters and Agence France-Presse, the successor to Havas. News originating from 'Third World' agencies represents only a tiny percentage of the total. While there are many national news agencies in Latin America, they lack the resources to develop a continental, much less an international service of their own. LATIN operates in a number of Latin American countries, 'but it has been created by Reuters and obtains its material through Reuters' (Smith 1980: 71). Generally Latin American newspapers do not even have foreign correspondents in the capitals of neighbouring countries and rely almost completely for coverage of them on international news agencies.

Analysts note that international news agencies have developed a particular style of news, although one that necessarily reflects the demands of different national markets. Certainly critics of the agencies, and of western news media more generally, argue that the western concept of news emphasizes, in its chief selection criterion, information of 'war, crime, corruption, disorder, fire, famine and flood' (Smith 1980: 70). This serves to 'systematically distort' international knowledge of the cultural, political and economic progress of the Third World and emphasize its negative aspects. What makes this even more galling or vexatious is that 'Third World' countries are obliged to receive news of themselves through the 'distorting mechanism' of the four major western news agencies. They can turn to news agencies in the socialist world such as Tass and Novosti, Hsin Hua and Ceteka, but such agencies are hardly major sources of information about the advanced capitalist or industrialized world and operate according to political ideological criteria which are not necessarily acceptable to some 'Third World' governments (Smith 1980: 70).

The major 'Third World' initiatives have been in the setting up of alternative news exchange mechanisms (Samarajiwa 1984: 119). A clear manifestation of this was the establishment in 1975 of the Non-Aligned News Agencies Pool on the basis of the Yugoslav Tanjug pool. The News Pool was brought into existence by a decision of the Fifth Non-Aligned Summit Conference in Colombo in August 1976 in which the eighty-five nations agreed to share information from their respective agencies in order to

> achieve the broad and free circulation among themselves of news, information, reports, features and photographs about each other, and also provide objective and authentic information relating to non-aligned countries and to the rest of the world.
>
> (Quoted in Smith 1980: 105)

The expressed intention was to break down the dependence of 'Third World' countries on 'biased, inadequate and distorted information' produced in countries which dominated international news collection and flows.

Smith (1980: 105–6) wryly observes that such a declaration revealed a little insincerity when it is considered that in many countries, certainly those outside Latin America, the news from the transnational news agencies is usually thoroughly vetted by government agencies before it reaches the newspapers or radio stations of their countries.

Transnational news agencies are essentially commodity (that commodity being news) -producing and -distributing companies operating on a worldwide basis. The news with which they deal is a commodity whose significance for many 'Third World' countries derives from its political and cultural nature rather than from its commodity status. Such agencies specialize in the 'production, transmission and marketing of spot news' which ultimately flows into domestic and worldwide outlets – newspapers, radio, and television. Transnational agencies such as Reuters and UPI are characterized by maintenance of extensive worldwide communications systems which move news reports from the outer centres of their news production to processing centres and ultimately to media and other buyers throughout the world. Such agencies have high volumes of news flow, generally employ large numbers of journalists and other personnel, have high revenues, and, with the exception of Reuters, serve as domestic news agencies in their home markets as well (Samarajiwa 1984: 120–1).

News is sold to other news agencies (national as well as regional), newspapers, broadcasters, and government agencies and corporations on a continuous service rather than a news item-by-item basis. Two main types of news dominate the output of the agencies: general news items which are used as producers' goods by media organizations and specialized news reports which are usually purchased by corporations, financial institutions, foreign exchange and commodity dealers, and government agencies.

The production and distribution of information by news agencies involves a distinction between the costs of initially producing information, and getting it to the theoretical first buyer, and replication costs involving the storing, reproduction, and distribution of information. The initial, or 'first copy costs', account for between 80 and 90 per cent of the total costs of a transnational news agency (Samarajiwa 1984: 123).

AP, UPI, AFP, and Tass serve as domestic news agencies while Reuters, with its substantial ownership by the domestic news agencies of Britain, has a major indirect access to the British domestic market. The affluent domestic media markets represent the principal source of revenue for the agencies, with revenues from foreign general news sales quite small in relation to the total. This ability substantially to recoup the costs of production in large domestic markets provides the transnational agencies with considerable pricing flexibility in international markets – a situation somewhat akin to the international marketing of many American television programmes whose basic production costs have been met in the domestic market.

It is possible for transnational news agencies to provide services to newspapers in 'Third World' countries at a fraction of the cost of major domestic provision of services. The relatively low cost of the service does not represent a loss to the agency since costs have been recouped in other markets. Without such pricing discrimination many newspapers in 'Third World' countries could not afford such services. For the agencies provision of low-cost services not only contributes to overall generation of revenue, but also serves to 'shut out present or potential competition' (Samarajiwa 1984: 125). This amounts to 'dumping' of news services in many markets, including some in the advanced capitalist world. Given the nature of media funding through advertising in the advanced capitalist countries, media companies in them are generally able to expend far higher outlays on world news reports than their counterparts in 'Third World' countries.

Attempts by 'Third World' newspapers, broadcasting organizations, and governments to 'break' the dominance of the transnational news agencies essentially founder on economic grounds. The market structure and conditions of entry into worldwide production and distribution of news are such that under present conditions they have little chance of challenging this dominance successfully. The first principal barrier to entry by a newcomer in the world news market is the capital cost of establishing the production and distribution system.[1] This is dependent on substantial investment in a basic infrastructure of bureaux, correspondents and stringers, and on the development of 'an efficient, fast and reliable telecommunications system to move information from the bureaux and correspondents to the processing centre'. There is also the need for computer-based information storage and retrieval facilities at the processing centre, and an efficient system for moving processed news to buyers. On top of these costs there is the need for investment in necessary buildings and administration. The second principal economic barrier is the problem of meeting recurrent expenditure on personnel. Unlike the major news agencies – with the partial exception of Reuters – any new news agency would not be able to rely on a national market capable of providing a sustainable financial base. Samarajiwa notes that

> This market is the one with the least buying power. The extreme heterogeneity of this home market will impose additional burdens on its modest resources. If this political, cultural and linguistic heterogeneity is not catered to, the new mechanism will lose whatever hold it has on its base. In addition, dumping by established TNAs will seriously affect its ability to set realistic prices.
>
> (Samarajiwa 1984: 127)

Further, the association of new 'Third World' agencies with 'Third World' governments, whether imagined or real, would serve to discredit such a newcomer trying to break into the major news markets (the United States, for example); news emanating from such an agency would invariably be touched by a 'bias' not their own. However, it is the vertical integration of the major news agencies with their home buyers which represents the principal structural barrier to entry to the major news market. To a substantial extent the major agencies are owned and 'controlled' by these buyers. Such vertical integration basically serves to keep prices low and enable profitability at the newspaper production or broadcasting organization end to be maximized (Samarajiwa 1984: 128).

The first international news agencies, Reuters and Agence Havas, were originally specialized agencies concerned with the gathering and distribution of commercial intelligence. General news business was added as a response to the expansion of mass media production. Although specialized news gathering has continued to be an important part of the operation of the major agencies (with the exception of AFP), its importance has been reaffirmed as part of the global expansion of information industries, and especially industries specializing in the production and distribution of information commodities for business, administration, and economic and political policy-making purposes. The introduction of computer-based techniques of information production, storage, and retrieval has encouraged agencies such as Reuters to establish different types of specialist financial information services, including networking-type ones where users of the services are at the same time producers of information for the service. Such a 'diversification' into the specialized news and information business provides an additional, even lucrative source of revenue, which requires no substantial additional capital investment in production. Advanced information technology link-ups with stock markets and commodity exchanges are required but do not represent great additional costs. The greatest costs are incurred in the distribution phase where investment in computer hardware and software has to be made. Essentially, however, in the provision of these specialized services agencies such as Reuters are able to make use of the same news production structure and telecommunications system required for their general news production.[2]

'Third World' agencies could venture into the specialized field, especially through provision of news originating in the 'Third World'. There are, predicably, numerous stumbling blocks in this path: much of this type of information is already gathered and distributed through the internal international communications networks of transnational corporations (transborder data flows), through transnational advertising agencies and market research organizations, and through specialist transnational research and information distribution companies. Further, most of the key decisions regarding the world economy are taken in the advanced capitalist economies where the major specialized agencies have already established market dominance and 'tied up' the principal sources of information. 'Third World' buyers would generally be few in number and would most probably prefer to continue to use a transnational agency service on the grounds that it provides a better, more comprehensive range of information (Samarajiwa 1984: 129).

Samarajiwa notes that the negative-sanctions type stance adopted by governments and media in many 'Third World' countries, and expressed through the United Nations and its agencies such as UNESCO, does little to address the basic problem of the development of alternative news suppliers. Positive action would hinge on the establishment of higher levels of co-operation between governments and the media of different states to allow both a pooling of resources and the formation of a sufficiently large market to give them leverage in their dealings with the major transnational news agencies. Such a high level of co-operation would be difficult, if not impossible to achieve, since it is predicated on co-operation between states with quite different media systems and relations between the media and the state. In some instances the only common denominator, apart from some hostility to the major agencies and the unequal international flow of information, would be a basic suppression of the media in conformity with dominant or ruling interests. Taking as an example East Africa, it would be difficult to see how a sufficient level of co-operation and collective action on the part of the Kenyan, Tanzanian and Ugandan governments could be achieved. The notion of collective and co-operative action by governments and media in 'Third World' countries is also predicated on the assumption that they have essentially the same set of problems with regard to transnational news agencies and media from the advanced capitalist countries. This, as we have seen, is definitely not the case.

During the decade of the 1970s the role of communications in the relationship between the industrial and 'developing' worlds moved to centre stage in international conference debates (Boyd-Barrett 1981: 247). While from the 1950s concern about the international news agencies was voiced, it was relatively subdued and did not form part of a more general and coherent critique of neo-imperialism or dependency. In the 1970s, however, the criticism became more strident and theoretically informed. The critique was partly the product of the 'radicalization' of the social sciences in Europe and

North America, as well as of the development of a collective self-interest in the 'Third World'. Boyd-Barrett suggests that

> This political consolidation was achieved mainly in the non-aligned movement and the headquarters of UNESCO secretariat in Paris. It found important practical expression through the genesis of the concept of 'new information order', the establishment of the nonaligned countries news agencies' pool, and the setting up of UNESCO's International Commission for the study of Communication Problems.
>
> (Boyd-Barrett 1981: 247–8)

By the beginning of the 1980s the critical preoccupation with the international news agencies and the international flow of news had largely fizzled out. This is clearly illustrated by the report of the MacBride Commission (MacBride1980) which did not dwell on the news agencies. The issue by this time had largely been overshadowed by the more complex and 'colourful' ones involving transborder data flows and direct broadcast transmission. As part of media imperialism and cultural dependency analysis, critical attention was directed much more at the whole context of information production and distribution. The issue of news agencies and news flow became part of a much wider discourse about information and relations between the advanced capitalist countries and those of the 'Third World'. In addition, a reassessment of the nature and role of the major international news agencies had occurred; they 'could no longer be depicted as the unambiguously wicked villains of existing imbalances in the flow of international news' (Boyd-Barrett 1981: 248).

Much of the criticism of the international news agencies has been based on the premise that the content of their services is somehow politically, culturally, and morally alien to the values of 'Third World' governments, media organizations, and media publics. Such content supposedly conflicts with ill-defined national interests and the struggle for national cultural autonomy. Hamelink, whose views have been influential in intellectual and media quarters in a number of African countries, argues that

> the role of international news in transferring values should not be underestimated. The selection of news by the few large international news agencies undoubtedly reflects the values of metropolitan countries. Most developing countries are dependent on this choice for their information on events outside their

country. They receive international news about themselves via the news centres in New York, Paris, or London.

(Hamelink 1983: 9)

More specifically the criticism is that, first, the agencies are basically preoccupied with the affairs of the developed world to the neglect of the 'Third World; second, that the particular 'western bias' of the news emphasizes the news of the exceptional (famine, war, tribalism, disorder, corruption) rather than 'development news'; and third, that the general western bias associated with the news agencies 'corresponds with the policy objectives of the governments of those countries in which the major Western agencies are based (Boyd-Barrett 1981: 255).

Empirical studies certainly do not provide any conclusive support for the three-pronged criticism. Tracey (1985), along with other critics, has questioned a number of the basic assumptions upon which rests the case for a NIIO, certainly as it applies to international news flow and the role of the international news agencies in them. Stevenson, after reviewing the *World of the News* study, concluded that 'too much of the NWIO debate has focused on assertions that were probably never true and certainly are no longer true. This study helps clear the air of pseudo debate' (Stevenson 1984: 137). The *World of the News* study found that despite substantial differences in levels of development and a variety of political perspectives and institutional arrangements, 'the overall pattern of attention paid to certain kinds of events was remarkably similar' (Tracey 1985: 31). Although politics dominated international news 'everywhere', regional news coverage occupied a dominant position; in most cases the region to which a service is directed gets more coverage than any other region (Boyd-Barrett 1981: 253). Thus, in the flow of news stories directed to Latin America, Latin America is normally the single most important source of such news.

According to Tracey (1985: 31) the frequently made assertion that western news agencies and mass media ignore the 'Third World' is 'simply untrue': 'about a third of foreign news stories in northern media systems originate in the Third World; in the Third World, about 60 to 75 per cent of all foreign news is from other Third World countries' (see also Boyd-Barrett 1981: 255–6). Where major gaps in news coverage occur is in the relative dearth of non-regional 'Third World' news (Latin American media have little coverage of African affairs, for example) and the lack of coverage given to Eastern Europe (Tracey 1985: 32).

Throughout the 1960s and 1970s the major western news agencies increased their regional coverage, including that of the 'Third World' (Boyd-Barrett 1981: 256). In the case of Reuters this was partly a result of a high-level directive to give more attention to a 'regionalization' for the markets of the 'Third World'. Reuters established more specialized African services, an Arabic service for the Middle East, a Caribbean service, and provided assistance with the setting-up of a co-operative Latin American agency, LATIN. This 'regionalization' has met with only limited success principally because the major clients in the United States in particular, and elsewhere throughout the advanced capitalist world, are reluctant to relinquish their reliance on the 'Big Four' agencies for an international news dependence on news agencies based in non-western countries (Boyd-Barrett 1981: 256).

Musa argues that much of the debate about the NWICO has been constrained by its location in dependency theory (Musa 1990: 330). Continued reliance on a centre–periphery model ultimately only obfuscates analysis by diverting attention from the basic internal dynamics of news and information production, selection, distribution, and control in 'Third World' countries (Musa 1990: 331). Undue emphasis on dependence 'underplays the domestication of the capitalist institutions and relations of production' in them and leads to the neglect of domestic pressures for a new information and communications order.

Ruling classes in 'Third World' countries have a vested interest in producing some reconstruction of the international information and communications order which will allow them and their policies to be positively portrayed in western media,[3] while providing them with the 'exclusive right and access to better information' (Musa 1990: 331). This does not involve addressing internal contradictions, especially vigorous, often ruthless suppression of dissent and tight control over the flow of information. In 'Third World' countries, just as in those of the advanced capitalist world, governments and corporations constantly interfere with the final news products that go out for public consumption,[4] as well as with information activities which could work against their interests (Musa 1990: 328).

Increasingly alternative news agencies in Africa and elsewhere are being forced into the financial data area as a way of survival where state subsidies are being cut and pressure exerted to privatize them (such as in the case of the News Agency of Nigeria). Increasing interest in financial data services on the part of executives of alternative agencies also reflects the extent to which the principal new agencies are the major agenda-setters for other agencies (Musa 1990: 335). The development of news agencies into big businesses exhibiting structures similar to other corporations, and their major role in the provision of financial data and business services, increasingly locks them into the corporate sector and a basic role in the internationalization of capital (Musa 1990: 340). This development tends to give rise to an information hierarchy where the public 'is offered some kind of concoction of news, entertainment, advertisements and some government image making products in the form of public relations' while financial and business information is fed into more exclusive publications and subscription services (Musa 1990: 340–41). In Nigeria and some other African countries, as well as throughout Asia and Latin America, this information goes into financial pages and supplements, and specialist publications, which for reasons of cost, literacy levels and language, are generally inaccessible to the wider public. As news agencies and mass media in 'Third World' countries increasingly perform such a dual role, and provide services for both local and international capital, the call for a NWICO either loses some of its urgency, or else becomes one where local agencies, media, and government have an expanded role in the provision and receipt of information of vital relevance to the conduct of business and private capital accumulation.

TRANSBORDER DATA FLOWS

The development of largely unregulated transborder data flows represents a strong challenge to older notions of cultural, economic and political sovereignty. Informatics, rather than being neutral, 'bears within itself the culture that produced it. The language, in its synthetic and semantic aspects, will receive extraordinary influence from the automatic retrieval systems and information services' (Joubert de Oliveira Brizida, quoted in Wigand et al. 1984: 159). For 'Third World' countries in particular this concern about the challenge to sovereignty embraces a contradiction: on the one hand they are anxious to have a greater exchange of information resources, if necessary as part of a free flow of information doctrine; but on the other hand, that greater exchange runs up against the superior capacity of the information-'rich' to produce and distribute information.

Governments throughout the industrialized world, as well as the industrializing such as Brazil and India, have expressed some apprehension about the expatriation of information about natural resources (perhaps secured by remote sensing), agricultural yields, and economically important and relevant data, being sent through private international communications networks for use in decision-making by transnational corporations. In Brazil state concern to control access to strategic information resources has led to the implementation of policy designed to eliminate the 'geographic separation between the decision-making process and the productive process' (Joubert de Oliveira Brizida, quoted in Wigand *et al.* 1984: 161).[5]

Some critics, such as Hilary Ng'weno in Kenya, have argued that while the freeing-up of the international flow of communications is necessary, even more urgent is the task of establishing an internal free flow of information in many countries. This is not simply a case where foreign transnational corporations, or others, have monopolized the production, storage, selection, retrieval, and distribution of information, but where governments restrict the flow of information for political and other reasons. This often assumes the form of the denial and suppression of public policy debate – about communications, including mass media policies, as well as more generally about the nature of economic policies to be implemented. Schiller (1979) suggested that the existing international flow of communications, by exacerbating information or communications gaps, contributed to growing inequality in 'developing' countries. The new computer-based information technologies and telecommunications both reinforced existing class divisions, and encouraged new ones (for Schiller they were actually a source of class division). Certainly there is little doubt that initially the principal beneficiaries of such technologies are the manufacturers and suppliers (invariably foreign transnationals, except in countries such as India and Brazil), national and transnational business users, and privileged, urban-based strata which have private uses for them.

The principal economic issues for 'Third World' countries regarding transborder data flows relate to the consequences of computer communications for economic productivity, investment, and structural change, as well as for balance of payments, employment levels, and threat to the growth and survival of fledgling local information industries. For the transnational corporations engaged in substantial use of such flows, the principal economic issues revolve around restriction of competition and market entry through tariffs, prohibitive pricing, monitoring, and other enforcement of privacy legislation. The economic issue of increasing concern to many countries, or at least potential concern for some, is the protection of information industries at a time when production and employment have undergone major restructuring. The importation of substantial remote processing and data storage services is likely to have serious implications for the job market, with some jobs lost to locations elsewhere. This is the case with Canada, where proximity to the United States and a 'dependence' on data bases there, is seen to have serious implications for the Canadian economy and expansion of employment in the information sector (Rada 1981: 55).

The economic analysis of transborder data flows poses major difficulties, mainly because most are of an intracorporate nature.[6] Transnational corporations are both large-scale, intensive users of transborder data flows, and the principal producers of the information technologies employed in them (hardware, telecommunications networks and data flows).[7] The decentralization of information-intensive industries such as banking and finance, insurance, tourism and transportation, has increased the demand for information facilitated by instantaneous transmission channels available at decreasing cost. Transborder data flows also take place through the commercial marketing of computing power and information contained in data bases. The growth of enterprises specializing in the sale of financial, accounting, inventory control, procurement, marketing, and scientific-technical research, and offering remote computing services on a global scale, has contributed to the formation of an expanding data industry and data market.

ALLOCATION OF THE RADIO SPECTRUM AND SATELLITE PARKING

A key issue which has become increasingly important in debate about the NIIO is the struggle for access to the natural resources required for efficient satellite communications; that is, access to effective slots or parking positions in the equatorial or geostationary orbits. This issue has been added to the earlier and continuing one of the allocation of space on the radio spectrum. Both are ultimately concerned with the immense advantages which the advanced capitalist economies have been able to obtain through their virtual monopoly over the development of modern communications systems, and thus, their restriction of opportunities for others to gain entry.

The electro-magnetic spectrum is 'the resource upon which the exploitation of all information resources (or almost all) depends' (Smith 1980: 118). Throughout the twentieth century more and more of the spectrum has been used for sending information and entertainment either through broadcasting to general audiences or from point to point. Different communications technologies make use of different quantities of spectrum or different amounts of 'bandwidth'. New developments in communication technologies have involved the use of more available frequencies (as well as the abandonment of others which are no longer required) with the result that there is a need for international regulation to avoid the squandering of spectrum space. This has been accomplished through the International Telecommunication Union (ITU), the world's oldest international organization which began in 1865. The ITU, unlike other international agencies, 'exists only through its members' and makes unanimous decisions 'from decade to decade on how to govern the use of this flexible resource of nature' (Smith 1980: 118).

In addition to the allocation of different quantities of the electro-magnetic spectrum, there is the issue of the parking of geostationary satellites. Such satellites have to be 'parked' in a way that enables them to send signals to the entire world – or at least to the national and regional markets being served. This type of technology, and certainly the capacity to launch satellites, has been restricted to a relatively small number of countries. Despite this, the number of satellites launched poses some problems as far as the cluttering-up of the orbit is concerned. In the case of satellite communications/telecommunications the allocation of a space in the orbit has to be accompanied by the right to use a frequency along which data can be sent to the satellite and another frequency to transmit that data back to a receiving station located in a suitable place on the ground.

The allocation of the spectrum through the ITU has become an intensely politicized process and expresses the way in which controversies surrounding information rights and creation of a NIIO have penetrated the ITU. The politicization is bound up with substantial inequalities between countries – and their corporations – in the ability to develop and exploit new communications technologies, and thus to make use of the electro-magnetic spectrum. Apart from the implications for economic domination, and fears of further social and cultural subordination, there is the fear that by the time that many 'Third World' countries are in a position to use the advanced technologies either the best locations will have been taken, or they will not be available. Further, the dominance of a few countries and their corporations enables them to set the basic parameters of the international communications system, forcing others to fit in with their arrangements, whether their 'national' economic or other policies determine so or not.

The response of many 'Third World' countries has been to demand spectrum rights even where they are not in a position to use them (Smith 1980: 122). Although a number of 'Third World' countries now have domestic communications satellites (Brazil, China, India, Indonesia, Mexico) it will be decades before others have them – especially African countries. While the United States government and communications interests have opposed this, the concern of 'Third World' governments has been that of trying to 'restrict the technological advantages which accrue to countries which develop early the economic and industrial capacity to exploit a world resource' (Smith 1980: 122).

A significant development occurred in 1988 with the convening of Space WARC[8] to consider and achieve the equitable access by all countries to the geostationary satellite orbit (Rones 1989: 26). Space WARC was requested by 'Third World' governments basically as a way of ensuring access to suitable parking spots. Generally the 'developed' countries were opposed to Space WARC on the grounds that rigid planning of the orbit was unnecessary; few 'Third World' countries had the immediate capacity to own and operate satellite systems, with some possibly never having that capacity (Rones 1989: 26).

In the 1985 Space WARC segment 'Third World' countries sought to wrest control from INTELSAT and the advanced capitalist countries by abolishing the first-come, first-served principle which had always favoured the economically and technologically advanced countries (Rones 1989: 26).

That session decided which space services and frequency bands would be planned; established principles, technical parameters and criteria for planning; and established guidelines for regulatory procedures with respect to services and frequency bands not brought under planning.

(Rones 1989: 26)

At the 1988 Space WARC an Allotment Plan emerged which created 480 national slot allotments. Provision was also made in the Plan for the development of sub-regional systems that would enable countries to bypass INTELSAT and to have the opportunity to own and control a satellite jointly (Rones 1989: 27).

Critics of INTELSAT have argued that its ownership by western governments has basically served the interests of western transnational corporations. INTELSAT services have discriminated in 'favour of the western countries who hold major shares in the organization'. With membership of the board of directors of IN-TELSAT tied to levels of capital investment, African and other governments have been denied any role in the management of the organization (Ya'u 1987: 129–30). For such critics INTELSAT is part of the control exerted by western countries and their transnationals over international communications; it contributes to the perpetuation of the global imbalance of information and the tying of 'Third World' communications systems to those of the imperialists (Ya'u 1987: 130). While satellite communications may contribute to 'national development', they have represented part of the drive by transnational electronic corporations, in conjunction with educational foundations, and American university centres, for the transfer of new communications technologies (Mattelart 1983: 5–7). For example, from the late 1960s there was a strong American push for the expansion of satellite telecommunications in Latin America, supposedly as a way of solving many of the basic educational problems, but also to provide a communications system indispensable for the operation of government and business. American efforts in Latin America foundered in the late 1960s when a number of governments recognized that an American-controlled regional satellite system, relying very much on American programmes, would undermine their cultural and educational self-determination (Mattelart 1983: 6–7).

INTELSAT's entrenched position makes a challenge to its services very difficult. It is used extensively by countries for domestic and regional services, as well as typical international applications (Rones 1989: 27). In many instances the introduction of sub-regional systems would simply duplicate existing services at greater cost. Available evidence would suggest a likely under-utilization of transponders at least in the short term (McAnany 1989: 8). The social, educational, and cultural benefits which have always been used to justify the introduction of domestic or sub-regional satellites have rarely, if ever, been a major priority after their introduction.[9] In Brazil (Mody 1989), India (Fernandes 1989), Indonesia (Lent 1982), and Mexico, the principal beneficiaries have been television (whether commercial or commercialized 'state'), urban telephone users, and national and transnational corporations. This is scarcely surprising, McAnany (1989: 8) notes, when such technologies reinforce existing power structures. Additionally, in many countries the very structures of development ministries 'do not allow for significant applications of communications technologies (McAnany 1989: 8). The costs of social applications are likely to be more expensive than originally projected. In Mexico, for example, national budgetary cuts in 1986 and 1987 led to the cancellation of plans for educational applications.

The carefully worked out regulatory net devised by the United Nations to ensure that nations control television signals within their borders is under challenge. This challenge comes not just from communications corporations in the advanced capitalist economies, but also from corporations based in the 'Third World' as well. The introduction by the Hong Kong company Hutchison Whampoa of an Asian regional satellite system, with amongst others channels for international news, music and entertainment, sports, and Japanese-language programmes, clearly poses threats to national sovereignty, at least in any state's claim to control television within a nation's borders, as well as to establish television monopolies in them (Scott 1990a: 34). The jamming of satellites is difficult, and the banning of satellite dishes poses real problems for government policing. While satellite television, especially news services, may serve as a catalyst as well as a chronicler of events, the principal concern of those associated with the establishment of an Asian television network is to build a viable commercial enterprise (Scott 1990: 35).

CONCLUSION

Since the 1970s when the issues of the NWICO were first articulated, the complexity of international and national economic and communications relations has challenged the theoretical assumptions and analytical frameworks within which much of the debate occurred. Any presentation of the advanced capitalist countries on the one hand, and the 'Third World' on the other, as monolithic blocs with similar communications systems and problems and concerns has been effectively undermined. Countries such as Brazil,

Mexico, and India, clearly have quite different communications capabilities and concerns than most others in the 'Third World'. The internationalization of capital, with the transnational corporation its most conspicuous manifestation, has exposed the extent to which there are conflicts between national regulatory frameworks and transnational corporations. Problems of cultural imperialism and domination once thought peculiar to 'Third World' countries have been given greater attention in advanced capitalist countries as a result of shifts in ownership and investment, including a greater role for international capital, and the development of satellite communications/telecommunications systems and international data storage, processing, and retrieval systems which render older notions of national sovereignty problematic. Recognition has increased that while the international dimension of communications flow is still of basic importance, and inextricably linked with international movements of capital, the state and dominant classes in 'Third World' countries are both capable of modifying relations with international capital, and at the same time having strong interests in existing communications and information flows whether at the international or national levels.

Chapter 6

Data: technological 'dependence' and communications

The ability to produce the basic means of modern communications is concentrated in corporations throughout the advanced capitalist world, and in the United States and Japan in particular. Even where there has been relocation of the production of such technologies to other countries, or their application to manufacturing production in them, there is still a heavy concentration of innovation, and the development of communications and information technology, in the advanced capitalist economies. This is partly a product of the high levels of expenditure on research and development by corporations and the state in such countries, as well as the concern basically to provide the technological parameters within which others will work. Certainly the technical criteria of the communications/telecommunications technologies employed in 'Third World' countries are largely determined by the dominant external producers and suppliers of hardware and software, even if they are adapted to local usage.

TECHNOLOGICAL DEPENDENCY

In a strict sense there is a technological dependency. There is a substantial monopolization of technical invention and technological innovation, as well as the production of electronic media and information technology, by the advanced capitalist world, and by the United States and Japan in particular. Where local production has been undertaken in many 'Third World' countries, it has been carried out either under a licensing agreement, or by local subsidiaries of metropolitan-based transnational corporations. In many instances it has only involved the assembly of relatively simple products such as radio receivers, with the design specifications determined elsewhere. Much of this production has occurred as a result of state import-substitution policies, although in Asia (Hong Kong, South Korea, Taiwan) major transnational manufacturers have been able to take advantage of a combination of relatively low cost, often skilled labour, and advanced technology, to produce sophisticated electronic communications equipment. Where this type of industrialization has occurred, it has frequently been labelled a 'dependent capitalist development', with metropolitan interests still retaining control primarily through the production of the means of production (the capital goods required for production), financial structures, and marketing and distribution.

Following Mattelart (1979b), Boyd-Barrett (1982: 177) notes that the pace of technological change may be 'related to the development and commercialization of innovations in the defence and aerospace industries of the major economies'. Certainly the dominance of United States electronic industries, as for example in mainframe computer production, was established during the 1950s as a result of the close relationship between the electronic and aerospace industries and defence expenditure. While defence and aerospace industries obviously continue to be crucial to the pace of technological change, perhaps more important since the late 1970s has been the challenge which Japanese computer and communications producers have posed for United States and other industries.

Satellite communications, which were developed primarily for defence purposes, clearly had commercial applications, and introduced 'the growing potential for direct broadcast television and greatly complicate[d] the task of global allocation of communication space' (Boyd-Barrett 1982: 177). The introduction of satellites for telecommunications and television broadcasting perhaps more significantly led to intense competition between capitals, between those with substantial investment in terrestrial telecommunications systems for domestic purposes and those pressing for domestic satellite telecommunications, and between the state and private capital over the allocation of access to broadcasting satellites. In countries such as Australia and Britain the introduction of national satellite systems was caught up in strong moves for the greater privatization and deregulation of communications, with concerted pressure coming from the principal business users, whether national or transnational, and communications interests which saw satellites as presenting an opportunity for establishing much greater market reach and control, and greater vertical integration. The fact that the rapid development of satellite communications occurs so unevenly exacerbates the conflict between those with the capacity to exploit such communications technology and those who, lacking such ability, would nevertheless like access to be preserved for further use.

The development of computer technology and digital communications, which has basically been dominated by corporations in the major capitalist countries, has increased the capacity for the international flow of data at a pace beyond the 'ability of international bodies to regulate' (Boyd-Barrett 1982: 177). Since World War II the number of activities dependent on different forms of information (business decisions, research and development, state administration, legislation, political decision-making, marketing and consumption) has grown exponentially. Employment in industries concerned with the production, collection, storage, retrieval, and dissemination of information has grown correspondingly. The 'spillover' from the United States military and space programmes, as for example in high-performance integrated circuits, satellites, and laser technology, combined with the large potential market for information, has been instrumental in improving the price and performance economy of the information 'package technology' which encompasses components, computers and telecommunications (Rada 1981 : 45). This is reflected in the development of memory chips with a great density of components, microprocessors, and microcomputers. While the economies in electronic calculators, computers and processors have been tremendous, in telecommunications and related equipment there have been similar reductions. The use of satellites has decreased the cost of telecommunications since the distance of a communication has virtually no effect on price (Garnham 1982: 30). The number of telephone circuits carried by satellites has increased dramatically over the last two decades, while the cost per circuit per year has been reduced some twenty-seven times in the same period (Rada 1981: 45). The cost of launching satellites may still be prohibitive, and launchings characterized by frequent failure, but ground stations are relatively inexpensive, and small receiver-only ground stations or dishes are cheap.

Accompanying the decreasing costs there has been a remarkable increase in the speed of transmission, as a result of the digitalization of messages. The development of fibre optics, which consist of tubes of self-reflecting glass no thicker than a human hair which carry messages in digital form using laser beams, has immense applicability to telephone and cable television systems.

There has been a great deal of concentration of manufacturing and service capabilities in the information industry. Numerous small firms, often highly innovative, have been important in the microchip and business systems areas (frequently involving customizing systems using hardware produced by others), as well as in software production where capital costs have generally been less. The nature of much of information technology is such, and the cost of its development sufficiently expensive, that its economic viability is very much geared to high-volume production and exploitation of a world market. In the component, computer, telecommunications, and software and machine services, the industry is highly concentrated and transnational. This concentration, which assumes an international dimension, involves both the horizontal and vertical integration of a great many different activities under the heading of 'information processing' (Mattelart 1979b). Computer giants such as IBM have moved into telecommunications through Satellite Business Systems. Rank Xerox has moved in the same direction, while AT & T has extended its activities into computer terminals and related equipment, as well as into *viewdata* or *teletext*. Some European private companies and PTT have also moved in this direction. British Telecom, even before its privatization by the Thatcher government, had developed the Prestel viewdata system, and established links with IBM's Satellite Business Systems, thus 'becoming IBMs ally in its attempts to break Europe's public telecommunications monopolies' (Garnham 1982: 32).

Concern has frequently been expressed by critics about the implications of the information technology revolution for 'Third World' countries. Rada, for example, contends that the readjustment policies of 'industrialized countries', together with their development and 'mastery' of information technology, is simply reinforcing the present international division of labour through substantial increases in productivity and concentration of information-intensive sectors in them (Rada 1981: 43). Advanced industrial or capitalist economies control an 'all-pervasive technology' which has both changed their economic production and services sectors, and reinforced their major advantage in science and technology. Any theory of comparative advantage has been effectively undermined by the microelectronic revolution, with the assumption that 'Third World' countries would industrialize on the basis of labour-intensive industries challenged by the increased and widespread adoption of 'high technology' by most industries in the advanced industrial or capitalist economies (Rada 1981: 44; Kaplinsky 1982). If there is no longer a need for labour, Kaplinsky asks, where does the comparative advantage for developing countries lie?

Since the mid-1970s there has been a major economic restructuring in advanced capitalist countries. This was provoked by competition between national capitals, lower growth prospects and falling levels of profitability, high and rising levels of unemployment, high energy costs, and competition from some 'Third World' countries in the production of manufactured goods (Taiwan, South Korea, Hong Kong). Central to this restructuring process has been the adoption of new technologies, particularly microelectronics, for the upgrading of products and processes (Rada 1981: 49). The restructuring, at the same time, has added considerably to rates of technical invention and technological innovation.

Some writers suggest that the introduction of microelectronics into sectors such as electronics, design, machine tools, and textile and garment manufacture substantially reduces the value to producing firms of relocating production in 'Third World' countries. In the case of the electronics industries, offshore installations have been used for a considerable time for the assembling and wiring of 'chips' (Rada 1981: 49). However, as a result of the development of automatic techniques, the industry has developed a new generation of plants in the advanced capitalist countries. For the companies involved, automation has been the only way of minimizing costs, increasing the output and productivity of workers, maintaining employment levels, and being closer to the vast majority of users. Major investments in the field of *integrated circuits* have taken place in the United States, Japan, England, Scotland, Ireland, France and West Germany. This does not mean that some operations will not remain in 'Third World' countries to assemble and test relatively simple 'chips' where the production value does not justify automated plants, and to exploit regional markets. There have been, however, some shifts of plant from higher-cost Asian countries such as Hong Kong, Singapore, South Korea, and Taiwan, to the Philippines and Thailand in an effort to reduce costs further (Rada 1981: 49).

Microelectronics offer innovating firms very substantial advantages. The combined effect of automation and electronic-based innovations pushes the transition of industry as a whole towards the 'high-technology' category strongly oriented towards research and development and the production of software. As far as product is concerned this often places new, improved, differentiated commodities on the market with significantly reduced lead-times (Kaplinsky 1982). There is also likely to be the optimization of materials utilization, such as steel and energy, as well as improvements in the production process. The application of microelectronics offers the additional advantage of significantly increasing the flexibility of production lines, and allowing for greater variation of product type. A move away from high-volume standardized production and economies of scale may follow from this. The effort to achieve higher levels of automation has led to the multiplication and strengthening of links between machine manufacturers and electronic/computer firms, and 'end producers' (Rada 1981: 50).

The concentration of manufacturing capability in the information industry has been accompanied by a similar concentration in information storage and retrieval. This concentration is associated with the development of fluid international interactive networks which are not inhibited by national boundaries. These networks provide immediate access to information regardless of location. Information can be stored in remote computers and retrieved from a great many different places. The fact that 'strings of ones and zeros' can be used to transmit documents, voice, or image over telephone lines, microwaves and satellites, and can be ciphered and manipulated, combined with the sheer number of users, makes monitoring, even for the most advanced, highly problematic (Rada 1981: 53). The economic, political and cultural ramifications of these data flows are of immediate and immense concern to governments in states which see themselves as 'dependent' *vis-à-vis* the advanced capitalist or industrial world.

The development of digitalized information networks means that specialized information can be retrieved through electronic systems without the use of conventional print media such as newspapers, or radio, and the mass media more generally. The alternative to this is to have an adaptation of the new information technologies to the traditional media of communication. This occurs when the increasing fragmentation and localization of specialized items is combined with the beaming of increasingly centralist editorial, political and international functions to the local press. The former is the one most used by business and government, with specialized organizations producing and storing information in central data banks and bases. This escapes traditional forms of monitoring and social control, and is probably more influential in helping to determine policy than the traditional media. The latter opens up the possibility of much more centralized selection and control of the 'content', with the metropolitan or 'mother-newspaper' dictating the editorial line and much of the content to many provincial or even foreign newspapers.

The concentration of data banks and bases in the hands of a few transnational corporations and countries is viewed by many 'Third World' and other critics as reinforcing the dependence of 'Third World' countries. The dominant position of the advanced capitalist world in international news reporting, together with their news agencies, has met with often fierce attack throughout much of the 'Third World'. Computerized information leads to a different form of exchange and interpretation. The figures and data retrieved 'do not provide for the social context or political realities' (Rada 1981: 54). Rather, the concepts or categorizations which order the computerization of references and data reflect the interests of capital in the advanced industrial states, and contribute to a 'further normalization and quantification of the social-political analyses'. For example, commonly used indicators such as growth in GNP and per capita incomes, and in the balance of payments, are of little value in trying to determine the extent of structural change or its necessity. According to Rada 'the normalization of information does not lead to its "objectivization"; rather the apparent scientific or technical status of the information in the same manner as using an average leads to a figurative representation and to false reproductions of reality' (Rada 1981: 55).

It is likely that the interactive information systems will be the main source of information for news, education, scientific work, and political decisions. The great concern of dependency theorists is that the concentration, organization, and control of data banks and information, and of information technology hardware, in the advanced capitalist countries especially, will further reproduce the old patterns of dependency and domination (Rada 1981: 54). This dependency is likely to be deepened, they suggest, by the vulnerability of dependent countries to decisions made in the countries holding the data – it is very noticeable that dependency writers are still locked into relations between nations rather than the different circuits of capital and capital accumulation processes. There are several reasons why this dependency should deepen. Routine data processing can be done more economically using the data processing facilities of highly industrialized countries. Such data centres may possess expertise not readily available in, and contain information which is unobtainable in, the dependent country. According to this argument, the very structure of the flow of information within transnational corporations contributes to this dependence. The manufacturing, financial, and marketing policies of these corporations, which are determined on a worldwide basis, ensure that the raw data which provides the basis for decisions flows towards the headquarters, while data containing already-taken decisions flows towards subsidiaries often located in dependent countries. This is exacerbated by the shift in the information content of goods and services. Previously the service sector was regarded as the principal locus of information processing, but the 'information intensity' of capital and consumer goods has fundamentally challenged this.

Concern about the implications of transnational data flows for growing dependence is not simply restricted to the 'Third World'. It is also to be found in countries such as Canada where foreign, particularly United States, capital is substantial, and where data banks tend to be located in the United States rather than domestically (Rada 1981: 55). Under certain conditions, such as economic war or the deterioration in political relations between countries, the retention or selective use of data can be used as a weapon. In the United States the so-called Jackson Amendment of 1974 gives the State Department the power to regulate the transfer of United States knowledge, software, and equipment. This type of power, and indeed of those who control data services, hardware, manufacturing, and machine and software services, increases in direct proportion to the diffusion and widespread use of information technology.

The implications for employment are also of major concern. The mainly intra-corporate shipping of data to centres in advanced capitalist or industrial countries for processing either leads to a loss of jobs or perhaps more important, a loss of job-creation potential. Of course the implications for employment are not simply international; the concentration of information capabilities in a limited number of centres in the advanced capitalist economies has basic implications for employment and unemployment in other areas. A 1977 government report in Canada estimated that 7,500 processing jobs and about $300 million in revenue were being lost because data processing was being done abroad, mainly in the United States. The projection for 1985 estimated losses of 23,000 jobs and $1.5 billion in revenue. The implications for employment and unemployment have also to be seen in relation to the decreasing costs of communications, and their concentration, in the advanced capitalist economies. According to Rada it is becoming cheaper for 'Third World' institutions and enterprises to 'send their design problems, calculations, research and routine data abroad rather than to assemble and develop local teams' (Rada 1981: 56).

Some writers have noted that while many 'Third World' countries have successfully addressed the basic problem of international news flow, and have done a good deal to redress the imbalance in it – especially through the establishment of national and regional news agencies – they have not seriously addressed basic policy issues which arise from the nature of the new information technologies themselves (Bascur 1985). Part of the explanation for this omission stems from a preoccupation with the 'content' of communications, which is perhaps readily understandable given subjection to European colonial powers and the ability of corporations in the advanced capitalist economies to penetrate their mass media and cultural markets, including education. This preoccupation, however, has contributed to a failure to grasp the way in which developments in communications technologies, and the establishment of new connections, often between older media, have led to a rapid convergence of all information channels and flows. New and different connections have been established between the print media, conventional electronic media (radio and television), telecommunications, and business information systems. Instead, Bascur (1985: 356) notes, 'developing countries stick to a sectoral view of mass media, telecommunications and informatics'. In addition, the concern with mass media content has contributed to the failure to formulate policy in the area of specialized information (transborder data flows, access to dataa banks) which may have a much more important bearing on their economic development. Further, the emphasis on content contributes to the negglect of the way in which the communications infrastructure and contents have become increasingly inseparable: 'when it comes to international bargaining in communications the Third World takes into account mainly contents' (Bascur 1985: 356).

Osakue (1988) raises a number of policy issues regarding the funding of communications, and the establishment of funding priorities in African countries. Communications development (radio, television, telecommunications) requires both substantial initial capital investment and increased investtment. The production of communications technologies is essentially restricted to a small number of advanced capitalist economies – Japan, the United States, Britain, France, and West Germany. As a result much of the investment involves scarce foreign currency. This scarcity is exacerbated by worsening terms of trade, falling commodity prices, and international indebtedness, and cannot be offset by increased sale of services since that occurs in local currencies. Domestic mobilization of capital for communications investment is a possibility. However, it is restricted by two major factors: first, state or public ownership and legal constraints which provide no opportunity for large-scale private participation; and second, the unattractiveness of investment in restricted areas unlikely to provide high levels of profitability and opportunities for substantial expansion.

> Even where an open door policy exists, it is doubtful if private investment can be fully mobilized because the market structure and pricing policy that could emerge may conflict with certain social goals designed to integrate the rural communities with the rest of society and preserve culture. Public monopoly and financing thus become inevitable.
>
> (Osakue 1988: 129)

In Nigeria, largely as a result of the 'petro-dollars' boom of the mid-1970s, a significant increase in investment occurred in the communications, and in particular, telecommunications infrastructure. As revenue from oil exports dwindled, financial cartels were put together by Nigeria's 'foreign friends' in Europe and America to provide extended credit facilities. The projects financed under these arrangements involved the transfer by the loan provision of the machinery and maintenance technology required (Sonaike 1989: 2). The prominence given to telecommunications in the 1960s and 1970s was very much the product of the application of a 'development-through-modernization' paradigm in which the mass media, and communications more generally, were held to be major catalysts for change. It is highly likely, as Sonaike (1989: 3) observes, that members of the Nigerian ruling class were attracted by some advanced aspects of telecommunications (televideo broadcasting and satellite-assisted telephony), which they had come in contact with abroad and were anxious to introduce at home.

Greater public investment in advanced communications systems has first, usually increased indebtedness, especially foreign indebtedness; second, helped to produce a redistribution of spending so that crucial areas such as health, water supply, and education, receive a smaller share of total public spending; and third, benefited relatively small sections of the population able to take advantage of the extended provision of communications/telecommunications services. In the case of the last it is not difficult to demonstrate the vast differences between the urban and rural areas in access to and ability to use radio, television, and telecommunications services. While communications/telecommunications have become increasingly important in developmental strategies – a fact reflected in often greatly increased expenditure – many of the initiatives for the adoption of the more advanced technologies and extension of facilities have come from users, principally private and public companies involved in radio and television broadcasting and production, telecommunications services, and business enterprises. This applies to pressures for the introduction of national satellite systems. Although the justification is usually couched in terms of the enormous social benefits (education, public health and information programmes in rural areas) likely to flow from the introduction of such satellites, in countries such as Brazil, Mexico, India, and Nigeria they have been used essentially for commercial purposes or by state instrumentalities involved in the extensive use of telecommunications. Generally the social benefits have been restricted to a relatively small part of the population.

Certainly in many 'Third World' countries (and others) the fear is expressed that if substantial investment is not made in the most advanced communications technologies, including telecommunications satellites, they will fall even further behind the advanced economies. The problem with this position is that the less technologically advanced communications infrastructure may be, at least in the short term, much more important for economic development. In most African countries, as well as many Asian and Latin American ones, the basic communications infrastructure of roads, railways, and ports suffers from both a lack of investment and reach. The ability to take advantage of national and international markets for agricultural commodities and a range of manufactured goods is often severely limited by an inadequate road system, or the lack of fit between road, railway, and air transportation systems. Poorly developed communications infrastructures often represent a major impediment for the distribution of conventional media products such as newspapers, magazines and books, and hinder the distribution of electronic hardware such as radios and television sets.

Some of the drive for the introduction of advanced communications systems has come from local manufacturers likely to be able to supply the expanding industry with components. Indeed in a small number of countries (Brazil, Mexico, and India) the substantial investment in an advanced communications infrastructure is an integral part of a longer-term industrial strategy designed not only to expand local electronic goods production but also to improve the competitiveness of major areas of industrial production through the introduction of information technology and use of computer-aided design, engineering and manufacture. In India, for example, while significantly increased state expenditure on communications has added to both international and local indebtedness, it has also been a considerable spur to increased investment in local electronics production.

> The liberal import policy is also responsible for the phenomenal growth in production in electronic components and equipment in India. Within the manufacturing sector, electronics had registered the highest growth rate.
>
> (Fernandes 1989: 31)

One of the major actors in telecommunications planning and the drive for more advanced communications systems in the 'Third World' is the World Bank (International Bank for Reconstruction and Development). Although Bank lending for telecommunications development still only represents a small share of total lending, it has nevertheless considerably increased in Asia in particular (Sussman 1987: 92). As with other sectoral programmes, the Bank's policies on telecommunications are based on strong preferences for private investment and enterprise, foreign investment, limited state expenditure and adoption of the user-pays principle, and trade liberalization (Sussman 1987: 92).

In the case of the Philippines substantial telecommunications developments, including the introduction of a domestic satellite system, and the creation of an advanced communications infrastructure, have involved the major participation of transnational corporations such as RCA, ITT, and Cable & Wireless (Sussman 1987: 94). The emphasis on advanced telecommunications, whose principal beneficiaries are business, tourist, and affluent residential district users, has led to the neglect of other telecommunications services which are primarily used by the rural and urban labouring classes (Sussman 1987: 103). The expansion of private involvement in telecommunications has been justified in terms of their role in producing general advancement within the global political economy. Sussman (1987: 103), following writers such as Schiller (1976; 1979) and Hamelink (1983), views such telecommunications developments in the Philippines as effectively disconnecting 'most Filipinos from information lines and social mobility'.

COMPUTER INDUSTRY

'Third World' countries account for only a relatively minor share of total world production and export trade in computers. This is the case even when the off-shore assembly of low-end computer and peripheral equipment is considered.

O'Connor (1985: 311) suggests that initially it is 'useful to differentiate between two types of policies relating to the computer sector'. The first type, information policy, is concerned with both computer applications and the 'whole range of actual and potential applications arising from the convergence of computer and communications technologies' (O'Connor 1985: 312). Such an information policy may be worked out in a country which has no domestic computer-manufacturing industry. The second type of policy is specifically concerned with the creation of conditions likely to facilitate the local development of computer, software, and peripheral equipment production. It seeks to identify the technical, economic, and competitive global environmental factors which basically act as constraints on the development of computer and related industries in 'Third World' countries. O'Connor is careful to identify the different possibilities offered by microprocessor, software, and component (semi-conductor) production, as well as clear differences between 'Third World' countries in their ability to enter into viable production in any one of these areas.

The development of an indigenous computer industry hinges to some extent, first, on capacity in hardware and software design which has become increasingly standardized, and second, on 'the design of interfaces between different components of the system' (O'Connor 1985: 313). The different components – peripherals such as keyboards, terminals and monitors, tape and disk drives, printers, X-Y plotters, and modems – have to be integrated in effective ways. The interface often involves linkages between the computers themselves, especially where microcomputers are linked with host mainframe computers in local area networks. Major producers of computers rarely produce all the peripheral equipment. Rather they contract with outside suppliers and ensure compatibility of the different components by revealing their 'interface specifications' (O'Connor 1985: 313).

For 'Third World' countries, and others seeking entry into the computer industry, it is microprocessor design and manufacture which probably represents the greatest technical and economic problem. Software design, on the other hand, is governed by different economic requirements. It is a more labour-intensive than capital-intensive activity which is not marked by the same high levels of obsolescence. Intense market competition in microprocessor design and manufacture dictates constantly new generations of computers. In the case of software production the turnover time of investment is generally much longer, this being determined by the logic of the market. Software users would baulk at the cost of investing in new operating systems (purchase of system, training of users) with every change of hardware, while equipment manufacturers predicate the production of new, advanced models on 'an accumulated base of applications software and accompanying documentation' (O'Connor 1985: 314).

The principal barrier to entry into software production is its increasing standardization, with basic operating systems such as MS-DOS and CP/M having established an international dominance. Although standardization of operating systems may represent a barrier to entry, there are particular idiosyncrasies of national software markets which could provide local software manufacturers with market niches (O'Connor 1985: 315). This is likely to be the case with accounting and financial analysis software able to take into account the specific features of a national economy and the corporate and other users.

According to O'Connor the systems integration route perhaps represents the best means of entry for 'Third World' countries. This has been the route for 'developed' economies such as Australia which have lacked the means, especially the large domestic market, to engage in competitive high-volume hardware and component production. The systems integration route involves the adaptation of standard hardware components supplied by other firms in combination with software packages which have either been designed specifically and produced for such purposes, or modified to suit the specific purposes of the user. Systems integration, in other words, allows for specific or customized systems to be produced for end-users. Such system integration can serve either horizontal markets where an application (for example, inventory control) is common to a range of industries, or vertical markets where the system is geared to users within a particular industry. It is perhaps in the area of industrial process control that the greatest opportunities for systems lie. A particular advantage of systems integration is that the inability to engage in high-cost local research and development, and hardware production, is not necessarily a barrier to entry. There is still the possibility of producing highly innovative systems using the hardware manufactured elsewhere.

'Third World' countries are generally severely limited in their ability to develop the type of research and development infrastructure required for computer hardware production. This is clearly underscored by the fact that in most cases their total research and development annual expenditure is less than the research and development budgets of major American computer firms such as IBM, Hewlett-Packard, and Unisys. Countries such as Brazil, Mexico, India, and South Korea, which are by 'Third World' standards major investors in research and development, are still only able to devote to them a fraction of the expenditure of the advanced capitalist economies.

SOFTWARE DESIGN AND PRODUCTION

Whereas opportunities are restricted for 'Third World' country entry into the manufacture of computer hardware other than for a 'narrow range of components and subassemblies, or to routine final assembly operations' (O'Connor 1985: 321), they are greater in software production where the market is still much more segmented. Software standardization has increased, but still not to the extent that both horizontal and vertical applications have been completely excluded. Different language groupings, for example, provide possibilities for substantial horizontal application.

Direct foreign investment (transnational corporation investment) in software production is unlikely unless the size of the national market, and perhaps some export opportunities, warrants that investment. In general partnership or sub-contracting arrangements are more likely in software production, with the foreign companies largely determining the technical specifications. This is essentially the arrangement in the advanced capitalist economies where microcomputer manufacturers generally rely on 'independent' software houses to write programmes run on their machines (O'Connor 1985: 321). It is more difficult for software producers in 'Third World' countries, using partnership or sub-contracting arrangements, to break into the major overseas national markets, usually because there is a lack of sufficient familiarity with end-user requirements in them. However, there are instances where this has successfully occurred. The United States-based Burroughs Corporation (now part of Unisys) entered into an export-oriented software joint venture with the Tata Group in India. Further, some Japanese computer firms have also entered into contracts with Indian software companies 'to write English-language software and documentation for their machines' (O'Connor 1985: 321).

One of the advantages for foreign computer firms entering into joint ventures with Indian companies is that they are able to take advantage of relatively low labour costs in what is a labour-intensive area of production without sacrificing high levels of technical skills and training. It has been possible for computer firms to carry out low-skill, routinized tasks in low labour-cost areas, while reserving the more creative, design tasks for home-based production. For 'Third World' countries this poses a problem since these tasks are increasingly automated. O'Connor is careful to warn that software production, while offering some opportunities for 'Third World' producers, does not provide them with an untroubled panacea. Systems software, rather than applications software, offers the greatest market potential since it essentially involves a one-to-one relationship with the computer, but this is also an increasingly standardized and high-cost area of production substantially monopolized by companies in the advanced capitalist economies.

COMPUTER INDUSTRY IN INDIA

In India there has been a long-standing concern with the fundamental role of new technologies, and in particular information technologies, in the modernization of administration and the domestic economy, and in increasing the international competitiveness of Indian industry. Under the Rajiv Gandhi administration, in particular, this became a major priority with attention given to ways of assisting and accelerating the growth of the domestic computer

and data-processing industries. Indigenous enterprise in semi-
conductors, telecommunications, computers, and computer software received considerable promotion (Singhal and Rogers 1989:
155). In order to overcome some of the problems of antiquated and
uncompetitive technologies, Gandhi's administration entered into
special funding arrangements (Singhal and Rogers 1989: 168–71),
with economic liberalization measures permitting the easier acquisition of necessary components from overseas or local sources,
depending on need (Delapierre and Zimmermann 1989: 567).
Further assistance was provided by the Indian government's introduction of a massive computerization campaign in the public
sector, including major commercial undertakings (Mahalingam
1989: 2376).

By the mid-1960s Indian policy towards the international computer industry and its relationship to India had been clarified. There
was concern, first, that India should participate in the ownership
and control of foreign computer subsidiaries, and second, that by
the end of the 1960s wholly Indian production should be able to
satisfy most of the major domestic computer requirements. Foreign
units would still be required temporarily to supply large and more
exotic systems, and it was to be hoped that India would have access
to and be able to 'participate in the manufacture of the most
advanced systems available internationally' (Grieco 1982: 612).

The pursuit of these policy objectives bound up with self-
sufficiency brought the Indian government into conflict with the two
foreign computer firms which effectively dominated sales: IBM,
and Britain's International Computers and Tabulators (ICT), which
in 1968 became a part of International Computers Limited (ICL).
IBM resisted pressures for local participation, arguing that centralized co-ordination and control was required for its
internationalized and interdependent operations. In the early
1970s, when the international and domestic environments had
changed, ICL complied with Indian government pressure for an
Indian share in ownership. In the mid-1970s Burroughs was interested in establishing a wholly-owned subsidiary, but gave way to
enter into a joint venture with Tata Enterprises in 1977. IBM still
resisted such pressure and withdrew its operations from India in
mid-1978 (Grieco 1982: 615).[1] The 1970s in India were thus marked
by the withdrawal of IBM, the consolidation of the operations of
ICL and Burroughs, and the emergence of a number of Indian

enterprises which were not under the direct control of the central government.

The implementation of information technology development objectives has been affected and constrained by a multiplicity of factors, some of which stem from the nature of Indian state structures. Certainly as Grieco's analysis of the Indian computer industry demonstrates, the different phases in the development of state policy, organizational responsibility, role of international producers and suppliers and relations with international capital, and production, indicate something of the complexity of state policy formulation and implementation and work against any simple notion of the state, including a *dependencia* one. The growth of the Indian computer industry is characterized by often intense conflict between different government departments and authorities over responsibility for planning and production and the best strategies for the development of the information technology industries (Grieco 1982: 626–30). The government protection designed to protect fledgling local suppliers has often been challenged by major users as well as other indigenous enterprises anxious to break into production, while the licensing system which has allowed importation of equipment by different firms has in many instances restricted the diffusion of competences from one sector to another (Delapierre and Zimmermann 1989: 563). There has been concern about the likelihood of unemployment with the widespread introduction of the new information technologies in service industries; banks and transport industries have voluntarily limited applications to preserve employment.[2] The narrowness of the Indian market for computers and information technology has also been a constraining factor.

One of the principal barriers to the rapid expansion of new computer-based information technologies has been the inadequacy of the basic telecommunications infrastructure which has inhibited the development of telex, facsimile, and electronic mail services (Singhal and Rogers 1989: 200–1).[3] Electric power provision is still relatively expensive, unavailable in some areas, and subject to strikes and breakdowns in ways which interfere with the functioning of computers.

BRAZILIAN COMPUTER INDUSTRY

In Latin America it is really only Brazil that has emerged as a major manufacturer of microcomputers, although in Cuba an effort has been made to formulate and implement a national policy geared to the establishment of a national industry (Mattelart and Schmucler 1985: 105). In Mexico there has been some development in computer hardware and software production. However, while there has been a rapid expansion of consumption of computer technology and data-processing activities, this has not been accompanied by the corresponding growth of domestic production. The expansion of the market for computers has been greatly assisted by the role of the Mexican state, especially through the use of computer resources in an expanding parastatal sector (Mattelart and Schmucler 1985: 93). The administration of public services such as health and education which deal with large numbers of people has also increasingly relied on computers. In addition the highly concentrated, monopolistic, industrial, commercial and financial sectors have increasingly adopted modern data-processing and computer technologies in ways which have consolidated their power (Mattelart and Schmucler 1985: 94). Although Mexican state policy has clearly been geared to the widespread adoption and dissemination of computer technology,[5] this has not been extended into local production; there is no control over national computer development and indeed the Mexican market in this sector is effectively monopolized by transnational corporations (Mattelart and Schmucler 1985: 94).

Brazil's emergence by the mid-1980s to the position of a major manufacturer, while partly due to the 'rise of nationalistic technocrats who began in the mid-1970s to implement a series of regulations that made it possible for Brazilian manufacturers to monopolize the domestic market for minicomputers and microcomputers', was much more the result of the involvs-2ement o-3f at least three generations of engineers and scientists in its development (Langer 1989: 95).

The idea of a domestic computer industry based on local talent existed for decades before the development of any commercially viable computer. Civilian universities and military academies provided Brazil with the scientific infrastructure and personnel to enter into computer and other information technology production. Some of the engineers and computeer scientists also had considerable experience in North American universities and electronic industries. According to Langer (1989: 96) the failure of a number of high-technology projects in the 1950s and 1960s was instrumental in bringing together a 'small group of highly nationalistic individuals in key positions in academe and state agencies'. This group was able to take advantage of 'a juncture of developments in computer technology and Brazilian politics to bring about a domestic information industry' (Langer 1989: 96).

Somewhat paradoxically, although military interests played an important part in information technology development, the military coup of March 1964 represented a major setback; it changed the atmosphere at the Instituto Technológico da Aeronautica and led to the dispersal of the civilian faculty and students who were vital to such development (Langer 1989: 99).

The development of computer policy in Brazil 'has its roots in the history of its telecommunications' as well as in the basic model of economic development and industrialization which took shape from the early 1960s. In contrast to Mexico, and other Latin American countries, the advent of computers in Brazil has been accompanied by a concerted effort at a state-supported industrial development of this sector (Mattelart and Schmucler 1985: 105). The Brazilian state has played a key role in the development of domestic telecommunications and computer industries, in establishing the respective spheres of national and transnational capital, and in establishing the basic regulatory framework within which both domestic and transnational interests operate. Nevertheless the history of Brazilian telecommunications, including the development of a domestic computer industry, has been shaped by a series of contradictions: between military officers and civilians; between those anxious to establish some national autonomy in telecommunications and those more closely identified with the interests of transnational corporations; between the diverse institutions involved in the constitution of a national system of communications and information; and within the greatly expanded strata of professional and technical workers. This set of oppositions has been played out 'within an ideological space where two powerful poles of attraction intervene: national identity and national security' (Mattelart and Schmucler 1985: 101).

After a period of dispersal, lack of co-ordination, and insufficient networks, and some foreign company responsibility for telecommunications, the Brazilian state set about establishing a clearer regulatory framework and the basis for a national telecommunications system. While radio and television were uniformly regulated as private operational spheres, telecommunications were increasingly brought under co-ordinated state control. By the early 1960s the Brazilian military was aware of the role of telecommunications in the 'integration' of an otherwise dislocated country and there was certainly increasing recognition that an extensive telecommunications network was indispensable to national investment and industrial strategies. The creation of TELEBRAS in 1972 was the 'culminating point of effort' to unify the telecommunications system (Mattelart and Schmucler 1985: 102). However, by the early 1980s private capitalist interests were seeking to expand the private communications sphere by reducing TELEBRAS's function and creating private networks.

In the years after the coup the military government, in its quest for foreign capital, was generally unsympathetic to domestic manufacturers of relatively sophisticated technology. This period, for example, saw the demise of the television-manufacturing industry which was located primarily in Sao Paulo (Langer 1989: 100). By the late 1960s a shift had started to occur in which the Brazilian navy showed an interest in developing a domestic computer industry (manufacture and servicing). This shift was brought about primarily as a result of the purchase of British frigates which used Ferranti computers. Concern was expressed that in the event of war the supply of computing equipment may not be available. This concern was also extended to the imposition of limitations on the importation of expensive foreign goods.

CONCLUSION

For many countries in Africa, Asia, and Latin America, investment in modern telecommunications and information technologies poses a dilemma: their economic development seems to be predicated at least partly on the expansion of modern communications and information systems which they are generally unable to develop and manufacture themselves, and whose purchase usually involves substantial increases in international indebtedness. The introduction of such systems, however, means incorporation into international communications and information systems over which they have little if any effective control.

The countries of Africa, Asia, and Latin America differ enormously in their capacity to develop and use modern communications technologies. The differences are bound up with the scale of the different countries, and especially of domestic markets, and above all with their levels of industrialization. The drive for the introduction of advanced communications systems has come from many different sources: from local manufacturers of components and systems; from the military in countries such as Brazil and India; from major national and transnational business users who are anxious to maintain their competitiveness; from privileged private urban users; from international telecommunications and computer suppliers; and foreign governments anxious to ensure the expansion of markets. The drive for the introduction of advanced communications systems has also been linked with privatization pressures in many countries, although major international telecommunications and computer manufacturers have not been opposed to the expansion of state communications/telecommunications systems which make use of their products.

The development of communications and computer-manufacturing capacity in countries such as Brazil and India has been contingent upon particular forms of state intervention, including industry assistance and tariff protection, and the provision of substantial, guaranteed markets. State intervention, however, has not been uncontested, especially where principal local users, including industrial manufacturers, have regarded local production as increasing their costs and reducing their competitiveness.

Chapter 7

Advertising

This chapter examines the role of advertising as the source of finance for other media as well as a key source of images. In many analyses of 'Third World' mass media, emphasis is placed on the role of advertising in presenting types of 'development' which serve international capitalist interests rather than allowing for alternative, non-capitalist or socialist development. This is achieved through the subversion of local history and culture, the integration of local ruling classes into dominant capitalist relations, and the formation and shifting of consumption preferences and tastes in accordance with the interests and activities of transnational corporations. Transnational advertising agencies play a key role in this process, often adopting national history and myths for such purposes where the local configurations of class forces require rationalization of images in local idioms (Mattelart 1979).

Although relatively small-scale advertising existed throughout much of Africa, Asia, and Latin America prior to the 1960s, it was during this decade in particular, when American-based transnational corporations and advertising agencies were associated with the rapid expansion of the global accumulation of capital, that the penetration of advertising markets in Latin American countries, and in Africa and Asia, increased significantly. African countries, with a few notable exceptions such as Egypt, Nigeria and South Africa, remain relatively unimportant in international advertising and per capita expenditure. In Asian countries such as India state controls restrict levels of transnational advertising agency investment in accordance with general industry and investment policies, and the protection of local agency accounts. Tunstall (1977: 56), amongst others, has observed that the global expansion of advertising, especially that associated with United States-based transnational corporations and advertising agencies, has been part of the drive to produce greater privatization of the electronic media where public broadcasting has been the dominant model.

The appearance on a substantial scale of American advertising agencies has . . . three major consequences. First, the total size of the media industry (in terms of revenue and of audience time) is increased. Secondly, the advertising agencies play a major part in switching revenue towards – and hence expanding the output of – commercial broadcasting. Thirdly, these agencies play a decisive part in swinging entire national media systems towards *commercial*, and away from traditional *political*, patterns.

(Tunstall 1977: 56)

This drive has been important in Western Europe and to some extent in Asia, and has certainly been pronounced in Latin America where a substantial United States stake has been developed throughout the twentieth century. In African countries, and many Asian ones as well, privatization pressures could only lead to greater access to public broadcasting organizations, since advertising markets were and still are unable to sustain electronic and print media. Print media – newspapers, magazines – are heavily dependent on state/parastatal advertising, although in countries such as India the advertising and mass media markets are now sufficiently large and diversified to allow for magazines (not newspapers) which are not principally dependent on state advertising.

Advertising, as the source of funding for other mass media, provides a paradox: where it is absent, or dominated by agencies of the state, the possibility for any media 'autonomy' and critical activity is severely circumscribed; where there is considerable development of commodity production, especially of consumer goods, and privately owned mass media, the critical news functions are subordinated to the interests of private capital accumulation.

ADVERTISING AS THE SOURCE OF MEDIA FUNDING

Advertising provides the principal financial base for commercial mass media. In many countries it is also an important source of revenue for public broadcasting systems and state-owned print media. It is this dependence on advertising which makes the media highly sensitive to economic downturn, recession and depression, and which has brought about the demise of often large-circulation newspapers and magazines and contributed to increased concentration of mass media ownership and control. The redistribution of advertising expenditure between media, as for example between print and electronic media, obviously has profound implications for the financial viability of particular media enterprises as well as processes of concentration of ownership and market concentration.

As Garnham (1979) clearly recognizes, the economic 'determination' of the mass media is direct, even if the media's reproduction of ideology cannot simply be reduced to the economic. The 'determination' is direct in the following ways: first, in the nature of capitalist ownership and control of media production; second, in the dependence of the commercial media (and non-commercial media to a considerable extent in many countries) on advertising revenue; third, in the links of the mass media with the remainder of the corporate economy through conglomerate ownership, reciprocal investment and interlocking directorates; fourth, in the role of the media in the reproduction of generalized and expanded commodity production and exchange; and fifth, in the reproduction of what Smythe (1977) refers to as the 'audience commodity' and labour power.

Smythe departs from the more 'conventional' Murdock and Golding (1973) political economy of mass communications by returning, like Marx in *Capital*, to the commodity as the starting point for theorization and analysis. It is not that he is uninterested in questions of media ownership and control, the dimensions and processes of concentration and monopoly, the advertising base of the commercial mass media, and the role of the mass media in ideological production and reproduction. However, prior to these aspects of media analysis is the nature of the commodity which must be grasped in both its abstract and concrete forms. According to Smythe, while mass media production is central to commodity production and consumption, the principal commodity being produced and exchanged is the audience, or more specifically, the predisposition of the audience to devote time to the media and to consumption. The selling of the audience commodity necessarily involves the reproduction of labour power, as well as more general commodity production. It is the nature of the audience commodity, more than any other factor, that determines what is possible in media production and distribution, as well as in the construction of advertisements.

This is the crucial point usually ignored by those associated with the view that the media are concerned with the imposition of a dominant ideology, or with manipulation and control. Media companies, or the institutions of the mass media, are ultimately restricted in their development, market reach, and rates of capital accumulation, by the nature and construction of the audience commodity. This does not mean that audiences are necessarily able in a strict sense to 'determine' media content or force the institutions of the mass media into the construction and reproduction of ideological practices antithetical to the interests of capital. The construction of the audience commodity and the determination of programming in accordance with that construction, is a basic way of ordering the world according to particular categories. While in a certain sense analysts such as Windschuttle (1988) are correct to stress that audiences are largely getting what they want (notwithstanding the usual objection that they are not in a position to propose alternatives since they are locked into well-established conventional categories), the programmes for obvious reasons remain within capitalist social relations and a capitalist ideological framework. The construction of meaning engaged in by audiences (and reading publics) may involve class affiliations and conflict, and particular sub-cultural ties, which provide the basis of a challenge to the 'preferred readings' of the text, but the whole, continuous development of the media, and their conventions, institutional arrangements, values of practice, and role in the construction and reproduction of ideology and culture is always constrained by their capitalist nature.

The expanded reproduction of commodity production is dependent on expanded and increased consumption. Since the last quarter of the nineteenth century substantial and increasing investment has occurred in the promotion of consumption and the formation of taste. This has been most conspicuous in the development of advertising and associated industries (marketing, public relations, opinion surveys) and advertiser-funded media. Modern communications media, including those which are state or publicly owned in capitalist societies, are both 'dependent' on commodity production (including the construction, definition of the audience commodity), and consumption, and are fundamental to its expanded reproduction. This great capital investment in the production of meaning or signifying practices is a crucial part of the constant, continuous redefinition of 'need' and use value.

In 'Third World' countries the problem of the construction of audience commodities tends to be compounded by a host of factors: language and literacy differences, and enormous inequalities, including great differences in the amount of disposable income which can be devoted to mass media use and commodity consumption. While, as we shall see, advertising strategies employ different media and techniques to reach and to construct markets, much advertising and media effort is really only devoted to the perhaps anticipatory socialization of mass publics. This has been understood by some as a 'revolution of rising expectations' (Vilanilam 1989: 489), but it is more accurately a case where diverse peoples are constituted as a media, advertising, and consumer-goods public often long before they have the disposable income to devote to such consumerism.[1] In Brazil, for example, the provision of cheap credit for the purchase of television sets dramatically expanded the television viewing public without being accompanied by corresponding increases in real incomes.

The expansion of United States advertising agencies into foreign markets has been driven by 'the expansion of industry itself'. Weinstein's study (cited in Janus 1981a: 299) of the expansion of the fifteen largest United States agencies found a significant relationship between the time and pace of industrial expansion and that of advertising. In order to protect their accounts, advertising agencies have either followed their transnational clients into new national markets, or opened overseas offices at their request. This latter practice developed in the early decades of this century. In 1927, for example, when General Motors assigned its account to the Thompson agency, that agency opened an office in every country where General Motors had a manufacturing plant or assembly line. In the same year McCann, at the request of Standard Oil of New Jersey, opened offices in Paris, London, and Berlin.

Before the expansion of the transnational agencies in the 1960s, manufacturers expanding into foreign, and in particular Latin American, markets were generally faced with a limited range of advertising and marketing services.

> Corporations doing business internationally after the war and even into the 1960s were faced with a very difficult advertising problem: multiple agencies turning out campaigns of uneven quality, little or no control over the company and product image on a world scale, accounting problems associated with multiple

agency relationships, and media and advertising statistics that
varied across countries.

(Janus 1981a: 292, 294)

The global expansion of industry during the 1960s, or rather, the
increasing character of capital accumulation on a global scale or
through global circuits, has required the development of a global
communications system. As United States, European, and Japanese companies have set up manufacturing and distribution
facilities in foreign markets, and increasingly provided financial,
accounting, and information services, they have sought 'dependable communications and marketing facilities capable of handling
their global operation efficiently' (Janus 1981a: 299). The transnational advertising agency has been able to provide these dependable
facilities, utilizing the most advanced communications skills and
techniques. Furthermore, Janus (1981a: 299) suggests, 'the transnational agency facilitates the consistent policies of media selection
and the use of the advertising campaign materials'.

Mattelart (1979b: 251) identifies three major, and essentially
intersecting, strategies of the internationalization of advertising
agencies: first, the imperial model; second, 'nationalization by
consent and other subterfuges'; and third, the diversification of
production. The imperial model refers to the way in which agencies
such as J. Walter Thompson and McCann-Erickson have extended
their operations throughout the world and endeavoured to maintain
full ownership of their subsidiaries even if the personnel in them is
recruited locally. They have substantially relied on clients of the
same nationality; in Mexico, for example, 25 out of 27 of J. Walter
Thompson's official clients were American transnational corporations (Mattelart 1979b: 255).

The second strategy, internationalization by consent, is partly a
response to government opposition to entry by foreign companies.
Where there is local resistance the best means of gaining access and
expanding operations is through acquisition of a share in a national
company (Mattelart 1979b: 257). Association with a national
agency is not simply advantageous from the point of view of entry,
but is also extremely useful in developing greater understanding of
local markets and avoiding 'chauvinist attitudes when they exist'.
Mattelart (1979b: 258) observes that association 'fits the par-
ticularities of the national market thanks to the presence of natives
who know the ways and customs of the country'. This strategy has
become increasingly important as a way of penetrating national

markets with the passing of 'the epoch of complete networks'. Minority participation perhaps inevitably leads to moves for greater control. Even where this is not forthcoming, the participation of the transnational agencies has a great influence on the nature of local industry and the models and styles it adopts.

In ASEAN countries transnational agencies, while retaining a dominant market position, have responded to localization pressures using various elements of the second strategy. During the 1970s there were strong pressures for the localization of advertising through ownership and legislation restricting the operation of foreign agencies and their commercials. Certain types of advertisements were banned and in countries such as Malaysia there was an insistence on the use of local artists in advertisements (Lent 1982: 183). In Indonesia during the 1970s the principal television advertisers and programme sponsors were transnational corporations, and the principal advertising agencies were transnational. Faced with competition from such agencies representing transnational corporations, the large number of Indonesian agencies exerted a good deal of pressure on the Indonesian government to prevent foreign ownership. Realizing the likely government prohibition of foreign ownership, the transnational agencies entered into consultancy arrangements with local agencies without greatly diminishing their influence (Lent 1982: 184). In Malaysia, where the largest agencies were foreign-owned, local corporations entered into mutually beneficial arrangements with foreign agencies to protect and increase their market share substantially. The Malaysian government in 1973 imposed a surcharge on foreign-made commercials and in the following year passed a bill requiring commercials to be produced in Malaysia using local personnel (Lent 1982: 185).

The third strategy adopted by transnational agencies has been a diversification of production. This has predominantly taken the form of 'the creation of a complete chain of services relating to modernized advertising work' (Mattelart 1979b: 262). Such diversification has been into public relations, the setting up or absorption of firms concerned primarily with the promotion of particular types of production such as pharmaceutical and medical products, and commercial research based on a 'spread of interdisciplinary knowledge, especially economics and psychology'. This type of diversification has increasingly brought advertising agencies into competition with specialist firms in the public relations, management consultancy, auditing, market research, and employment agency areas. The combined activities of the advertising agencies with their expanded range of services, and the internationalized specialist service bureaux, help form 'an immense complex of precisely adjusted research services' which is of great use to the transnational corporations (Mattelart 1979b: 265–7).

ADVERTISING IN AFRICA

Head (1974: 336) suggests that when African broadcasting systems 'sought competent advice on how to increase advertising revenue, billings have gone up – often dramatically'. This happened, for example, in Kenya, Ethiopia and Malawi in the late 1960s. One of the major obstacles to government-controlled broadcasting organizations in Africa realizing further earning potential from advertising stems from the adoption of a public broadcasting model largely unsympathetic to advertising. There is sometimes a staff indifference, even hostility, to the possibilities of increasing advertising revenue in state-funded broadcasting organizations. This has not been helped much by the tendency of governments to require that advertising revenue from broadcasting should flow into general revenue 'while the broadcasting systems that earn the revenue operate on inflexible annual budgetary appropriation'. Problems are exacerbated when often arbitrary government action interferes with programming and thus commercial schedules. Television in African countries tends, Tunstall (1977: 114) notes, 'to be used as the President's personal public address system to the local elite'. Where this is the case broadcasters are forced to respond quickly to political directives, even if this leads to a significant loss of audience.

The problems have been compounded, certainly for those who would like to see a much stronger commercial orientation of African broadcasting media, by either the ineffectiveness or the virtual absence of advertising agencies. Agencies which are able to offer a full range of services, including research and production, can contribute to programming variety (even producing such programmes) as well as advertising volume. Such agencies tend to be either transnational or their local affiliates.

In African countries, where advertising expenditure is slight in comparison with the advanced capitalist world and countries such as Brazil, Mexico, and India, the largest single advertising agencies are American. This is the case in Ghana, Kenya, and Nigeria. Lintas has dominated the market in Ghana, Sierra Leone, and Nigeria, although the agency it established in Kenya in the early 1960s only lasted for three years (Abuoga and Mutere 1988: 93). The picture which emerges in Kenya is of American agencies in the 1960s establishing a stronger presence in a market which had previously been dominated by relatively small companies run mainly by British expatriates. The relatively small size of the market, possibly combined with a lack of detailed knowledge of it, led to frequent collapses, takeovers, and absorption into transnational agencies. Shifts in relations between transnational agencies, as part of the trend towards much greater international concentration of the industry, had a decisive impact on the Kenyan market. Ogilvy and Mather, for example, the market leader, bought another international agency, S.H. Benson (East Africa) Limited, in 1962, and took over their accounts. Another American agency, Grants Advertising, was established in Nairobi but was sold to McCann-Erickson. Other international agencies have established offices in Kenya, only to withdraw after a few years of operation. This was the case with D'Arcy, McManus and Massius Worldwide Inc., which teamed up with Peter Colmore Limited and acquired the accounts of Union Carbide and Colgate-Palmolive (Abuoga and Mutere 1988: 92–4). At present advertising is almost entirely controlled by international capital. Of the eleven Nairobi-based advertising agencies, four are subsidiaries of transnational corporations, and six are local corporations with a large share of foreign capital. Only one is Kenyan owned (Jouet 1984: 441).

ADVERTISING AND THE SHAPING OF MASS COMMUNICATIONS SYSTEMS

Advertising has not only had a profound, if difficult to specify, effect on the shaping of consumption preferences; it has also played a role in shaping mass communications. This has been the case in advanced capitalist societies where modern advertising has developed in almost a symbiotic relationship with the mass media. The dependence on advertising of media has largely determined their organizational structure, programming, and relations with audiences or publics. This influence has been extended to public broadcasting organizations such as the BBC which have been increasingly forced to respond to market pressures in order to justify continued levels of state funding in audience terms.

It is more difficult to ascertain the role of advertising in shaping mass communications systems in many 'Third World' countries. This is not simply because in socialist or communist countries such as China and Cuba the media have been seen as important agents of revolutionary transformation and mobilization, or have been substantially government-owned and dominated by public broadcasting values. Rather, it has been that in so many countries, especially in Africa, the advertising market has been so undeveloped that it has been incapable of making more than the slightest difference to radio and television broadcasting.

Although many African government-controlled radio and television stations accept advertising, and in some instances sponsorship, this appears to have made little difference to broadcasting systems which are heavily dependent on state subvention. Advertisers would clearly like to be able to associate their products with successful programmes, whether local or imported, and establish more precisely the nature of target audiences, but are constrained by, amongst other factors, the economics of broadcasting. This includes the importation of high-cost programmes. The push for greater commercialization, even privatization, inevitably runs up against the limited media and advertising outlets. Advertisers are not necessarily interested in privatization; the question of ownership is essentially irrelevant if markets can be reached effectively through government broadcasting. It is likely to be only where government programming and funding policies reduce the ability of advertisers to reach expanded audiences and market segments that such interest increases.

Some governments, like their counterparts in advanced capitalist economies, have been anxious to reduce state expenditure by further opening up public broadcasting to private capitalist interests while retaining firm control over programming. Receiver licence fee systems, especially for radios, have generally proven unworkable and in some instances have been abandoned. Both the political and economic costs (administration, collection, policing) of fee systems have been unacceptable, although alternatives other than direct subvention have been limited.

In Latin America the strong advertiser drive for the transformation of radio broadcasting began in the late 1930s, and in the case of television at the end of the 1950s. United States exporters to Latin America were quickly aware of the enormous potential of radio as an advertising medium. Towards the end of the 1930s United States government trade promotion officials were extolling the advertising advantages which Latin American radio stations offered North American businesses. United States broadcasting companies such as NBC and CBS were also interested in penetrating Latin American markets through direct broadcasting advertising.

> Allowed by the FCC in 1939 to sell commercial time on their shortwave broadcasts to Latin America, NBC and CBS both inaugurated plans for a Latin American network of affiliated stations which would rebroadcast local programs and advertisements transmitted to those stations via shortwave.
>
> (Fejes 1980: 46)

After World War II the major North American networks encouraged the growth of commercial television in Latin American countries. They were clearly attracted by the possibility of setting up 'a centralized hemispheric broadcasting network' which would enable North American advertisers to reach Latin American audiences. The North American networks extended capital, organization, and technical assistance, as well as programming, to developing television stations 'which would then act as affiliates' (Fejes 1980: 46).

The attempts to create inter-continental networks failed, partly as a result of competition from the internationalizing advertising agencies. The principal drawback for the networks was that their centralized system of advertising production and distribution could not adequately take into account the needs of transnational corporation clients in specific markets. Transnational advertising agencies, sometimes through local affiliates, were invariably better able to provide the detailed local knowledge and careful planning of advertising required. The growth of television in the 1960s meant that advertisers increasingly directed their spending to the electronic media; by 1977 the transnational agencies were spending an average of 65 per cent of their advertising budget on radio and television advertising. As they required literacy, and lacked the reach of radio and television, the print media quickly lost ground in the competition for transnational advertising revenue.

In most Latin American countries the amount of time and space devoted to advertising by different media is high and tends to increase (Janus 1981a: 310). This is as true of print as it is of electronic media. A study of twenty-two major Latin American newspapers conducted in the late 1970s found that an average of

49.9 per cent of their space was sold, with some selling as much as 65 per cent of their space (Brockmann 1978). Television stations in some countries often carry as much advertising as programming content. In the advanced capitalist countries such as the United States print media (newspaper and magazine) dependence on advertising revenue has generally increased. Although there is no comparable and precise data for 'Third World' countries, it is probably safe to assume that there has been a corresponding increase.

While mass media in general, including public broadcasting systems in many countries, show a greater dependence on advertising revenue, the importance to media of transnational advertising has also grown. Brockmann's 1970s study of twenty-two large Latin American newspapers found that if the three government-subsidized newspapers were excluded, between 20 and 50 per cent of advertising space was purchased by transnational corporations. A similar situation obtains in the case of the twenty-five largest women's magazines of six Latin American countries in which an average of 59.7 per cent of advertising space is devoted to the promotion of transnational products. Broadcast media in countries such as Mexico have also shown a high dependence on transnational advertising. A study of Mexican broadcasting found that

> of the 270 commercials transmitted in one day by a popular radio station, 84 per cent advertised transnational products. Similarly, of the 647 commercials transmitted by the five television channels in Mexico City that day, 77 per cent carried transnational products.
>
> (Janus 1981a: 311)

ADVERTISING IN BRAZIL

The development of the mass media – television in particular – and the growth of advertising in Brazil have been strongly influenced by protectionist policies designed to restrict foreign, mainly American, influence. Seven of the ten largest advertising agencies in Brazil are domestic, primarily as a result of a government policy granting advertising accounts only to national agencies. The growth of the Brazilian mass media, and of advertising, has obviously been tightly linked to economic growth and industrialization (Mattos 1984: 211). Advertising expenditure through agencies in Brazil (excluding advertising sold directly to the mass media) grew from US $150 million in 1959 to $1,920 million in 1980, making Brazil one of the world's major advertising expenditure countries.

Not unexpectedly Brazilian television accounts for by far the largest share of advertising expenditure, this having grown from 24.7 per cent in 1962 to 57.8 per cent in 1980. While the share of newspapers has remained relatively constant, that of magazines has dropped significantly since the early 1970s. It has been radio, however, which has experienced the greatest drop in share of advertising expenditure. As Mattos (1984: 213) notes, the organization of Brazilian television in national networks contributed to the growth of television's share of advertising expenditure by facilitating the work of the agencies. In other words, the establishment of national television networks has been a key factor in the nationalization and homogenization of the masses.

In Brazil, government at federal, regional and local levels has become the largest single advertiser. This has often given it considerable power over the mass media without formal legislative intervention. The largest group of advertisers is composed of transnational corporations which allocate between 60 and 95 per cent of their advertising expenditure to television. Of the eight largest advertisers on Brazilian television in 1980, six were transnational corporations such as Gessy Lever, Nestle, and Johnson and Johnson (Mattos 1984: 211). Brazilian economic growth and industrialization policies of the 1960s and 1970s were predicated on the importance of foreign technology and substantial foreign investment. These policies increased the role of United States-based transnational corporations in the Brazilian economy. Predicably major transnationals such as Colgate-Palmolive sponsored and 'also encouraged the importation of American programs'; indeed Colgate-Palmolive in the early 1960s hired Brazilian writers to adapt specific United States television programmes for sponsorship purposes (Mattos 1984: 214). The stimulation of mass consumption occurred initially, as it did elsewhere throughout the 'Third World', in the food, health, and consumer goods areas. The most advertised products included toiletries, groceries, savings-and-loans, drugs, cigarettes, banking, automobiles, alcohol, shoes and cleaning products, many of them produced by the subsidiaries of transnational corporations.

GLOBAL ADVERTISING

The transnationalization of capital accumulation, markets, and advertising, has clearly contributed to the development of the 'global campaign', with an emphasis on a single advertising theme for use in all the local markets where the product is available. The ultimate logic of this tendency is the rationalization and homogenization of consumption habits around the world. Many Latin American analysts have understood this, as we have already seen, as the intersection of transnationalization and the combined processes of the nationalization and homogenization of the masses; in other words, the constitution of the 'masses' as a national market open to transnational influence, primarily through the agency of television.

The creation of the global consumer is 'rarely spontaneous' (Janus 1981a: 300). As in the societies which first underwent a major consumerist phase, consumers or potential consumers in 'Third World' countries usually have to undergo a prolonged education in the uses and advantages of new products. Clearly the constitution of the global consumer meets resistance from consumers used to local products and who have well-established preferences. Resistance is also likely to come from local business interests engaged in competition with the transnationals for market share. Global strategies have to meet the well-entrenched cultural peculiarities or configurations in which marketing takes place. Often-cited examples of advertising strategies requiring significant cultural change include: first, overcoming local prejudice against instant coffee consumption in a major coffee-producing country such as Brazil; second, encouraging mothers to use milk formulas and baby food products produced outside the home; and third, persuading people to accept fast foods produced by transnational corporations such as McDonald's and Kentucky Fried Chicken.

Sinclair (1987), Mattelart (1979b), Mattelart, Delcourt and Mattelart (1984) and other writers emphasize the way in which the transnationalization of advertising and agencies operates through the peculiarities of national cultures. This emphasis can perhaps lead to the neglect of the importance of local agencies, marketeers, and producers of consumer products, especially in countries where there has been substantial industrialization and development of a local bourgeoisie. In India, for example, there has been a significant expansion of advertising geared to electronic and electrical appliance and expensive household goods consumption. The principal producers of such goods are Indian companies – in some cases subsidiaries of transnationals, in most local companies working in conjunction with transnational corporations through various types of technology transfer and licensing agreements. It is national capital which is paramount, even if it operates through co-operation with international capital and local state structures. Clearly the intended consumers of the advertised products are the Indian bourgeoisie and petty bourgeoisie which are numerically large and have a strong international orientation (Clad 1990).

The expansion of the consumption of electronic goods (radios, stereo systems, television sets, video cassette recorders, personal computers) and electrical appliances (washing machines, clothes dryers, refrigerators, food processors, juice extractors, air conditioners) represents part of the transnationalization of markets and commodity culture. In many advertisements immediately recognizable local settings and people are used, but always with some international referent to indicate that consumption is part of an international phenomenon. For example, a recent Indian magazine advertisement for International Lux relies on the connection between national and international images and appeal. Set against the backdrop of the Manhattan skyline of skyscrapers and flashing lights (it could just as well be Bombay) is the centrally located pocket with a portrait of a 'film star' as well as the elongated, oval bar of soap with 'Lux' engraved in it. In the left-hand corner, and occupying the most prominent position, is the Indian film star 'Sreedevi'; her picture is considerably larger than that of the international star, her appearance highly Europeanized or 'westernized'. Immediately she is associated with an international setting (she merges into Manhattan), international stars, and international products which stars and others use. She is made to exclaim: 'The favourite complexion care soap of 70 countries is my favourite too!'

Another interesting example of internationalization is provided by the Dinesh clothing advertisement featuring the Indian cricketer Sunil Gavaskar – a person who epitomizes success, international connections, and widespread recognition. This advertisement depends on the identification by the observer of Gavaskar as an internationally famous cricketer at home in an international setting. The linkage between cricket and baseball is established without any direct references to cricket; Gavaskar is so well known for his cricketing prowess that no further explanation is required. In the main picture Gavaskar, the height of sartorial elegance in his suit and overcoat, and with a scarf loosely tossed around his neck, is signing a baseball bat for a large, slightly podgy American. An attractive young woman, left hand lightly, perhaps even intimately placed on Gavaskar's shoulder, her other hand held against her face, watches the autograph-signing and experiences pleasurable surprise. In the first of the smaller pictures located vertically on the right-hand side of the advertisement Gavaskar holds the baseball bat and demonstrates his grip; he is watched by three children with whom he shares a joke, and the attractive woman. In the second of these pictures Gavaskar is autographing the bat for, and sharing a joke with, the children while the attractive woman looks on. In the third, Gavaskar, at three-quarters length, stands alone displaying his Dinesh clothing.

While these two advertisements are clearly derived from models and a lexicon of images and practices well established in the major national advertising markets of North America, Western Europe, and Japan, the driving force behind them in any direct sense has not necessarily been international capital or the transnational corporation. The products and services being advertised are the same as those available in the most advanced markets, but they are produced by national firms. Increasingly the drive for such advertising, coupled inevitably with the drive for expanded production and consumption, comes from national as well as international forces.

Advertising in the African, Asian, and Latin American regions, despite national variations, manifests striking similarities in imagery and meaning. This is partly bound up with the transnationalization of advertising, as well as the adoption by local advertising agencies of the models and values of practice associated with the major agencies; in other words, they could be seen as part of cultural imperialist, and imperialist relations more generally. It is also simply the result of the basic function of advertising which is to sell by making consumers believe they are in some way inadequate and can transform themselves through particular types of consumption. Advertising does this by the constant reworking of significant meaning within particular cultures.

Some advertising simply involves substitution: in an Omo or other washing powder advertisement, for example, whether for television, cinema advertising, or print media, essentially the same advertisement is used but with the substitution of local people. Two black Kenyan women, rather than American or Australian 'house-wives', meet in the local supermarket and discuss the virtues of Omo. A little surprisingly, the construction of the nuclear family has become almost universal in advertising – certainly in processed foods, beverages, and household appliances. This would appear slightly odd in societies where extended family and other kinship relations are of great importance, or where different types of family arrangements have been worked out, as for instance in the *barrios* of major Latin American cities. This may yet again be simply a cultural imperialist transference of values, or a recognition that the nuclear family or an equivalent represents the principal consumption unit in a capitalist society; if it does not exist, then it should, or eventually capitalist social and economic transformation, with advertising playing a key role, will produce it.

CRITICS OF TRANSNATIONAL ADVERTISING

Critics of transnational advertising often assert that the most vulnerable to the appeal of advertising are the marginalized who lack the financial means to purchase the advertised commodities and who are in the worst possible position to assess critically their usefulness or otherwise. Most advertising is not explicitly directed at such people for obvious reasons, even if they do come across it on billboards, in cinemas, and on radio and television. Access to advertising in print media is restricted by literacy, as well as the financial means to purchase a newspaper, magazine, or perhaps a book. Access to television is also greatly restricted in many countries, although throughout Latin America, and especially in countries such as Brazil and Mexico, there is a very high per capita usage. Radio, which often reaches larger audiences than print media and television, is clearly a major advertising vehicle, certainly in countries where both television and the print media have only a very limited reach.

The rationale has frequently been advanced that advertising plays a key role in economic growth by 'creating and mobilizing the demand and disposable income of lower-income groups so as to create a vast market for goods' (Fejes 1980: 44). The satisfaction of this demand supposedly leads to increased investment in productive capacity and the creation of new jobs. As a result, the living standards of the lower classes are raised and the extremes of income and wealth characteristic of 'Third World' countries decreased. Critics, however, note that usually the new investment generated is directed into more capital-intensive forms of production which directly employ very little additional labour (Fejes 1980: 44). Few jobs for the lower-income groups are created, and the increased income is used for additional investment in machinery, distributed to shareholders, or in the Latin American case, it may go into repaying substantial loans, including international ones. Increased income does not necessarily flow through into higher wages at all and the concentration of wealth may be greater than before.

Critics in Africa in particular, as well as elsewhere, constantly assert that advertising contributes to the dominance of 'consumption-oriented models of development' in countries where even the most basic needs cannot be satisfied. Writing of Africa, Jerry Domatob (1987: 281–2) suggests that 'advertising creates a consumption syndrome and unleashes untold expectations in one of the world's most backward regions. At times the desires created by advertising lead to crime, greed and corruption'. Such critics reject the assumption made by Walter Rostow, Ithiel de Sola Pool, and other modernization writers, that advertising may be a powerful tool of development by stimulating demand for goods which can ultimately be produced through expanded local, import-substitution industrialization, by emphasizing its role in reproducing underdevelopment, extreme inequality, and penetration by transnational corporations. Domatob argues that transnational corporations, rather than being 'great levellers and great equalizers',

> actually reinforce the sharp class cleavage that exists in all poor sub-Saharan states. The principal targets of most transnational companies are the enclaves of affluence within destitute sub-Saharan African societies. The expensive capital goods (sic) such as automobiles, luxuries such as fine watches and cameras and costly services such as plane rides to New York, London and Paris are available to only a tiny fraction of the population in sub-Saharan Africa, although it obviously represents a sizeable market.
>
> (Domatob 1987: 286)

In African countries the consumption preferences emphasized and stimulated by transnational corporations and their advertising agencies represent a drain on foreign exchange, especially when there is continuing deterioration of terms of trade and currency devaluation. For critics such as Domatob (1987: 286) the mobile upper classes of Africa, through their adoption of the eating, clothing, and travelling habits of the 'American upper middle class', essentially live 'imported lives'. Thus, in much African criticism links are established between the consumption model provided by the transnational corporations and their advertising agencies, and which is held out to the upper classes in particular, and a cultural unauthenticity which had its origins under European colonialism. This unauthenticity has been deepened and intensified in the postcolonial period, with advertising helping to create 'false needs' which divert attention, and more importantly, resources from basic developmental problems. The distinction is frequently made between 'real psychological and social needs' and those associated with transnationals and advertising. 'Real' needs are associated with cultural authenticity as well as with development.

The criticism is developed that transnational corporations and advertising agencies promote a completely inappropriate consumption ethos when what is desperately needed is a production ethos. Transnational advertising facilitates cultural dependence. Transnational corporation investment priorities contribute to the 'disarticulation' of economies in Africa and elsewhere throughout the 'Third World' (Domatob 1987: 288). Further, the transnational encouragement of particular types of consumption through the mass media – cigarettes, soft drinks and alcoholic drinks, cosmetics, and household appliances – discourages domestic savings and the indigenous accumulation of capital (Domatob 1987: 288).

Vilanilam (1989: 481) develops a similar critique of television advertising in India, emphasizing the way in which advertising is a key part of the development and spread of a global corporate culture which 'cuts at the roots of cultural autonomy of politically independent countries'. In his dependency model the Indian ruling classes acquiesce in the model of development proposed by transnational corporate interests, and are part of a transnational consumer culture which is largely unrelated to the real needs of the vast majority of Indians who are sunk in 'poverty, illiteracy, malnutrition, superstition and unemployment' (Vilanilam 1989: 487). In the case of television advertising the messages which reach the 'elite' are overwhelmingly about new types of processed and packaged foods, clothing, and shelter, but never address the immediate needs of the vast majority of people. Vilanilam acerbically notes that for advertisers

Housing is no problem in India; the problem is how to keep the mansions and bungalows already constructed by the affluent class disinfected, deodorized, shiny, sanitized and fragrant, decorated with natural or artificial flowers and foliage, covered with paint of varied hues, and polished with the best wax and varnish in the world. The lawns are to be kept trim, adorned with sprinklers and fountains. The driveway should sport, if possible, the imported car.

(Vilanilam 1989: 488)

In a country where there is an 'acute shortage of safe drinking water', nutritionally useless aerated soft drinks are extensively advertised, with their consumption often linked to international values (Vilanilam 1989: 491).

CONCLUSION

Advertising is both an important source of finance for other media and a key source of imagery in 'Third World' societies. The expansion of advertising can be seen as part of the global expansion of capitalism in which transnational corporations and advertising agencies have played a key role. This expansion has frequently been considered by critics as a major part of the ideological apparatus of imperialism and a significant part of the ideological penetration of 'Third World' societies. Critics have condemned its role in promoting inappropriate consumer-oriented models of development which do not address basic problems of inequality and human need and in arousing expectations which cannot be met given current levels of development.

Advertising's drive for expansion has been linked with the greater privatization of electronic media where public or state broadcasting has been the dominant model. However, to see this as simply driven by international capitalist forces is to underestimate the extent and importance of national capitalist industrialization and expansion of consumer markets, as well as the formation of local capitalist classes whose interests both coincide and clash with those of international capitalism. The drive for privatization of electronic media is often retarded by national political factors, as well as by an advertising financial base which is insufficiently large to allow for their complete extraction from the state or governmental sphere.

Chapter 8

News

In their call for the institution of a NWICO, governments and critics in the 'Third World' have emphasized the unidirectional flow of international communications, the dominance of 'bad news' reporting of 'Third World' countries in the media of the advanced capitalist societies, and the role of the major news agencies in perpetuating this state of affairs. The establishment of national and regional news agencies to redress the international imbalance and provide greater control over the flow of communications about the 'Third World' has run up against financial problems as well as the basic difficulties in Africa in particular of setting up comprehensive news-gathering networks.

Apart from wanting to redress the imbalance in international news flow, and condemning the 'free flow of information' doctrine as part of the penetration of 'Third World' countries by advanced capitalist societies and their transnational corporations, many critics have been anxious to construct different concepts of 'news' which are not simply replications of those which are dominant in the commercial media of the advanced capitalist world. This redefinition has been complicated by a host of factors: often uneasy relations between the print media in particular and party and state; the use of the media for presidential 'image building' and political purposes; and the supposed demands of nation-building and national unity which usually amount to major intellectual suppression. Within news organizations there have been conflicts over whether journalists should pursue advocacy and investigative journalism, development journalism, or adhere to the values of practice such as objective reporting and detachment which are dominant in the media of the United States and some other advanced capitalist countries.

The press has probably represented the area of most intense controversy and conflict over news redefinition and relations with state and party. This is partly due to its colonial origins in African, Asian, Latin American and Middle Eastern societies, association with nationalist and anti-imperialist struggle, and subsequent difficulties in post-colonial societies adapting to demands of party and state. It is also partly due to the fact that the press has much deeper, longer roots, and values of practice that are much more thoroughly ingrained in intellectual and political culture than radio and television broadcasting. The intensity of conflict involving the print media, and not just daily newspapers, stems to some extent from the premature emergence in many societies of a division between the older cultural apparatus with its intellectual practices and institutional bases (universities and colleges, journals and reviews, some publishing houses, professional associations, and particular modes of political-intellectual discourse) and modern culture industries.

During colonialism, and even in the early years of the post-independence period in some countries, there were important links between those who could be considered part of a cultural apparatus and the mass media. In many instances the press provided important intellectual outlets (poetry, short stories, criticism) where few others were available. A combination of different types of state repression and basic changes in the nature of the press, especially as a result of its dependence on advertising and key part in the commodification of production, has meant that it is no longer a major vehicle of intellectual expression – if that is understood in a narrow sense. Increasingly 'news' has become constructed in its entertainment and commodity functions, as it is in the advanced capitalist countries, or constructed in ways which support particular ruling interests, state institutions, and developmental strategies.

In the case of radio and television the particular or dominant construction of 'news' is bound up with the different 'models' of radio and television production and distribution adopted, including the industrial structures and organization of finance (whether dependent on state funding, commercial advertising, or a direct part of the state or party apparatus as in China) and the dominant forms of programming. It would appear to be the case that when electronic media, including state- and publicly-owned radio and television, become more dependent on advertising revenue, important changes occur in programming. The entertainment function becomes more important as a way of attracting audiences, and the programming takes on more of the structure of that of the major commercial media in the advanced capitalist countries. This has consequences for news programming, and news definition, which become more subject to entertainment criteria.

DEBATE ABOUT JOURNALISM: SOCIALIZATION AND PROFESSIONALIZATION OF JOURNALISTS

Despite strong, frequent criticism of foreign domination of mass media in African countries, journalism education programmes are still largely patterned on those in Europe and the United States (Murphy and Scotton 1987: 12). Prior to independence nearly all Africans working in journalism had received their training on the job. While in South Africa and Rhodesia apprenticeship schemes were operated by some newspapers, elsewhere Africans were taken on as assistants to help with the production of material for African audiences. For many, on-the-job training was provided in the African newspapers and news sheets which were vehicles and voices of nationalist struggle. Many of the trainees 'certainly absorbed the professional attitudes' of the European-controlled publications for which they worked, even if their political views diverged sharply.

The advent of independence produced a demand for substantially increased numbers of trained media personnel, including journalists, editors, and technicians. This was partly the outcome of the departure of European personnel, as well as of the rapid expansion of the media, especially broadcast media, which were seen as having a vital role in the establishment, dissemination and implementation of development goals. The United Nations, and governments such as the British and French, provided funds and technical assistance for the rapid expansion of facilities. Broadcasting was given particular priority, primarily because it was seen as a way of reaching large, dispersed audiences, by transcending the barriers of illiteracy.

Tunstall (1977: 208) argues that before UNESCO's identification with the attempt to institute a New International Information Order in the 1970s, the 'triumph of the "value-free" American ideology of the media was nowhere more remarkable than in UNESCO'. In a real sense, Tunstall suggests, UNESCO was effectively captured by American media doctrines and interests. It became associated with the propagation of American notions such as the 'free flow of information' which 'inevitably favour the major media exporting nations'. Much of the research which guided its discussion and formulation of policy was based on American models and findings which reflected the peculiarities of the American commercial media systems. This was partly a function of the predominance of American mass communications studies, although critical, essentially European alternatives were available.

The first serious UNESCO media effort coincided with the great wave of newly independent countries in the early 1960s. In 1958 the United Nations General Assembly had voted for 'a programme of action for developing national media systems' (Tunstall 1977: 209). Major conferences on Asian, Latin American, and African media were held in 1961 and 1962. UNESCO policies were imbued with an optimism which did little to address the basic economic and other problems affecting the introduction and development of sophisticated media systems (Tunstall 1977: 210). The view was rampant that many of the problems associated with illiteracy and generally poor communications distribution in African and other countries could be surmounted by the rapid development of electronic media which would serve as a major educational force – notwithstanding that educational television in the advanced capitalist countries was poorly developed and dependent on tiny budgets!

Journalism training was an important way of extending 'a potent Anglo-American influence in other countries' (Tunstall 1977: 214). This influence took the form of particular notions of professionalism among journalists, broadcasters, and others in communications occupations. 'Professionalism' in communications predicably involved the assertion of the principle of autonomy, or independence from either political or commercial direction. This principle fitted comfortably with functionalist communications and media analysis in which a clear separation is made between communications and other systems. Pye (1963: 78), for example, noted that 'the mass media dimension of the modern communications process not only is comparatively independent of other social and political processes but also constitutes a distinctive industry in both an economic and social sense. Both as an industry and as a profession the modern field of communications tends to generate an ethos and a relatively distinct set of norms for guiding its functions'.

In the case of journalism and other occupations the claim for professional autonomy and concomitant professional standards tends to be made through professional training establishments, and especially schools of journalism (Tunstall 1977: 214). By the 1950s the vast majority of such schools were in the United States; a UNESCO document claimed that in 1952–3 only 95 of the 645 journalism training programmes were outside the United States. The export of American journalism education had begun much earlier: in Latin America, especially throughout the 1930s, and in China, and in Egypt through the American University in Cairo. In many respects American journalism schools – professional training institutions, as well as mass communications research traditions and methodologies – represented the largely unchallenged model which UNESCO effectively adopted during the 1950s. International training centres based on the American model were established in France (at Strasbourg, for the training of African communications personnel), Ecuador, the Philippines, and in Senegal (Tunstall 1977: 216).

The spread of American-style journalism education was also facilitated by CIESPAL, a partly UNESCO-supported centre in Ecuador. From the perspective of American journalism educators this was 'the linchpin of a new structure of "professional" journalism education in Latin America'. It was able to provide the professors who could teach at the large numbers of university-based schools of journalism established throughout Latin America in the 1960s in particular – by 1970 there were sixty-eight. Financial aid to journalism education in Latin America also came from many other sources: the Ford Foundation, the USIA, the Inter-American Press Association, and before its receipt of CIA funds was revealed, the Inter-American Federation of Working Newspapermen's Organization (Tunstall 1977: 215).

The spread of American styles of journalism education, and American media knowledge, is also to be found in Africa, Asia, and Western Europe. In Nairobi (Kenya) the International Press Institute's journalism training programme (now part of the University of Nairobi) was financed at its inception by the Ford Foundation and directed by a British journalist. In Nigeria the American influence is conspicuous in the training of journalism educators – indeed, many did postgraduate degrees in the United States – the structure of journalism programmes, and research methodologies employed in media analysis. Despite the adoption of radical dependency perspectives, there is surprisingly little familiarity with the more critical European culture and media analytical traditions.

In many countries the pressures for the increase in the training of communicators were political. In Nigeria, for example, after the

Biafran secession and the civil war, the creation of a new federal structure with nineteen separate states led directly to substantial increases in the demand for media personnel, the federal government having 'promised each state radio and television facilities and a newspaper' (Murphy and Scotton 1987: 16). By 1972 there were at least thirty training programmes in journalism and mass communications in Africa, with approximately two-thirds of them in sub-Saharan countries. The extension of training facilities and programmes immediately led to debate over the forms of training and non-African domination at all levels. In Nigeria often vigorous debate revolved around the advantages of academic as opposed to professional-technical training, with the former gaining increasingly widespread support throughout Africa. While this is still important, the ground of the debate has shifted very much to the issue of the relevance of training. The non-African basis of training has been increasingly criticized for its perpetuation of western cultural influence, although clearly many African political leaders prefer existing training programmes to continue rather than have develop the disruption of oppositional journalism (Murphy and Scotton 1987: 17–18).

The African 'dependence' on western media models and mass communications research methods is demonstrated by the almost complete dominance of content analysis in empirical research studies (Murphy and Scotton 1987: 20). Although many African mass communications writers and researchers work within cultural dependency and media imperialism concepts, they nevertheless remain wedded to research methods and theoretical precepts which seem more characteristic of the dominant, conventional American mass communications tradition than of the more critical European traditions. As such, this is a major legacy of their training in American or American-influenced institutions. African journalism texts published during the 1980s have not pushed much beyond the well-established values of practice and the dominant definition of news to be found in standard American journalism texts (Murphy and Scotton 1987: 22). The edited collection, *Reporting Africa*, published in 1985, does shift slightly towards the values of 'new journalism', with Michael Traber, for example, calling for an awareness of 'alternative' news values which involves giving coverage at times to non-prominent people who often make good news and features sources. There is also a need, according to Traber, for the African journalist to use 'alternative language' and to give attention to stories which emphasize social processes rather than simply events.

In *Reporting Africa* many of the contributors are still committed to notions of journalistic detachment and objectivity which they hold to be common within the 'worldwide' fraternity of journalists (Murphy and Scotton 1987: 24). However, critics of such a position reject the idea that journalistic values and practices can somehow be 'culturally neutral'. The supporters of advocacy or 'new journalism' have dismissed the ideal of objectivity as both an impossibility and as undesirable.

It is frequently argued by critics that the dominant values of practice of 'western' journalism that have spread to African countries directly contradict earlier, essentially pre-colonial, communications models and practices. The communicator in 'traditional' society was engaged in socially purposive communications, and not objective reporting, and was as such involved in the shaping of messages to produce agreement and acceptance (Golding 1977).

Although the advocacy position has been adopted by many journalists in Africa it is by no means universal among professional journalists, many of whom are still strongly committed to the older professional values of American and other western journalism. Exchange programmes for student journalists, combined with the literature readily available to them, have served to maintain such professional values and practices. In Africa the advocacy model runs up not only against the objective model, but also against development journalism. Whereas in the United States and other western capitalist countries advocacy journalism has been attached to causes and the exposure of governmental corruption, and not identified with any political party, in African countries it is usually understood by journalists as a commitment to economic and social development and the governmental institutions concerned with bringing about such development. While African journalists and media analysts frequently assert that the journalist's developmental role embraces criticism, this is rarely what happens, especially when the press media are government-owned and often tightly controlled by politicians.

TANZANIA

In Tanzania often fierce conflicts between the press, party, and the state, indicated the extent to which there was contestation of what was meant by socialism and socialist journalism. This is clearly illustrated by the turbulent and interesting period of the early 1970s in which Frene Ginwalla, a South African-born Marxist lawyer and journalist, occupied central stage. Ginwalla became editor of *The Standard* and *Sunday News* after the nationalization of the first in 1970. After independence *The Standard* had, under its British editors, adopted a sympathetic stance to the government, but the sale of its parent group to Lonrho rendered it more suspect in Tanzanian government eyes and it was duly nationalized. This nationalization was part of the post-Arusha Declaration wave of nationalization designed to give Tanzania greater control over its own resources, to break the 'dependency' links with the major capitalist economies, and disengage from imperialism. Greater control of the news media was considered a necessary stage in this process.

Ginwalla started work with a Presidential Charter whose message was to stimulate constructive debate within the country and to promote the Arusha Declaration. However, Ginwalla's sustained attack on the notion of objectivity as a fiction shocked many of the journalists who had been reared in the British journalistic tradition (Barton 1979: 114). The shift at the time of the nationalization of *The Standard* from a reliance solely on the news agency Reuters to AP from the United States, Tass from Moscow, and Hsin-Lun from Beijing, put pressure on the sub-editors who often had reports from four different sources with which to cope. At the same time journalism training was combined with the development of political orientation both in the classroom and on the job (Barton 1979: 114–15). In addition socialist foreign feature material came from Prensa Latina, the Cuban-based agency, *Granma*, the Cuban newspaper, the American Liberation News Agency, and the Africa Research Group, and was published in *The Standard* and the *Sunday News*. For many journalists the political orientation distracted from other aspects of their training, and there were problems of non-cooperation with the training methods.

Ginwalla's Marxism-Leninism gave *The Standard* a strong international orientation. Tanzanian socialism was often critically examined against the backdrop of international socialism. Wide coverage was given to liberation movements in Southern and Portuguese-occupied Africa, as well as in South Vietnam. Eastern European and Latin American affairs received considerable attention, as did the Black Power movement in the United States. Debate

at the domestic level was concerned with the danger of the emergence of class divisions, and with the extremely critical analysis,
often in unsigned articles by European expatriate academics and
radicals, of parastatal organizations such as the National Development Corporation, the 'great sacred cow of the state'. *The Standard*
questioned whether Tanzania really had socialism or state capitalism (Barton 1979: 119). Two particularly important, and at times
vitriolic debates – those involving tourism and *ujamaa* versus capitalism – were carried on in its columns. These debates had the effect
of opening up the paper to the ideas of a number of young intellectuals, mainly from the University of Dar es Salaam. At this time a
distinctive feature of *The Standard*, and more generally the Tanzanian press, emerged. Contributions were encouraged from non-
journalists, university academics, secondary school teachers, and
state administrators, who were able to use the press to disseminate
their ideas to a broader public.

The development of the African press and journalism was, like
that of Asia and Latin America, intimately linked with political and
social reform and the birth of nationalism. In East Africa early
newspapers and broadsheets were generally the mouthpieces of
political associations or political parties which possessed sufficient
funds, distribution means, and educated personnel to establish and
maintain them. Such papers served important organizational purposes, exerted leverage on colonial governments, and provided a
coherent interpretation of events for their supporters/readership.

At the time of independence, which in Africa was predominantly
throughout the 1960s, there were two distinct press traditions. The
first was the dominant European or foreign-owned press which was
generally concerned with slow constitutional advance and the protection of settler interests in countries such as Kenya and
Tanganyika. The second was principally an African political press
which was poorly financed and technically ill-equipped, and which
in countries such as Kenya and Uganda had been battered by the
colonial administration's repressive measures during the 1950s –
banning, closure, and court actions for sedition and libel. The two
coexisted uneasily, but only temporarily. In Kenya, for example, the
political party press rapidly withered under pressure from the two
major privately owned newspaper chains and government policy
was concerned much more with controlling the private, largely
foreign-owned press, than with establishing its own. In Tanzania the
state of coexistence persisted until 1970 when *The Tanganyika*

Standard was nationalized. The ruling party TANU had established its own papers *The Nationalist* and *Uhuru* for the purpose of disseminating and discussing TANU policy and counteracting the influence of the foreign-owned local press, *The Standard* in particular. The Swahili daily *Ngurumo* continued to operate under private-citizen ownership until its demise.

The independent press throughout Africa was initially used by the tiny petty bourgeois intellectual stratum as a vehicle for its dissent from major aspects of colonial society and to establish a broader social base for its nationalist, anti-colonial dissent. The press, however, whether party or non-party, also provided an important outlet for creative writing, including poetry, essays, commentary, and social, literary, and aesthetic criticism, at a time when other outlets were either in incipient stages of development (publishing houses, academic journals) or unavailable through the colonial nature of their control.

During the colonial period throughout Africa the distinction between writer, journalist, and politician was a difficult one to make. Writers and journalists were generally committed to the furtherance of the anti-colonial struggle, usually as part of a political party or association and had no truck with professional standards of detachment and non-partisanship. At independence many of those who had been actively involved in the founding and operation of the independent publications abandoned journalism for political careers.

In Africa the development of a professional journalistic ethos became, in Pye's terms, 'deeply enmeshed in the general problem of the writer's emergence from a traditional role'. Pye suggests there is 'tension between the writer's tradition of involvement in life, of commitment to ideas, and of passion for causes and principles and the journalistic standards of detachment and non-partisanship' (Pye 1963: 81). African journalists, despite professionalization movements, including establishment of schools of journalism, are still disengaging themselves from the tradition of the writer, although many would clearly prefer not to. This disengagement is hampered by the intrusion of a political legacy and social and political forces which impinge upon the journalist's work and make acceptance of values of detachment and objectivity unlikely.

FREEDOM OF THE PRESS

It is in discussion of 'press freedom' that some of the most blatant ambiguities and contradictions appear. Ng'wanakilala, in *Mass Communication and Development of Socialism in Tanzania* (1981), draws a distinction between a 'free press' and 'press freedom'. While it is possible for the latter to exist, the former may not if the press is 'rented' and in 'bondage' and depends on 'foreign patronage and domestic interests'. In this case 'the media operate through the context of foreign and domestic contracts and bonds and not through media objectivity and the available facts'. In Africa the concept is often dismissed as irrelevant, merely a neo-colonial residue which helps perpetuate subordination to the major capitalist powers. Under European colonialism the privately owned press, especially that which belonged to major overseas press groupings such as Lonrho, Thomson, and the Mirror Group, was usually seen as opposed to majority African interests and supportive of colonial policy. The historical picture in countries such as Kenya and Nigeria was clearly much more complicated. In Kenya some sections of the press were identified with settler interests, others with colonial policy and African nationalist aspirations. Such complexity, however, is often lost in the sweeping dismissal of the press as colonial or neo-colonial. Ng'wanakilala (1981: 46) refers to the 'destructive' nature of the colonial media and their opposition to the interests of the majority unless they happened to 'coincide with their own'. The media also appeared to thrive on 'friction' between them and the establishment.

It could be argued that the dismissal of the concept of 'press freedom' invariably rests on a failure to recognize the particular historical conjuncture in which it emerged.

The Kenyan editor-publisher Hilary Ng'weno in 1968 argued that in conditions of 'poverty, illiteracy and disease' such as to be found throughout Africa, Asia, and Latin America, 'it would be sacrilegious to talk about press freedom, for freedom loses meaning when human survival is the only operative principle on which a people lives' (quoted in Mytton 1983: 60). The press had a responsibility 'to encourage greater national unity' where disunity and tribalism were widespread and threatened the very security of the state. The dilemma for Ng'weno, and many others, was how the press could reconcile this role and a critical one, especially when 'in most countries governments tend to treat themselves as the sole judges of what constitutes the national interest'. Ng'wanakilala

(1981), while dismissive of the notion of the free press, is also acutely aware of the contradiction where the media and state and party organization claim to be representing the interests of the people and the national interest. Where the party and state institutions serve particular interests, and the media are state-owned, this is non-sense, and is basically little different to privately owned media which are closely aligned with ruling fractions and representative of particular interests.

African writers on the mass media, as well as politicians, almost invariably argue that the particular, momentous problems facing African countries render irrelevant or inappropriate the mass media practices, values, and institutional arrangements of the advanced capitalist world; after all, they are a key part of the colonial and neo-colonial legacy which is being fought against. Although some more astute observers are aware of the pitfalls there is surprisingly widespread agreement that the mass media, reconstructed in appro-priate ways, should join with government in contributing to national development and the struggle for 'self-reliance'. The concept of 'development' is usually taken as given, as unproblematic, and therefore not something that is open to contestation and the subject of major political, including class, struggle. In few analyses is the struggle to define development seen in relation to struggle for control of the state apparatus and the competition between different interests to determine state policy. The constant emphasis on national development, and the need to break the shackles of continuing political, economic, and cultural dependency, serves to deflect attention from the more basic, problematic aspects of 'de-velopment'. Thus the mass media, and the press in particular, are very rarely seen as part of that process whereby 'development' is defined and policy determined. Rather the media accept and oper-ate within the parameters of a development which has been defined and accepted as given.

More recent criticism of the media in African countries is that they have become strongly centralized. This originally occurred during the colonial period but has intensified in the post-independence period. The media have thus been used by govern-ments to disseminate centrally initiated 'developmental' policies to the masses in the countryside without giving them an opportunity to respond. Boafo suggests that the

> notion of democratizing media systems in Ghana is predicated on
> the rationale that centralized media are poor and inadequate

tools for fostering a self-reliant development. The centralized model of managing and operating media systems is non-participatory, hierarchical and non-conducive to the development needs of the country.

(Boafo 1987: 29)

Many of the proposals for the decentralization and 'democratization' of the media in African countries run directly counter to the media's very direct role in an ideological state apparatus and in some instances, where there is some private ownership and media funding through private advertising, the capital accumulation processes in which they are engaged.

CHANGES IN THE CONCEPT OF NEWS

A frequent criticism of African media is that their coverage, following the models of the advanced capitalist media and the international news agencies, is dominated by day-to-day events (Nordenstreng and Ng'wanikilala n.d.: 21). The 'hard news' concept of western media has been one emphasizing events rather than process, or the analysis of events-related news 'within an informed and politically enlightened context'.

In Latin America the concept of news has undergone a profound change very much in accordance with changes in the media of the advanced capitalist countries. In the middle of the nineteenth century the concept of news 'was originally understood as a current of opinion, with newspapers presenting ideological debates and political positions on the growth of new nations' (Matta 1979: 164). This concept was dominant in the 'serious' press of Europe and North America and represented part of the bourgeois public sphere or discourse. The changing economic structure of 'independent' Latin American countries, and the establishment of new economic links with, and forms of subordination to, Britain and the United States, gradually brought about a change in the concept of news. International news agencies played an important part in this change. The French agency Havas dominated from 1870 until 1920 when the first agreement was signed between United Press and *La Prensa* of Buenos Aires. Matta notes that 'new factors – an eager market, the need for information with impact, and an interest in the immediacy of information – these gradually affected the concept of news' (Matta 1979: 164). The growing dominance of the American news agencies strengthened the trend towards a basically different

news concept, and brought with it a stronger emphasis on 'professionalism' along the lines of the North American model. The result

> was a concept of news which moved from the task of interpreting
> events and presenting opinion to the daily process of selecting
> events deemed 'newsworthy' and commercially interesting.
>
> (Matta 1979: 164)

However, it would be misleading to see such a change in the concept
of news as simply the product of new types of dependency relationships. According to Matta, while some Latin American countries
such as Argentina, Brazil, and Mexico, have substantial media
industries and the capacity to set up a news-information structure,
they have not done so simply because their concept of news and of
the 'journalism industry' is primarily a North American one (Matta
1979: 165–6). While a change in the prevailing dependence on
United States news agencies in particular scarcely represents a
major objective for media owners and controllers, it is likely that the
very structure of the mass media-communications industries in
these countries is one which increasingly relies on this concept of
news. It may simply be the case, in other words, that the economics
of the media, and dependence on advertising, are such that a
particular concept of news derived initially from the United States
experience is the most 'appropriate' one. Thus 'interest in the
concept of news value currently in force is a commercial and
industrial concept of news' (Matta 1979: 168).

In Brazil, as in many other countries, the high-rating television
'news broadcasts are tailored to fit the usual working day' (Kottak
1990: 90). TV Globo squeezes its evening news between its most
popular *telenovelas*, and also provides major national news
coverage in the early afternoon when many Brazilian professional
workers are at home for lunch. Television news, compared with that
in the United States, Britain, Australia, and many other countries,
is marked by an absence of sports and weather segments. National
news items strive to portray Brazil as a large and important nation
participating in international events (this also tends to be characteristic of other countries where prominence in news programmes is
given to the participation of national leaders in international conferences or meetings with neighbouring and other state leaders).
Such reporting emphasizes the multiple links which Brazil has with
the rest of the world while indicating that this interdependence, at
least economically, is the source of many of Brazil's difficulties. The

news also reinforces the image of Brazil as a nation with major and virtually insoluble economic, political and social problems (Kottak 1990: 91). Local news examines the threats (crime, protests, strikes, pollution, traffic congestion) that the streets pose to person, house, family, and society. Once Brazilian television news coverage moves beyond national concerns it usually covers neighbouring states, Latin America, and only then Europe, the United States and the rest of the world (Kottak 1990: 93).

Musa (1990: 333) argues that news in Nigeria is increasingly being subordinated to the information as commodity function. As the old distinction is collapsed between news – especially 'bad news' – and information of relevance to business users in particular, the role of negative, accident/disaster-type news diminishes (Musa 1990: 334). In addition, the importance of 'image-making' news illustrates the growing reliance of news-making on state officials as key sources of information (Musa 1990: 337). News from such sources, including press relations departments in government ministries, tends to pass into the bulletin without major revision and criticism. Okigbo's content analysis of a number of Nigerian daily newspapers – *The National Concord*, *Daily Times*, *The Guardian*, and the *Daily Star* – found little to support the contention that 'bad news' is the predominant content of much of the mass media (Okigbo 1988: 137). His study found that 'bad news', apart from accounting for only 20 per cent of content during the survey period, was not 'disproportionately displayed on the conspicuous pages' (Okigbo 1988: 142). Significantly, and not unexpectedly, 'proportionately' more bad news was to be found in foreign news reports. Local news content was dominated by development news, accounting for 54.8 per cent of content in government newspapers and 28.7 per cent in the case of the privately owned (Okigbo 1988: 136). The prominence given to development news could be accounted for by strong political direction. This is clearly more important in the case of government newspapers, but also important where the privately owned press is heavily dependent on state advertising and subject to intimidation, banning, censorship, and other forms of interference. Many journalists also have a strong development orientation, which tends to be reinforced by a strong reliance on both governmental and international agencies as sources of ready-made news items.

It is clear that where advertising becomes increasingly important as a source of revenue for media, and entertainment packages of soap operas, music, and sports are central to attracting and con-

Chapter 9

Fictions

It is in the capacity to produce 'fictions' – novels, plays, comic books, photo-romances or *fotonovelas*, films, and television programmes, especially long-running series such as the *telenovelas* of Latin America – that the enormous differences between 'Third World' countries become most striking. In many African countries the problems of worsening terms of trade, deteriorating exchange rates, and international indebtedness, are such that they combine to make even the importation of cultural commodities a prohibitively expensive business. In countries such as Brazil and Mexico, huge, diversified, and horizontally and vertically integrated media conglomerates engage in high-volume production of *telenovelas* and other programmes for massive domestic markets and for export. Domestically produced comic books (Hinds 1979; Hinds 1980a; Hinds and Tatum 1984) and *fotonovelas*,[1] often produced under licence, sell in their millions, while film production, if in decline, still maintains levels higher than in most places.

Feature film production in many countries has been constrained by a multiplicity of factors: the unavailability of finance; lack of access to relevant technologies, and technical and creative personnel; the apparent absence of suitable musical, theatrical, literary,[2] and other traditions which can be drawn upon in film production; inadequate institutional arrangements for the reproduction of labour power, including state provision of film and television schools and film archives; the absence of state policy with regard to the importation and taxing of foreign films, taxation concessions and forms of financial assistance to local producers; censorship; and the unavailability of distribution and exhibition networks able to reach audiences with the disposable income and time to devote to film. The market can be severely constrained by language factors. This is especially the case in African countries where both vernacular and foreign-language publics are often insufficiently large to support feature film production.

There are major differences between Asian, African, Latin American, and some Middle Eastern countries (Egypt in particular) in production capacity, volume of production, the size of domestic markets and availability of export markets, and language factors. Film production in Africa suffers from a basic lack of infrastructure: 'the African film industry continues to be plagued by a chronic lack of capital, equipment, production facilities and effective distribution and exhibition channels, nationalization decrees notwithstanding' (Cham 1987: 13). In 'socialist' countries such as Angola and Mozambique which experienced long wars of liberation from Portuguese rule, there is a predominance of documentary works which reflects both the intention of harnessing film to revolutionary transformation and ideological purpose, and the financial and other conditions necessary for even sporadic feature film production (Armes 1987). African film-making is essentially a North and West African activity, with the 'Francophone' countries accounting for the 'overwhelming majority of productions'. This distribution is difficult to explain, but possibly has something to do with the greater centrality of film to a strongly French or Parisian-influenced intellectual culture.

Nigeria, which of almost all African countries would appear to have conditions suitable for sustained local film production, has only managed sporadic activity. The output has been disappointing and marked by

> lack of originality, imitation, commercialism and pandering to (instead of critically confronting) the tastes and sensibilities of an audience still numbed by a daily dose of the cheapest and worst types of escapist rejects from the West and East.
>
> (Cham 1987: 20)

Illustrative of this, according to Cham (1987), is Ugbona's *The Mask* (1980), which is an awkward imitation of a James Bond movie. In this film Major Obi (Agent 009), with Head of State's blessing, sets out on a mission to London to repossess part of Africa's cultural heritage from the British Museum.

There have been many less derivative and imitative Nigerian films. Ola Balogan, whose intention is the creation of a commercial cinema, has nevertheless tackled in his films a number of issues central to contemporary intellectual concerns. His film *Aiye* (1980) is an adaptation of a Hubert Ogunde play which itself is an adaptation of a Yoruba legend dealing with the triumph of good over evil. The Nigerian critic Osundere (1980) considered this film to be 'pandering to the glamorous but misguided call for the exotic in our culture, a facile glamorization of our disappearing past'.

In Asia, in contrast to Africa, there are major film production industries in China (Clark 1987), Hong Kong where martial arts exploitation films, Cantonese comedies, social satires, and historical movies based on episodic novels such as *Dream of the Red Chamber* have been common, Indonesia (Heider 1991), and India in particular.

The popular Indian film industry based in Bombay and increasingly Madras has, like Hollywood, relied on glamour and the lure of stars. Also like Hollywood, it has been dependent on commercial organization for its growth, although it has not had the same vertically integrated structure as the Hollywood studio system of the 1930s and 1940s (Armes 1987: 120). During the 1920s, despite a lack of protection by the colonial government, the Indian silent film industry expanded rapidly. The advent of sound during the early 1930s, and continued expansion of film production during the 1940s and 1950s, led to a split in the Indian cinema audience. While the all-India Hindi-language film based in Bombay continued to develop, there were also the regionally based films which used local languages and which helped to affirm regional identity. The Bombay-based Hindi sound film served to some extent as a national unifying force, and certainly played a key role in disseminating a simplified Hindi which was accessible to far more people.

It was within the regionally based film production, and Calcutta in particular, that the serious, critical, neo-realist film practice developed (in the work of Mrinal Sen and Satyajit Ray in particular). Nevertheless regional language cinema, like that of Hindi, has been characterized by its strong, popular commercial orientation. The need for Hindi sound film to tap a vast, disparate, and non-Hindi speaking audience was undoubtedly crucial in the emergence and the prominence of the Indian song and dance film (Armes 1987: 111; Valicha 1988). Despite a diversity of influences from both Hollywood film and indigenous theatrical, musical, and other cultural practices, the basic structure of Indian popular films has scarcely changed. They continue as 'largely a mixture of songs,

dances, fights, suspense, and comedy' with hardly any specialization (Valicha 1988: 37). The absence of specialized genres such as
thrillers, comedies, science fiction, and family dramas, is basically
the result of catering for a vast, heterogeneous audience located in
both rural and urban areas, as well as in Africa and Asia.[3]

Indian popular entertainment films, in contrast with those of the
new cinema, rely overwhelmingly on well-established conventions
and explicit codes. Lovers communicate with each other by singing
and dancing together (Valicha 1988: 10–11), although the convention of romantic love is mainly a middle-class preoccupation
(Valicha 1988: 48–50). The Radha-Krishna legend, with Krishna
serenading Radha with his flute, provides cultural support for this
film convention, and is used to 'convey the spiritual quality of Indian
music together with the innocence and idyllic romance of pastoral or
village life' (Valicha 1988: 47). Frequently in Indian films the songs
have no narrative significance; they merely have a phatic function
and serve to fill in time and provide noise. Popular films rely on
heavy melodrama, and frequently depend on coincidence and
misunderstanding (there is often the reuniting of long-lost sons and
daughters with parents). They usually rely on simple binary oppositions with archetypal themes rooted in the family. Valicha (1988)
and other writers suggest that popular Indian films provide for their
audiences a 'significant kind of confirmatory experience' of established attitudes to caste, to marriage, family, and gender relations,
and to manual work.

Where extensive borrowing from Hollywood occurs it is re-
worked within the conventions of Indian popular film. In recent
years strong elements of American spaghetti westerns, kung-fu
action, Rambo, and even Tarzan films have been incorporated in
Indian film without basically changing the structure. Indian film
music has also drawn extensively from, and indeed often directly
plagiarized, British and North American popular music (Malik
1990). The Amitabh Bachchan film *Sholay* (1975) provides a good
illustration of the borrowing from the American-Italian spaghetti
western formula, while at the same time producing shifts in the
dominant film conventions. The spaghetti western formula undergoes a major metamorphosis when its setting becomes one
involving peasants and a *zamindar*-like aristocrat.

> It is a society threatened by the presence of a dacoit who is out to
> destroy it and, significantly enough, his main target of annihila-
> tion is the *zamindar* and his family. The resistance to the dacoit is

represented by two hired killers who clearly belong to a more modern and egalitarian ethos.

(Valicha 1988: 71)

In *Sholay* there is typical thematic interest in romantic love and loyalty in friendship. However, there is a surprising absence of the values of the family – especially the middle-class family. The two heroes have no visible family ties; neither does the heroine Hemu Malini. Bachchan in this film is the first to create the image of the industrial man in Indian popular cinema. He is the professional, industrial man who is calculating, fierce, machine-like and efficient, and ultimately loyal to himself (Valicha 1988: 67).

In Latin America, as elsewhere, the distinction between fictional and documentary film has been an important one (Mosier 1986: 173). Also important has been the distinction between popular film intended for mass consumption, and film produced for, and appreciated by, an intellectual or cultural elite. Popular film has been dominated by foreign films (in particular those from Hollywood), and locally produced films such as the Mexican western which have relied heavily on foreign models. Indeed, as Armes (1987: 166) notes, the whole history of Latin American film production up to 1930 and beyond has to be seen against the background of an overwhelming Hollywood superiority in the absence of governmental barriers.

The Latin American commercial bourgeoisie invested in the infrastructure for film distribution and exhibition rather than in production (Armes 1987: 166). In Mexico relatively low-budget silent feature-length films were dominated by escapist melodramas. In Brazil many feature-length films were made between 1898 and 1930. The advent of sound in the 1930s produced mixed results. In the larger countries such as Argentina, Brazil, and Mexico it provided opportunities for expanded production able to make use of local accents, rhythms, and music. In smaller countries, the increased production costs represented by sound, combined with competition from imported Hollywood and Mexican films, served to undermine local industries.

During the 1930s changes in industrial strategies, especially the adoption of import-substitution industrialization policies, occurred as a result of depression and the weakening of ties with international capital. Despite some greater industrial capital investment in film production, and the development of a petty bourgeois concept of 'national cinema', the viability of Latin American film industries was dependent on the provision of state support. In Mexico this was associated with the founding of the Mexican Revolutionary Party and the introduction by the Cardenas government in 1934 of support for the film industry (Armes 1987: 170).

In Brazil the Hollywood model was adopted by Sao Paulo industrialists in the late 1940s and early 1950s (Armes 1987: 173). Brazilian film from the late 1930s through to the 1950s was dominated by the *chanchada* genre which was derived from a mixture of American musicals – particularly the radio broadcast musicals of the same period – and Brazilian comic theatre. However, it was not until the advent of Brazilian neo-realist *cinema nuova* that there was any decisive breakthrough in Latin American feature-length fictional film. This breakthrough had its paradoxical elements, Mosier (1986: 177) notes, largely because the film makers associated with it were anxious to break cultural dependence, and yet relied on foreign cinematic influences such as Italian neo-realism. In Cuba, the Cuban Film Institute, which was founded in 1959, 'sponsored the grafting of the socialist filmmaking of Eastern Europe onto native traditions' (Mosier 1986: 177).

TELEVISION FICTIONS

In many countries where feature film production has never really developed (most of Africa, for example), or basically collapsed (such as in smaller Latin American countries), the introduction and growth of television means that such production on any sustained basis is most unlikely. Even in countries with long-established film industries, high volumes of production, and in most cases state policies designed to support and protect them, the advent of television has placed enormous pressures on feature film production. In India film production has been affected by the growing popularity of television entertainment programmes, especially soap operas such as *Ramayana* and *Mahabharata*. As a result film production companies increasingly direct their activities to television rather than the uncertainties of the feature film market. In China the officially sanctioned growth of television has put pressure on film production associated with more troublesome political and ideological tendencies (Clark 1987). The result of such developments is that film production in many countries is assuming the character of an authorial second cinema which is dependent on the intelligentsia and on various forms of state assistance.

In the case of television many countries are either heavily dependent on imported programmes (drama series, soap operas, films, sports), or too poor to engage in any sustained local production. The problems of local production become exacerbated as viewing hours are extended and there is an increasing reliance on commercial advertising and programme sponsorship. As we have already seen, the structure of television programming in many countries begins to assume a uniformity which cannot simply be explained in media imperialist or cultural dependence terms. Foreign, especially American, models for television fictions are clearly important in local production, but undergo transformation in the light of the specific nature of local audiences, class configurations, and particular national cultural traditions and practices. This can be seen very much in the case of the soap opera.

SOAP OPERAS AND *TELENOVELAS*

Soap operas have become a central feature of sustained television production in many countries: in Brazil and Mexico, and other Latin American countries such as Argentina, Chile, Colombia, Peru and Venezuela; in China, Hong Kong and India. More sporadic production also occurs in many other countries, including some African ones. The antecedents for the soap opera are many, ranging from the serialized fiction and drama of Britain and the United States in the nineteenth century, the *feuilletons* of France, and the radio serial in the Anglo-American experience. The last has been the most direct influence on the development of the television soap opera. Indeed, despite quite different technical determinants, the television soap opera continues to employ the same formula as radio soaps: 'open-ended stories on the domestic concerns, daily hopes and despairs of more or less average middle class families,[4] living in small towns and suburbs' (Frey-Vor 1990b: 2). To some extent soap operas and *telenovelas* have been a 'female genre' since they were 'originally designed as advertising vehicles to attract housewives' (Frey-Vor 1990b: 9) In effect many of the day-time television soapies were little more than televised radio since they relied on interminable dialogue, and very little visualization and action. This restriction, which can be seen clearly in day-time soaps such as *Days of Our Lives*, *The Young and the Restless*, and *Bold and Beautiful*, was determined by tight production schedules and budgets.

THE LATIN AMERICAN *TELENOVELA*

The immediate predecessor of the *telenovela*, the Latin American variation of the continuous serial, was the *radionovela*. Initiated in the 1940s by the same United States conglomerates (mainly producers of soap, detergents, toothpaste, and other household goods) which had started radio soap opera in the North, it spread from Cuba to other Latin American countries where it exerted a strong influence on production. *El Derecho de Nacer* (1946) was one of the earliest Cuban *radionovelas* to be taken up in other countries, even being made into different television versions.

The Brazilian *telenovela* went through several stages before reaching its contemporary form (Mattelart and Mattelart 1987: 16). The first stage commenced in 1963 with TV Excelsior's daily *25 499 Ocupado* (Engaged). Adapted from an Argentinian scenario, it was written by Dulce Santucci who had previously worked in radio. This period of production was still dominated by scenarios imported from Argentina, Mexico and Cuba, as well as influenced by borrowings from and adaptations of *radionovelas* (Mattelart and Mattelart 1987: 16). The 1964 success of *A Moca que Veio de Longe* (The Girl who Came from Nothing) demonstrated the capacity of a *telenovela* to monopolize the television audience and established its firm place in the 8.00 p.m. timeslot (Mattelart and Mattelart 1987: 17).

In 1965 the second stage was ushered in with the sponsored *telenovela*, *O Direito de Nascer* (The Right to be Born). This *telenovela* was used by Jose Bonifacio de Oliveira, manager of a large advertising agency, to sell the products of a beauty company whose account was managed by his company (Litewski 1982: 12) The enormous success of *O Direito de Nascer* turned the *telenovela* into the major vehicle for Brazilian advertisers, with the result that the major manufacturers of toiletries, cosmetics, and home products sponsored at least one daily *telenovela* (Litewski 1982: 13). As the *telenovela* consolidated its position in Brazilian network television, Brazilian writers increasingly affirmed their autonomy and began to distance themselves from imported scenarios in order to explore locally produced ones (Mattelart and Mattelart 1987: 17).

Beto Rockfeller, shown in 1968, marked the beginning of the third stage of the Brazilian *telenovela*. According to Ismael Fernandes, *Beto Rockfeller* established the archetypal *telenovela*. Stilted, grandiloquent language gave way to a loose dialogue in which everyday speech was used. Acting became freer and more relaxed. There was greater improvisation and use of exterior locations shots, as well as a greater number of shots which increased the pace of the narrative (Litewski 1982: 13; Mattelart and Mattelart 1987: 17–18). *Beto Rockfeller* also initiated other changes by dealing 'realistically' with characters and creating social settings familiar to audiences. It introduced a new type of hero, or rather anti-hero, who was no longer the executor of vengeance and the embodiment of some Manichean device of good and bad (Mattelart and Mattelart 1987: 18). In *Beto Rockfeller* a 'lower middle class man tries to climb the social ladder using any available means. This anti-hero was characterized by insecurity, the search for self-affirmation and a need for esteem. The *telenovela* used a whole range of typical characters from different social classes, employing contemporary dialogues – something radically new in Brazilian soap operas. The world of the urban Brazilian middle classes with their dramas and aspirations was to become dominant in the telenovelas' (Litewski 1982: 13).

The Mattelarts note that *Beto Rockfeller* coincided with the first manifestation of the myth of the Brazilian economic miracle which had largely collapsed by 1973 (Mattelart and Mattelart 1987: 19). While this miracle brought benefits to the Brazilian middle classes, it was vital in instilling the model of consumption which has served as the reference for the aspirations of all other groups.

> This fiction, which signifies the entry of the novela into modernity, also inaugurated the meeting of a national genre with a definitively larger public recruited from all social classes, all income categories, all professional strata and all age groups.
>
> (Mattelart and Mattelart 1987: 19)

CONSTRAINTS ON THE PRODUCTION OF *TELENOVELAS*

The makers of Brazilian *telenovelas* work under a number of major constraints. Apart from pressures of production budgets, there are audience composition and detailed audience surveys, censorship, the intrusion of merchandising into the actual structure of the *telenovela*, and the monopolistic position established by TV Globo.

State censorship, combined with that exercised by television controllers for commercial and other reasons, restricts the producers of *telenovelas*. Authors, as elsewhere, have devised strategies for dealing with this censorship, including inventing episodes which capture the attention of the censor, and which can be deleted if necessary, without substantially affecting the structure of the work

(Mattelart and Mattelart 1987: 49). State censorship of *telenovelas* has undergone change in accordance with the shift from military to civilian rule. In two famous cases state censor mutilation of *telenovelas* was such that TV Globo preferred not to programme them despite the fact that considerable production of episodes had occurred. *Roque Santeiro*, after being censored and removed from the small screen in 1975, returned in a new version as a popular success in 1985–6 under the Nova Republic. In its new version *Roque Santeiro* more explicitly addressed the 'national situation' by dealing with a microcosm of Brazil in terms of a small town in which life revolved around a myth (Mattelart and Mattelart 1987: 47–8).

Apart from political censorship of any questioning of Brazilian reality in programmes such as *telenovelas*, there has been an obsession with moral censorship. At various times campaigns have been waged against pornography, eroticism, sexual emancipation, and any depiction of police violence (Mattelart and Mattelart 1987: 48). In relation to the last, for example, it is not possible to speak of crimes committed by the police. The result of this, as Sirkis has observed, is that censorship 'gives the green light to American productions which have violence as a natural ingredient. The programme which has been censored does not incite violence, rather the opposite' (A. Sirkis, quoted in Mattelart and Mattelart 1987: 49).

A case where TV Globo exercised its own censorship occurred in 1979 with the *telenovela* called *Os Gigantes* whose amorous theme was influenced by François Truffaut's film *Jules et Jim*. The action of *Os Gigantes* was situated in an interior region of Brazil, thus breaking with the usual choice of urban settings. In this region the author placed a dairy industry multinational which was frequently in conflict with local enterprises. Federal censorship focused on the amorous intrigue – the woman living with two men. After one hundred episodes, however, it became apparent that the issue of sexual morality was no longer the source of difficulty but rather the role of the 'wicked' multinational corporation. As a result the author of the series was forced to withdraw by the controllers of TV Globo.

The second major constraint on *telenovela* production is audience response and audience research. Audience research is a vital part of Brazilian *telenovela* and more general television production. Kottak notes that Brazil 'has well-developed market-research, public opinion sampling, audience targeting, and other techniques designed to spur consumption' (Kottak 1990: 23). Often detailed research is used to

> verify public attitudes and responses to a character or group of characters and indicate reaction to the new fashions introduced by the *telenovelas*. On the public's answer depends the destiny of characters or the way in which the plot develops. Authors writing a new text keep in mind the findings of the research which gives them an approximated idea of the viewers' desires.
>
> (Litewski 1982: 14)

TV Globo has a Department of Analysis and Research which plays a key role in determining the type of audience the *telenovela* will reach. It is constantly concerned with the monitoring and evaluation of reaction to its *telenovelas*, even to the extent of allowing such assessments of reaction to affect character and plot development (Kottak 1990: 32). The *telenovela* thus represents a 'semi-open work' whose development the audience often has a major role in guiding.

The third, and closely related constraint on Brazilian *telenovela* production is 'merchandising', that is, adapting the narrative to allow for the insertion of a product for advertising purposes. TV Globo even has its own sales agency APOI for merchandising. Specialized sales promotion commercializes the participation of products, brands, and services that appear in the output, and deals with the rights (slogans, logotypes, texts, characters) created by TV Globo's programmes. *O Primeiro Amor* (The First Love) re-introduced the habit of riding bicycles and enlarged their sales to young people. The Caloi bicycle company developed the project with TV Globo. Honda got together with TV Globo for the *telenovela* called *O Cavalo de Aco* (The Steel Horse), in which a Honda motorcycle could be seen in nearly every episode. Varig, the Brazilian airline, collaborated with TV Globo for *Carinhose* (Tender) in which Regina Duarte played a Varig air stewardess. Contracts stipulate that products must be associated with characters who are more likely to represent the marketing strategies of the companies concerned and not reflect badly on them (Leal and Oliven 1988: 85). Critics, especially authors, contend that merchandising has turned *telenovelas* into one long advertisement (Lauro Cesar Muniz, for example, quoted in Litewski 1982: 16). Predicably the view of TV Globo management is rather different.

Brazilian *telenovelas* appear six times per week and at night. Typically they have 150 to 180 chapters and run for six or seven months. In this respect they stand in sharp contrast to American soaps (Kottak 1990: 89). *Telenovelas* use the serial form to deal with a series of characteristic conflicts and problems, many of which involve status reversals, especially ones involving upward mobility. Usually they have urban rather than rural settings. Most are concerned with aspects of the urbanization and modernization of Brazil. Within settled, highly conventionalized narrative structures, they usually provide comment on current issues, trends, and fads (Kottak 1990: 41). Invariably they contain examples of upward social mobility, with the central character typically the ascendant figure. They are characterized by several romances and often end with a series of weddings. Although failed marriages are common (*Malu Mulher*, for example), marital infidelity, in sharp contrast to American soaps where it is central, is rarely dealt with. The sexual encounters between unmarried people which are also common in American soaps are almost entirely absent.

Telenovelas, nevertheless, are preoccupied with romance. Certainly they are frequently concerned with examples of wild, crazy love (Kottak 1990: 41). In some instances unrequited love, especially that involving a woman's hopeless devotion to a man destined for another, is dealt with. However, if inter-generational and inter-racial romances occur, they are rarely between central characters. *Crazy Love*, a 1983, 8 o'clock *telenovela*, embraces the types of relationships, issues, settings, and characters typical of *telenovelas* in that time slot. *Crazy Love* offered

> confused parentage (from a switch of babies), a sixtyish rich man's marriage to a fortyish lower middle-class woman, and a late fiftyish woman's marriage to a late thirtyish man. Also included were an interracial marriage (of a woman and her chauffeur), interracial adoption, two murders, and a detective. Add to all that the magazine industry, an alcoholic artist, several characters relentlessly pursuing money, and a status hungry mother.
>
> (Kottak 1990: 41)

Brazilian *telenovelas* are typically structured around series of binary oppositions: conflicts between rural and urban life; tradition and progress; old and young; archaic and contemporary structures; and the declining agrarian aristocracy and gentry and the rising urban bourgeoisie (Kottak 1990: 45). *O Bem Amado* (The Well-Beloved, 1973) was one of the most significant portrayals in the *telenovela* form of the clash between an agrarian and an urbanized way of life. This series, written by Dias Gomes, dealt with quarrels over political power between two factions in a town in Bahia. The mayor pursues his own interests to the detriment of the people and is opposed by the female police chief and the owner of the town's newspaper (Litewski 1982: 17). A later *telenovela*, *A Casaräo*, dealt with a similar conflict. Starting in 1900, this serial followed the move of a traditional family from large rural properties to Rio de Janeiro (Kottak 1990: 49).

Malu Mulher (Maria Luisa, the Woman), was set in Sao Paulo and had as its protagonist a divorced woman who lived with her mother and daughter. She has a degree in sociology but no steady job (Kottak 1990: 41). In a changed political climate *Malu Mulher* was able to deal with issues such as marital separation, divorce, single motherhood, machismo, and even female orgasm, which hitherto had been avoided. Jordao suggests that *Malu* arrived at the end of the economic 'miracle' and helped 'explain' the adjustments that would have to be made in the new economic climate (Jordao 1982: 8).

Malu Mulher, many critics noted, dealt with essentially the world of middle-class problems; in contrast, the vast majority of women are preoccupied with the harsh struggle for daily bread. For them, the struggles for a full and independent life, and separation and divorce, are unimportant issues.

HINDU MYTHOLOGY AND POPULAR FICTIONS

Not unexpectedly many Indian popular 'fictions' are taken up with stories from Hindu mythology: from the *puranas*, and the two great epics, the *Ramayana* and the *Mahabharata*. This applies to feature film to a limited extent (Barnouw and Krishnaswamy 1980; Ramachandran and Rukmini 1985), to popular literature and especially comic books (particularly true of Indonesia as well), and increasingly to television series where the *Ramayana* and the *Mahabharata* have enjoyed astonishing popular success.

Ramanand Sagar's *Ramayana* was shown by Doordarshan in 1987–8. Based on the religious epic, it attracted vast audiences (60 million on Sunday mornings) and substantial advertising revenue. The televised production of the epic, which celebrates Lord Rama's victory over the Demon King Ravana, stressed human values such as morality, obedience, discipline, and loyalty. While for many critics the series was a poor representation of the epic, for others it had the virtue of stressing values which would enable people to cope in a climate of often rapid economic and social change and moral uncertainty (Singhal and Rogers 1989: 70). The *chaupaiyans* (verses) of the epic 'were put to melodious music, each conveying a moral theme'.

The popular success of *Ramayana* led to the production of another Indian epic serial, *Mahabharata*, which began broadcasting in late 1988. The strength and popularity of the series is seen by some commentators as residing in its 'contemporaneous flavour', its realism in the sense that it deals with conflicts immediately familiar to its audience, including the 'most common cause of family disputes – property', and above all, in the way in which 'every episode seems like a leaf taken out of the routine happenings in any ordinary Indian family'.

Whereas soap operas had long been the most popular genre of television programming in Latin American countries, in India they did not appear on national television until 1984. The first of such serials, *Hum Log*, was a pro-development soap opera influenced by the Mexican model. After a lack of initial popular enthusiasm for the first episodes, and political criticism, a number of changes were made which increased its popular appeal.

> The family planning theme was diluted and themes such as the status of women, family harmony, and national integration became central to it.
>
> (Singhal and Rogers 1989: 95)

Hum Log's plot revolved around the joys and sorrows of a lower middle-class joint family, with a sub-story addressing political corruption and underworld activities. Masud (1985) notes that this setting had the advantage of securing a vast audience, while 'domestic or domesticated space is the perfect home for scenes of intimacy and confrontation'.

Hum Log was followed by series such as *Buniyaad* (Foundation) and *Khandaan*. Shown in 1986–7, *Buniyaad* was a historical soap opera which dealt with India's partition primarily through the examination of the life and times of a four-generation family. The saga focused on the tumultuous events following the partition with Pakistan. Some characters in common with the earlier *Hum Log* were clearly important in maintaining audience involvement and continuity. *Khandaan* is

> the rich man's *Hum Log* but is meant, like the latter, for the lower middle classes (as *Dynasty*, its original, is in America). However *Hum Log*, despite its gaucherie, has a certain innocence. *Khandaan* is all knowingness, contrivance and calculation.
>
> (Masud 1985: 55)

Apart from the *Ramayana* and the *Mahabharata*, since the introduction of television soap operas there has been a great diversity of setting and themes. Recently Vijaya Mehta's *Lifeline* (Jeevan Rekha) provided a realistic portrayal of life in a hospital. Col. Kapoor's *Fauji* was a semi-factual, semi-fictional account of life in the army. Ketan Mehta's *Mr Yogi* provided an initially irreverent take-off of the middle class and modern manners. *Doctor Sahib* dealt with a general practitioner with a heart of gold, while *Murjim Haazir* recreated a turn-of-the-century Bengali ambience.

Doordarshan's programming of serials has been regarded by its critics as always being with an eye to its political masters. One critic observed that in 1989,

> perpetually scared of incurring the wrath of the political bosses, the DD mandarins played safe by blocking out all that could be interpreted as critical of the government, at the same time trying to please the authorities by airing programmes that gave a boost to government objectives and policies.
>
> (D'Silva 1989: 43)

Boond Boond was dropped after it poked fun at village panchayats and its protagonist bore some slight resemblance to the then opposition leader – later prime minister – V.P. Singh. The Indian answer to Britain's *Yes Minister, Kakkaji Kahin*, was constantly butchered from the beginning. Storyline and dialogue were so extensively altered that 'ultimately, the Bhojpari-speaking political fixer named Kakkaji lost his identity and a promising satire was turned into a dull farce' (D'Silva 1989: 43).

Masud (1985), writing at the beginning of the wave of Indian television soapies, considered sponsored television in India to be the 'triumph of the middle class', certainly of middle-class culture. Threatened by labour disorder, urban lawlessness and overcrowding, this class has had a 'panic stricken admiration of "order" and "rationality"', a fascination for the consumer culture exemplified in television advertisements which provide a type of structured order which ultimately contributes to their subordination, and the 'celebration of celebrity' in which politicians such as Rajiv Gandhi, and stars drawn from the film world, provide release for their fears and aspirations. The middle classes have provided the publicists and writers – the literati in general – who have produced the 'celebrity culture' and the hegemony for the ruling classes of the industrialists, ex-landlords, top politicians and senior state bureaucrats.

BOOK PUBLISHING

In many of the countries under examination book publishing has been particularly subject to debates about cultural dependence and imperialism. Debates have usually revolved around the control of publishing and distribution, especially by transnational publishers, and the nature of the texts to be published and distributed. The ideological character of the work is particularly sensitive where it forms part of the educational curriculum.

The debates have been at their most intense where, despite linguistic diversity and the existence of substantial indigenous language groupings, local publishing and formal education have been conducted in the language of the former metropolitan colonial power. In many African countries, and some Asian, the continuing use of English and French – and Portuguese for that matter – represents for critics the continuation of colonial subjugation and the denial of some cultural authenticity. The Kenyan writer Ngugi wa Thiong'o's decision to write in Kikuyu rather than English is an expression of this. Such debates have scarcely touched Latin American countries: in Brazil and Mexico indigenous languages are spoken by few, and literary and cultural production is carried on in Portuguese and Spanish to the extent that it rivals or surpasses that of the former colonial powers. The mass coverage by centralized television production and transmission in these countries has also contributed to a basic standardization of language. In India language politics have been particularly intense and have revolved around not so much the position of English, as Hindi. Regional state governments have provided support for film production partly as a way of protecting their languages (Kerala with Malayalam, Tamil Nad with Tamil), while there has also been a concern to preserve and extend local language literatures.

In Tanzania the combined commitment of the government to socialist transformation and the concerted implementation of a Swahili national language policy led to the prominence of Swahili language publishing and Swahili language use more generally throughout the mass media.[5] Until recently the principal stumbling block to indigenous language publishing, and justification of English, French, and other European language publishing, was economic; local vernacular language markets were too small, fragmented, and poor to warrant high-cost publishing. Concern was often expressed that an emphasis on vernacular language publishing and cultural production would only exacerbate ethnic and regional conflicts and cut off African societies from the principal centres of knowledge production.

In the early 1970s a distinctly new phenomenon of Kenyan literature emerged – a popular, commercial literature, which was directed at a readership quite different from that of the earlier serious, intellectual tradition. This was the literature dominated by the urban experience which catered for the literate working classes. There was a precedent for this in the Onitsha market literature of Nigeria, but what was distinctive about the Kenyan popular literature was the quality of its production. Although this literature was initially published by the East Africa Publishing House (Charles Mangua's *Son of Woman* being the primogenitor), and a few small local publishers (David Maillu's Comb Books being the most important), it was not long before the major transnational publishers such as Heinemann, Longman, and Macmillan established their own series to capture a substantial share of the market. This vigorous movement into popular fiction publishing was probably partly forced by the encroachment of state publishing activity, and the Jomo Kenyatta Foundation in particular, on their previously highly lucrative textbook market.

The growth of this literature, while to some extent force-fed by publishers, was the result of a multiplicity of factors (Reeves 1984). It certainly must be seen as part of a more general expansion of material and commercial culture during the late 1960s and early 1970s when real incomes in Kenya increased and there was a substantial growth of consumer goods industries through import-substitution policies. It must also be seen as part of, and as preceded by, the rapid growth of newspaper and magazine publishing and journalism, and popular music production in the Swahili and Kikuyu languages in particular. The growth of the popular literature was also largely dependent on the increase in the size of the literate working class (heavily concentrated in Nairobi and Central Province), as well as petty bourgeois strata, with sufficient disposable income, established reading practices, and inclination to purchase such works. Reading practices were provided to an important extent through the school curriculum, by newspapers and magazines in both English and Swahili, and through the popularity of writers such as Mickey Spillane, James Hadley Chase, and Peter Cheyney. The literature was able to develop through the availability of publishing outlets which were not subject to strict ideological control or state repression, as well as through reasonably good distribution in Nairobi and Central Province.

The emergence of the popular literature aroused a good deal of Kenyan intellectual interest and opposition. For some it represented the continuation of metropolitan capitalist cultural domination by pandering to the language and the immorality of popular writing from the United States in particular. For others it represented the denial or negation of the literary tradition dominated by political commitment and national reassertion (Reeves 1984: 53–61). The focus on sexual immorality, prostitution, bar and nightclub life, urban squalor, the new materialism associated with capitalism and urbanization, the corruption of the new ruling classes, and extreme social inequality, was done in such a way that according to some critics it provided a form of escapism and acceptance of the social phenomena dealt with in the popular literature. However, although much of this literature does not directly engage critical political and social issues, and is produced primarily for entertainment, it can scarcely be dismissed as 'escapist' since the little audience information available suggests both an active reader engagement with it, and the part the literature plays in class-cultural conflict in Kenya (Wanjala 1980). In contrast to popular literature elsewhere, political concerns and critical social analysis have not been entirely absent. Certainly David Maillu's rambling, largely unstructured, voluminous poems, *The Kommon Man* and *My Dear Bottle*, provide a critical account of post-independence society within a rudimentary theorization of the transition from colonial to post-colonial capitalist society.

In Kenyan popular literature the accumulation of wealth, drinking, and having sex are the major preoccupations. Many of the protagonists – Matthew and Obonyo (Oludhi-Macgoye, *Murder in Majengo*), Reuben (Ruheni, *The Future Leaders*), Mwangi (Maura,

Sky is the Limit), Ngindi (Mutiso, *Sugar Babies*), Washington Ndava (Maillu, *No!*) – belong to the salariat or indigenous bourgeoisie. Rarely do such people work, although they must have completed secondary education and perhaps university degrees to move into the positions they occupy. One of the exceptions is Washington Ndava in David Maillu's *No!* who hardly had 'seven years of formal education' but who, as an ambitious 'genius', was 'highly educated through self teaching'. The passport to the conspicuous consumption life of the *wabenzi* (new ruling classes) lies much more in luck, opportunism, bribery, corruption, and the use of office for private accumulation.

The protagonists of Kenyan popular literature are aggressively masculine, their identity apparently dependent on sexual prowess. Virility is judged by the number and frequency of sexual conquests (*Son of Woman*, *Sugar Babies*), the size of the penis (*One by One* and *Sugar Babies*), and a high sperm count (Kahiga, *The Girl From Abroad*). In many of the popular works there is an interesting connection established between political power, wealth, and sexual power and privilege. Indeed in Maillu's *No!* wealth and power count for nothing without sexual prowess. This is also the case with politicians like Makola and Somboloya in Maillu's *The Kommon Man* who use their positions to seduce more-or-less at will the women with whom they come in contact. Their power is demonstrated by their ability to make the wives and secretaries of others as jealously guarded sexual property.

CONCLUSION

The differences in the ability of 'Third World' countries to engage in the production of fictions are considerable. Many countries in Africa in particular, Asia, and Latin America are unable to sustain any volume of fictional production, regardless of whether it involves feature films, television programmes such as 'soapies', and book, magazine, and comic publishing. Clearly the countries of the 'Third World' are characterized by an immense diversity of fictional forms which, even where imported, have been informed and transformed by indigenous cultural traditions and practices. In the major production countries fictional production is marked by growing differentiation of form or genre. While fictional forms which were established in advanced European countries and the United States have tended to predominate in the media of 'Third World' countries, they have usually undergone some significant processes of mediation and transformation in their transplanted settings. This is the case with the Latin American *telenovela*, as well as television series in India such as the *Ramayana* and the *Mahabharata* which are based on ancient Hindu epics. Even in film production, where the Hollywood industrial model and feature film genres have exercised considerable influence, films produced in 'Third World' countries have reflected both the peculiar economic conditions of their production and contradictions in their social relations and major cultural conventions. In India, for example, Hollywood influences have been strong in feature film production, but have been considerably modified to take into account the peculiarities of the audience, and major conventional practices and values which are fundamental to Indian culture and social structure. Undoubtedly many of the fictional forms, and their characteristic ways of dealing with social conflict, represent part of the expansion of imperialist culture and ideology; they also represent and express capitalist and dominant values in particular national societies but are never to be seen as merely ideologically unidimensional or homogeneous. Analysis of fictional forms as diverse as *telenovelas*, *fotonovelas*, and comics reveals them to be responsive to contradictory social relations and shifts in ideological positions.

Chapter 10

Sounds

The advanced capitalist countries, and the United States in particular, have been able to exert substantial influence, if not control, over the development of modern music production throughout the world. This influence in Africa and Asia occurred initially under European colonial rule and involved the control of the development and use of reproductive and distributive technologies, production and distribution of phonograms, capital investment (many local record companies have been subsidiaries of the major international record companies and have played a key role in the distribution of phonograms produced in the 'metropolitan' countries), and the formation of taste. The last, which is bound up with the essentially unidirectional flow of sounds from a few advanced capitalist countries to the rest of the world, represents a difficult area of analysis.[1] Usually it is seen as a major manifestation of cultural imperialism and transnational corporation dominance, but as Laing (1986) amongst others has argued, it may have contributed to the growth of new and oppositional musical tendencies in many 'Third World' countries. Certainly it is clear that musical tastes and forms of expression show a great many local or national variations which have to be accepted by major companies, whether transnational or national, if they are to continue their domination of markets.

As in other areas of communication and cultural production there are important differences between 'Third World' countries in respect of the diversity of their musical cultures, extent of penetration by foreign musical forms, levels of capital investment in production technologies (especially sound recording and record pressing facilities) and state policy towards music. Countries such as India, Brazil, and Mexico have highly differentiated popular music markets and industries which are linked with film, radio and television, magazine, and more recently, video production. In many smaller countries where few such links exist, and indeed where other sectors of cultural production are still at best in their incipient stages of development, there are almost insuperable problems with small markets and high costs. Countries such as Tanzania, despite the absence of local record production facilities, and shortages of imported musical instruments and phonograms induced by acute shortages of foreign exchange, have nevertheless been characterized by vibrant popular music cultures, partly as a result of state policies concerned with the development of national music cultures.

Added to the differences between 'Third World' countries in the scale, differentiation and volume of musical production, are often quite pronounced differences in state policy. Such differences clearly reflect different national historical experiences and constellations of class relations, as well as the time of the development of nationalist movements and the gaining of independence. While in many former colonial societies state music policy has been spurred by national cultural reassertion and nation-building considerations,[2] in others the nationalist concerns have also been harnessed to more strident anti-imperialism, and to socialist transformation and the development of socialist consciousness. In China, for example, this involved a rigorous adaptation of traditional musical forms, including children's folk songs, for socialist political and educational purposes, as well as for directing popular attitudes in the factional struggles within the Communist Party hierarchy (L. Chu 1978; Chu and Cheng 1978). In contrast, in Cuba, while state policy under Castro has been anti-imperialist and socialist, it has been much more flexible and accommodating; this partly reflects the strength of indigenous forms of popular commercial music, as well as the difficulty of screening out rock music influences from the nearby United States (Manuel 1987).

Frequently there has been a contradiction between state policy with regard to the promotion and development of 'national' music forms and the absence of other state policy interventions likely to foster the growth of local musical production.

The development of a music industry characterized by new social relations of music production and distribution, and new productive, reproductive and distributive technologies, has had a profound if uneven impact on indigenous musical traditions and forms of production. In some cases the indigenous traditions have lent themselves to adaptation for new commercial purposes; they have undergone changes in instrumentation (the adoption of western musical instruments), and been modified by electronic amplification and other electronic accessories. The industrial-organizational forms of the music industry in advanced capitalist countries have generally not been reproduced in 'Third World' societies. Under colonialism in the early twentieth century in Africa and Asia the new sound recording and reproductive technologies were introduced, but at best Asian and African countries, and Latin American ones as well, essentially remained secondary markets for the music industries in Britain, the United States, and France. There was basically no way that the industrial-organizational structure could be transferred and replicated in them.

Artists of the 'Third World', as previously noted, 'constitute a large reservoir of talent on which producers can draw to revitalize artistic forms' (Miège 1989: 103). West Indian music, especially *reggae*, has been successfully integrated into internationalized musical production and distribution, initially through the connection between substantial immigrant groups in Britain and the United States and home countries such as Jamaica. To see such integration into dominant musical production relations as representing an ideological incorporation of producers (singers, composers, musicians) and audience is misleading since it underestimates the role of *reggae* and other types of Caribbean music in identity formation and in forms of cultural contestation both in 'metropolitan' centres (Rastafarianism in Britain) and in Caribbean countries (Hebdige 1987). Popular commercial music in countries such as Indonesia may be strongly influenced by rock music – and thus seen as cultural imperialist – but nevertheless perform oppositional and liberating roles where lyrics are used in however veiled a way to develop criticism of ruling regimes and dominant social relations, and where the music may be identified with newly emerging youth cultures which cannot easily be contained within existing social and ideological relations (Frederick 1982; Harsono 1989; Yampolsky 1989).

Popular forms of musical expression, including traditional, noncommercial ones, have often been closely identified with anticolonial expression. In many post-colonial societies music has served as a vehicle of protest and satire, and in some instances has been part of anti-imperialist, oppositional, and revolutionary movements.

Wallis and Malm (1984) identify a number of common elements of change in musical cultures. Their scheme involves the identification of four principal changes: first, in the mode of performance; second, in music style and structure; third, in organization; and fourth, in the use and function of music. Undoubtedly there are a great many national variations in this change, certainly in its historical timing and sequence as a result of different rates of capitalist transformation and urbanization.

MODE OF PERFORMANCE

Graham notes that 'given the centrality of music to many aspects of everyday African life, it becomes almost impossible to conceive of a division between "classical" and "popular" music in Africa as obtains in the west' (Graham 1989: 9). In some countries a division existed between court musical traditions, where music was professionalized or involved hereditary strata of musicians, and popular traditions, while in contemporary societies there are divisions between popular commercial musical forms influenced by western instrumentation and orchestration and continuing traditional forms of musical expression which may have undergone significant change. In Latin America the division between 'classical' and 'popular' holds to a considerable extent, although contemporary forms of musical expression are a complex mixture of European 'classical', popular, African and Indian elements. The essentially European character of dominant classes in post-colonial Latin American societies ensured that European 'serious' musical traditions should be of great importance, with many modern Latin American composers such as Vila-Lobos associated with developments in modern serious music. In Asia, in India and China, and Indonesia, the 'classical' and 'popular' distinction held, with the classical forms of musical expression associated with the courts, and in the case of India, with particular religious practices and foundations of support.

As musical production shifts from spontaneity to more organized and disciplined performance – especially concert performance – it undergoes major changes (Wallis and Malm 1984: 13). The increasing integration of musical production into commercial relations means that it is arranged to suit the acoustics of halls, the nature of audiences, the demands made by organizers and sponsors, and the technical abilities and limitations of the musicians. Even classical traditions, whose social relations of production have changed, and which are increasingly dependent on market patronage rather than older religious and personal forms of support, are prone to this development. This is the case, for example, with Indian classical music (Ramakrishnan 1990).

Musical production has also undergone substantial organizational change. Wallis and Malm identify three sets of such changes, the first concerning the shift from 'traditional' venues for ceremonies and rites – from the court, village, and even the temple, to new, often urban venues such as community centres, concert halls, and *maisons de culture* (the example of Indian classical music referred to above). The second concerns the increasingly influential role of the state in the administration, organization, and funding of certain types of musical production. In many 'Third World' countries music, and the performing arts in general, has become a matter and instrument of state policy. This is distinct from state policy in the area of import quotas, tariffs, and state provision of recording studios and record pressing facilities which may have a crucial impact on modern musical production. Rather, it concerns the development of a national apparatus for music administration, the establishment of national folklore ensembles and national educational institutions devoted to the training of artists and the collection and recording of 'traditional' music. The third concerns the growth of specialization and the emergence of professional musicians, as well as the emergence of recording facilities, phonogram companies, and concert agencies (Wallis and Malm 1984: 14). The levels of specialization, professionalization, and industrial organization of musical production are clearly related to the extent of the development of the capitalist market and the formation of classes with the disposable incomes and interest to devote to music consumption.

USE AND FUNCTION

Clearly the use and functions of music change, often dramatically, as a result of the use of music as an instrument of state policy, the expansion of the market for music, and changes in the mode of performance. In the pre-colonial and pre-capitalist contexts music, in its localized forms, was inextricably linked with other activities. It was frequently integral to social and political action, and was associated with activities in which societies 'express or consolidate their interpersonal relationships, beliefs and attitudes to life' (Nketia 1966: 149). Much of the music was for public performance, whether for ritual, ceremonial or recreational purposes, although the centrality of music to collective experience did not preclude individuals from making music for their own amusement or as a means of subsistence.

Music is used increasingly as a symbol or means of establishing national identity, as well as identity for different groups, whether they are based on age, class, ethnicity, region, religion, or urban location. 'Folk' music is often a symbol for country and people: dominant classes and ruling regimes invariably prefer carefully orchestrated, choreographed, and selected 'folk' music and dance which has been expunged of critical content and made politically pliant or quiescent, and which can safely be used for international and national consumption purposes. Musicians frequently regard 'folk' music as a major source of inspiration, styles, lyrics, and national reassertion and identity, and in some instances source of style to be opposed to imported musical expression, ruling classes and the state. In Latin America, while 'modern' and commercial forms of music have been used for social criticism and political mobilization purposes, there is a long history of 'folk' forms being adapted for such purposes. The assertion of 'folk' tradition is in some instances bound up with the common 'left' position that modern, commercial forms of music are almost irredeemably tainted by the capitalist conditions and relations of their production; 'folk' represents either a pre- or non-capitalist form in which the musician is not alienated labour and in which a much closer identity can be established between performer-composer and audience.

Basic shifts in the social relations of musical production have led to the much greater use of music for the provision of political and commercial information. Apart from advertising, music is used for film and television soundtrack purposes, with the result that in countries such as India and Brazil there is a close connection between film and television production and the music industry; indeed, in Brazil the major television networks also own record companies.

In India popular commercial music has been closely associated with the cinema, and the Hindi cinema in particular. The introduction of sound film provided Indian producers with markets 'which foreign competitors would find difficult to penetrate' (Barnouw and Krishnaswamy 1980: 69). Of greater importance than the spoken word, however, was the song. Early Hindi and Tamil films had a profusion of songs as well as dance sequences.

> The Indian sound film, unlike the sound films of any other land, had from its first moment seized *exclusively* on music-drama forms. In doing so, the film had tapped a powerful current, one that had given it an extraordinary new impetus.
> (Barnouw and Krishnaswamy 1980: 69)

The importance of song and dance to Indian film was clearly the result of the strong persistence of folk music drama forms in the various Indian regions. This tremendous success in film 'meant an almost mortal blow to the *jatras*[3] and other kinds of folk drama' and helped bring about an often substantial transformation of folk song and dance (Barnouw and Krishnaswamy 1980: 71–2). Songs were changed through the introduction of new, often western rhythms, as well as new types of instrumentation.

At the time of independence the reform zeal concerned with the eradication of imperialist influences and practices overtook Indian film music (Barnouw and Krishnaswamy 1980: 140). A Bombay government body report on music education condemned film songs as corrupted by western influences and 'alien to the genius of Indian music'. By this time most film producers had adopted western instrumentation and combinations of instruments.

> Many Bombay producers were using lush combination of fifty or sixty instruments, foreign to Indian classical tradition, and film audiences responded with ecstasy.
> (Barnouw and Krishnaswamy 1980: 157)

There was also borrowing from American jazz and Latin American rhythms which produced a 'hybrid' music which was condemned as 'western' by Indian purists and regarded as Indian by western listeners.

By the early 1950s the film song had become a key to successful film promotion. Film songs were almost automatically made into phonograph records under the label of the Indian subsidiary of the British HMV company. The phonograph records were usually made during the production of the film, most often by simply directly dubbing from the film sound track, and released for radio air play shortly before the premiere of the film.

All India Radio was initially involved in the introduction of film songs. However, in 1952 AIR began a drive against 'hybrid music'

(Barnouw and Krishnaswamy 1980: 157). A combination of the desire of broadcasters to continue with Reithian public broadcasting traditions, and the concern of 'some Hindi-speaking politicians[4] [who] saw the radio as a key means of introducing classical Hindi and traditional Indian music to the masses, meant that AIR had little market orientation' (Tunstall 1977: 121). Few were interested in traditional Indian music or literary Hindi. Many were much more interested in the Indian film music broadcast by Radio Ceylon to its audiences in South Asia (Barnouw and Krishnaswamy 1980: 157–8). The Indian response was eventually to reply in kind; a popular music service – Vivrath Bharati – was introduced in 1957 to play mainly Indian film music (Ramachandran 1978: 27).

The removal of music from its 'traditional context' gives rise to changed attitudes to music. The specialization, professionalism, and adaptation of music to modern media renders it 'an independent phenomenon' which can be performed outside its original context (Wallis and Malm 1984: 15). Other art forms such as dance, drama, and sculpture also move to a more 'independent' status and 'together with music become known as "art" or "culture"' (Wallis and Malm 1984: 15). There are, however, exceptions to this. In India dramatic folk art continues essentially as an integrated form, while most experiments in popular people's theatre combine elements of music, dance, drama, and a whole history of proverbs. The incorporation of indigenous 'folk' musical forms into a new 'system' of musical production, combined with the adoption and adaptation of western art and popular music forms, contributes to a substantial rationalization of music. Wallis and Malm (1984: 15) suggest that the 'rich flora of traditional music forms has been rationalized to a limited number of standard forms'. This is manifested conspicuously in song lyrics where the tremendous range of concerns in traditional songs gives way in popular commercial music to songs about love and individual problems. There are of course major exceptions. In Nigeria, Kenya, and other African countries, as well as in Latin American countries, popular songs often retain a diversity of lyrical content. This reflects not only the importance of earlier popular forms, but also the way in which popular song is used for critical and oppositional purposes. As part of rationalization the modern versions of folkloric music take on nationalistic idioms, indicating the extent to which such music is bound up with state policy and the effort to form national cultures.

MUSIC AS OPPOSITION, CRITICISM, ANTI-IMPERIALISM

Throughout much of the 'Third World' popular forms of music expression, whether of rural or urban origins, or indeed of thoroughly commercial nature, have been closely identified with anticolonial and anti-imperialist struggles. In many countries musical expression has represented one of the few means of criticism and dissent where state repression and intellectual suppression have denied the possibility of others. If not explicitly oppositional, music in many places has become part of the means whereby groups establish a 'space' for themselves in relation to a hegemonic culture; it provides them with one of the bases of cultural contestation. Even sophisticated popular music which is not closely linked with oppositional politics, or a substantial base of dissent, may be concerned with the development of social criticism, at least drawing attention to the alienation characteristic of an urban, capitalist society marked by extremes of wealth; this is the case in Brazil with *bossa nova* and *tropicalismo*.

In China revolutionary songs were an important part of the communist struggle against Kuomintang and Japanese forces. After the revolution they were a key, conspicuous part of the new party and state communications apparatus and concerned with the propagation of socialist ideology and the mobilization of Chinese peasants and workers for development purposes. They became, in effect, an important part of the waging of class struggle.

In India nationalist-patriotic songs, often deriving from traditional folk and poetic forms, were an important means of nationalist and anti-imperialist expression (Baskaran 1981: 45, 49–57). Since independence, popular songs have continued as an important part of the communications systems of mass peasant, working-class, and radical anti-caste movements. For example the songs Omvedt collected in Maharastra state in 'a variety of settings ranging from peasant huts in rural districts affected by the so-called "green revolution" to trade union offices in Poona and Bombay' were drawn from a variety of popular sources: traditional village folk songs, children's songs, *raga* themes, and in some instances popular film songs. While invariably the singers were peasants and workers, the songs were often composed by radical students and educated Marxist organizers, as well as by peasants and workers themselves (Omvedt 1977: 244).

Throughout Africa 'traditional', as well as 'contemporary', strongly western-influenced contemporary commercial forms of music expression, were associated with anti-colonial nationalist movements and political parties. In Ghana, for example, there was active collaboration between the 'nationalist and itinerant drama troupes, guitar bands, and big band groups of the period' (Van der Geest and Asante-Darko 1982: 27–35; Agovi 1989: 195). The period of nationalist struggle was marked by the relatively harmonious, close collaboration of political leaders, creative artists, and ordinary people (Agovi 1989: 196). This was a period in which there was considerable sharing of 'national aspirations and yearnings for freedom, self-rule, and colonial emancipation'. After the initial post-independence euphoria, when Kwame Nkrumah was preoccupied with Pan-Africanism and the establishment of African unity, severe economic problems, partly induced by the particular development strategies adopted, engendered severe political and cultural dislocation.

In Kenya, for example, many Kikuyu songs and other forms of oral expression were utilized by the Land Freedom Army (Mau Mau) both for emphasizing basic demands and political messages, and maintaining unity and resolve in the population which provided its basis of support.[5] Usually traditional forms were retained while lyrics were changed for nationalist political purposes. Mau Mau songs were an anti-colonial expression which eulogized the heroism of Mau Mau guerrillas and leaders such as Dedan Kimathi, and all those who sacrificed their lives in the cause of the struggle. Many songs attacked as traitors the Home Guards and all others 'who betrayed the movement to the British imperialists' (Kinyatti 1980: 7). Interestingly European Christian hymns were also adapted for anti-colonial and nationalist purposes (Ogot 1977). After independence, when many of the problems and conflicts associated with uneven capitalist development became readily apparent, some popular musicians turned their work to satire and often bitter social and political comment. Perhaps the most important of these musicians has been Joseph Kamaru. Kamaru started singing in the mid-1960s and has exploited traditional Gikuyu rural imagery to deal with contemporary issues such as prostitution, drunkenness, landlessness, poverty, alienation, and the crime, theft, and corruption which have developed as part of capitalism and urbanization processes (Wachira-Chiuri 1981). After the death of the dissident politician J.M. Kariuki, Kamaru composed the heavily symbolic song *J.M. Kariuki Mwendo – miiri* (J.M. Kariuki was loved by all) in which he attributed the killing to a clique who were the enemy of the Kenyan people.

STATE AND MUSIC

State intervention in musical production and distribution may take a multiplicity of direct and indirect forms. The direct intervention ranges from censorship and suppression to legal regulation to protect local production, to the establishment of state institutions for the support of local music production.

> In many countries the government plays an increasingly active role on the music scene. Through legislation, subsidies, different bodies such as ministries of culture, cultural councils, music councils and committees for music policy-making, governments support and suppress different kinds of music. Government-supported institutions of different kinds are generally responsible for formal music education, both general and at an advanced level.
>
> (Wallis and Malm 1984: 58)

In some countries, state cultural policy is designed to restrict foreign musical influences and encourage the production of selected local musical forms. In others, state support and encouragement is provided for traditional folkloric and classical forms, and not for contemporary popular music forms which are seen either as saturated with foreign, imperialist values, or as critical of those who hold state power and thus threatening to public order – Kenya, for example. State policy with regard to music may reflect broader concerns with national culture and the 'cultural climate', as well as with conflict involving different groups with stakes in musical production and state assistance: musicians and unions representing them; composers; local record production companies; subsidiaries of transnational corporations involved in phonogram production and distribution; and local broadcasting interests.

Tanzania is one African country where state policy and the 'intellectual establishment' have encouraged the 'development of modern popular music trends' (Wallis and Malm 1984: 64). In Tanzania a multitude of different ethnic groups exists without any one being able to establish dominance. The ethnic diversity is replicated in the multitude of musical styles which were originally tightly integrated into their social contexts. As part of the emphasis on the development of a national culture able to bring greater unity to ethnic diversity, the Tanzanian government established Swahili as the national language. It also established, under the direction of the Ministry of Culture, a national dance and musical troupe which blended the different regional ethnic music and dance styles into the national *ngoma*[6] style (Wallis and Malm 1984: 219).

In the late 1960s and early 1970s the popular music scene was effectively dominated by visiting Rumba-style groups from Zaïre; local jazz groups were very much in the background. However, principally as a result of local radio support, Tanzanian jazz music greatly increased in popularity. The Zaïrean groups which remained in the country abandoned singing in Lingala and adopted Swahili for their performances (Wallis and Malm 1984: 64). The national radio ban on imported music meant that by 1973 Tanzanian radio was playing Tanzanian music exclusively. However, despite the crucial role played by radio, the music industry suffered from the absence of record pressing facilities and chronic foreign exchange shortages which affected the importation of musical instruments.

NIGERIA

Music, of all modern media, is perhaps the most difficult to analyse in media or cultural imperialist terms; certainly it would appear to be the least susceptible to the media imperialism thesis. Although it is clear that world music production is substantially concentrated in the advanced capitalist economies, the very nature of music production lends itself to often relatively cheap local forms of production and distribution which can compete with products controlled by the transnational phonogram producers and distributors. In many countries small recording studios, pressing plants, and labels cater for local markets, in some instances, such as in Nigeria, often being owned by the successful musicians themselves. Even without such facilities, music can be made widely available through performance in any number of venues ranging from the officially approved to the illegal. It is the capacity of music to resist and elude the normal means of state suppression and censorship that makes it an important voice of opposition and resistance.[7] Even where records are banned, radio and television airplay is prohibited, and musicians constantly harassed and even imprisoned, it is difficult to stifle musical protest and resistance completely. Musical expression becomes so closely rooted in and identified with particular social bases

– the urban poor, dissident students – that its influence is difficult to eradicate.

In music, as much as in other areas of cultural expression, there has been anti-imperialist and nationalist reassertion. Many Nigerian musicians, for example, have obviously been influenced by western musical styles, including their instrumentation, but have consciously sought to subordinate such influences to essentially indigenous forms. The depth, diversity, and vitality of traditional indigenous musical forms in Nigeria, as well as in other countries, has meant that they have provided the basis for contemporary popular music, even where imported sounds are strongly present and influential. Some of the most significant flows of musical influence have not been directly from the western capitalist countries; rather, they have involved musical styles in neighbouring states which have either come to dominate popular music taste and the market, or exerted a profound influence on the development of local styles. Zaïrean music, for example, has been of great importance in Kenya and Tanzania, while *highlife*, a form which developed in Ghana early this century, took hold in the 1950s despite the vitality and diversity of musical production in Nigeria. Clearly, strong, influential musical styles such as *rumba*-influenced Zaïrean music, and the Ghanaian *highlife*, have been at least conditioned in their development by western musical styles, but have undergone so many processes of mediation to be significantly different – certainly they cannot simply be reduced to the imported influences.

Nigeria, in contrast to most other African countries, possesses the resources to support a quite substantial music industry (Real 1985: 97). In the early 1970s there were twenty-four recording companies and labels, as well as an extensive radio network for the broadcasting of music. Despite the importance of local enterprises such as Tabansi Records, the two leading transnational companies – Polygram and EMI – accounted for the largest market share, and were the principal conduits of imported music (Robinson *et al.* 1991: 94–5). Nigeria also possessed a substantial economic base for producing and purchasing popular music, and cultural and economic policies which, if lacking overall coherence, were anti-colonial and concerned with the encouragement of indigenous cultural and economic enterprise.

Since Nigeria's independence in 1960, often rapid changes in government (successive military coups, return to civilian government, civil war, the restructuring of federalism), government cultural policy, and the general state of the world economy (especially drops in world oil prices), have had a profound effect on Nigerian musical production. The types of close patronage relations which have often existed between musicians and particular state administrations have invariably led to reprisals by subsequent administrations. Political instability, uncertainty, and successive changes of administration have meant that cultural policy lacks overall cohesion, and tends to reflect the position of particular favourites at any one time (Robinson *et al.* 1991: 92–3).

Throughout Africa radio is the most widespread mass medium and thus of fundamental importance to the local music industry, 'especially the recording, duplicating and distributing of LP and 45 rpm discs and tape cassettes' (Real 1985: 96). Nigeria is particularly well served by radio broadcasting; in the early 1970s there were eleven state and three national sets of programmes which relied on the substantial output of both indigenous and international music. Radio in Nigeria, and elsewhere in Africa, has been the key vehicle for vernacular language cultural expression – indeed, perhaps survival. This has been immensely important for traditional regional music expression. In Nigeria traditional regional music has been documented, the musicians interviewed, and selections of music played on radio (Real 1985: 98). Real's brief comparative study of Nigerian and Liberian broadcast music found that music of African origin accounted for 54 per cent of selection: 'The music of western origin was less exclusively North American than the Liberian sample, although it was also a mixture of soul, disco, reggae, middle of the road, gospel, and classical' (Real 1985: 97). However, much of the African music was of Nigerian origin. Nigerian radio broadcast music included the *juju* sound of Chief Ebenezer Obey and Sunny Ade as 'successors to the *highlife* tradition', *apala* music, the *sakara* sound of southern Nigeria, music influenced by the *Afro-beat* of Fela Anikulapo Kuti, *fuji*, and a variety of other popular styles.

The fact that Nigeria has a large, ethnically diverse population[8] has contributed enormously to the diversity of musical styles and to a fairly well-developed music industry (Graham 1989: 33). Some of the major cultural and musical differences can for convenience roughly be related to the principal regional divisions: the west, occupied by the Yoruba; the east, occupied by the Ibo; and the north, occupied by the Hausa-Fulani. The diversity and vitality of Nigerian culture and music is partly bound up with the maintenance of strong regional differences, reinforced through the regional state structure, and partly through state cultural policies which have encouraged the preservation and persistence of 'traditional' forms of musical and other expression. In contrast to many other African countries, in Nigeria many of the 'traditional' forms 'remain as potent and popular as modern urban varieties of music' (Graham 1989: 33) and are available on disc.

Although it is clearly impossible to categorize the different regional musics easily, that of the Hausa-Fulani dominated north tends to be characterized by ensembles comprising 'percussion of various types, male and female vocals and various trumpets and horns' (Graham 1989: 33). Yoruba music is dominated by drums. In the east, Ibo traditional music has featured percussion instruments, vocals and flutes, and xylophones and lyres.

Modern Nigerian music has been dominated by three principal styles. The first of these, *juju*, is a Yoruba twentieth-century guitar style from western Nigeria which has been the single most popular since the 1960s (Graham 1989: 34; Stapleton and May 1989: 78). The music has built up specialist followings in North America and Europe and demonstrates well the capacity of African musical cultures to absorb western ideas and instrumentation and rechannel them in ways which are distinctively African: 'its electric, even pedal-steel-guitars, for instance, are played in a manner which owes little to the guitar heroes of rock or country music, but a lot to the centuries-old court and social music of Yoruba culture. To compound the difficulty *juju*'s lyrics are sung almost exclusively in the Yoruba language' (Stapleton and May 1989: 78). It is essentially a combination of elements of traditional indigenous musical instruments – talking drums and other percussion instruments, and lyric subject matter and the electric guitar sound of the west. Although there is confusion about the origins of the term *juju* there is little doubt that many of the music's principal characteristics have very long historical antecedents. Stapleton and May (1989: 78) note that 'call and response vocals, rhythm patterns, the use of religious folklore in the lyrics . . . have been common to similar styles stretching back over several centuries'.

The second dominant Nigerian musical style, *fuji*, whose popularity has overtaken *juju*, first emerged during the 1970s as a development of various traditional Yoruba forms such as *apala*, *sakara*, and *waka* (Graham 1989: 46). *Fuji*'s popularity stems partly from its strong Islamic quality 'which offers a deeper African alternative to some of *juju*'s more western features: churchy harmonies and electric instruments' (Stapleton and May 1989: 91). It also has the advantage in a time of economic stringency of making use of acoustic instruments, as well as essentially being a street music which strongly appeals to ordinary people.

Fuji makes use of talking drums, *bata* drums, bells and *shekere* (*shekere* is a type of gourd rattle which is widely used in *fuji*, *juju*, and many other African musical styles), and has a vocal style which is strongly Islamic; indeed, *fuji*'s vocal lines are taken from the sound of the *ajimere*, an 'Islamic singer who wakes up the faithful each morning during the annual fast of Ramadan' (Stapleton and May 1989: 91). Some *fuji* musicians have shown quite a strong antagonism to western popular music. Haruna Ishola, for example, regarded the arrival of guitars, horns, and keyboards throughout most popular music in Nigeria after World War II as at best an irrelevance, at worst a threat to the Africanness of Nigerian music (Stapleton and May 1989: 92). The major *fuji* musician Wasiu Ayinde Barrister, suggests *fuji* music has a strong African identity: 'It's a pure Nigerian music. There is no Western influence. It may have started out as an Islamic sound, but now it's for everyone' (Stapleton and May 1989: 94).

In *fuji* music much of the lyric content of early artists such as Haruna Ishola (1918–83) came from traditional Yorubu proverbs. Some lyrics were praise songs, laments to departed contemporaries, and occasionally topical songs. Barrister's lyrics are heavily indebted to 'Yoruba proverbs, sing praise songs for wealthy clients, comment on topical events, including elections and economic programmes, and other matters of concern to all' (Stapleton and May 1989: 94). Alhaji Chief Kollington Ayinla (b. 1953) avoided religious and moral homilies to 'concentrate on earthier subjects such as politics and corruption' (Stapleton and May 1989: 91). As economic crisis deepened in Nigeria, Kollington's *fuji* lyrics became more critical of politicians and public waste and profligacy, praised teachers, and praised the arrival of the new military government (Graham 1989: 50).

The third major style of popular music is *highlife*. Popular throughout the English-speaking countries of West Africa – from Nigeria to Ghana and Sierra Leone – *highlife* is found in two main forms. *Highlife*, which had its origins in Ghana, arrived in Nigeria in the early 1950s following the successful tours of E.T. Mensah, the Ghanaian *highlife* king (Graham 1989: 52). After a period of great popularity in western Nigeria, where many musicians abandoned either western dance music or native blues to take advantage of the new musical style, *highlife* went through deeply troubled times as a result of the Civil War (Graham 1989: 53). Among the Yorubas in the West *juju* established an unchallenged hold while in the East, among the Ibos, *highlife* flourished. At a time when the popularity of *highlife* was waning in Ghana, it took hold among Ibo musicians who developed new styles which drew upon Congolese influences and '*makossa* overtones' (Graham 1989: 53).

The lyrics of *highlife* music in Nigeria have also assumed strong political dimensions. The controversial musician Fela Anikulapo Kuti (b. 1938) has identified his music with the plight of the 'common man' and as a result has been subjected to vilification, harassment, and even imprisonment by the Nigerian government. Associated with *Afro-beat*,[9] Fela consistently attacked military corruption, greed and waste, and social injustice to the extent that his compound, where he had his studio recording facilities, was attacked and burnt by the military government. Fela sang in broken English rather than Yoruba and established a large and loyal following among the urban poor in the shanty towns around the major cities. Fela sang about their problems in ways with which they could immediately identify and denounced 'the new ruling classes and their enforcers of law and order' (Stapleton and May 1989: 67–8).

LATIN AMERICAN MUSIC

In Latin American countries music has almost inevitably been caught up in nationalist, anti-imperialist, domestic oppositional and class-based causes and movements. In the 1920s cultural nationalism constituted an important part of the Mexican revolution when the writer and philosopher José Vasconcelos, as Minister of Education, implemented a far-reaching educational and cultural programme. National themes were introduced into music; active support was provided for musicians, the formation of orchestras and the teaching of music was encouraged, and native musicians and folk-singing groups were engaged. Mexican composers sought to recover Indian roots, including the use of pre-Columbian instruments, in their works.[10] Dance, especially folk dance, also received official encouragement, 'although the Ballet Folklorico de Mexico

was not officially recognized as a national company until 1959'
(Franco 1970: 91–2).

State involvement in music, while often manifesting nationalist
concerns, has more often taken the form of banning, censorship,
and suppression. This is scarcely surprising when, despite the
existence of popular commercial forms of music, including imported ones, many musical styles and forms have been closely
identified with resistance and struggle against authoritarian military
and civilian regimes and the imposition of cultural hegemony in
their interests. Even the *bossa nova* in Brazil in the early 1960s
underwent a politicization and showed an increasing social awareness as the authoritarian military regime seized power and tightened
its hold.

CUBA

Cuban music, which has retained certain dominant features of Afro-
Cuban folk music, has exerted an at times decisive influence over
the development of many popular musical forms throughout Latin
America.

> From the *habanera*, the *son cubano*, the *danza cubana*, and the
> *bolero* to the *mambo*, *rumba*, *conga*, and *chachachá*, Cuban
> music has either shaped the emergence of *criollo* music genres in
> other countries of the continent or been adopted in toto at
> various periods as fashionable dance music.
>
> (Béhague 1986: 45)

In socialist Cuba the market is still a key determinant in popular
music production and distribution. However, the supply of music to
the market is affected by state cultural policy, while demand is
affected by socialist forms of consciousness and class revolution
(Manuel 1987: 161) After the establishment of the Revolutionary
Government in 1959, many Cuban critics condemned the negative
effects of the North American music industry on Cuba. Some critics
denounced both the warping of Cuban music in the pre-
revolutionary period by foreign commercial influences and the
restriction of music education and patronage in the same period to
the urban upper and middle classes (Manuel 1987: 162). For such
critics the dominance of the market held out the bourgeois promise
of artistic freedom for the musician, but essentially denied it by

forcing him to commercialize and sensationalize his music to survive.

The internationalization of Cuban music was condemned by some critics on the grounds that it led to its adulteration, especially when mixed with anaemic non-Cuban forms. The inundation of the Cuban market by foreign popular music was an affront to nationalist sensibility, and part of the commodification process in which musical taste and ideology were deformed and used by the dominant classes to perpetuate the subordination of the Cuban working class.

> This situation encouraged a passive, consumerist mentality by means of presenting an escapist, artificial, inverted portrayal of reality – a portrait that obscured class antagonism and frustrated individual and collective self-realization.
>
> (Manuel 1987: 162)

A few years after attaining power the Revolutionary government nationalized most aspects of the commercial music industry including radio stations, concerts, and nightclubs. Cuban state cultural policy was predicated on the democratization of access to culture. Despite funding problems and severe shortages of trained teachers, considerable effort went into providing material facilities for cultural expression throughout the countryside.

In Cuba popular music has been regarded as a valuable and vital part of the national heritage and has received a great deal of promotion by the state. Whereas in the Soviet Union, and Eastern European state socialist societies, popular music was generally condemned (unless of course it was a carefully orchestrated regional folk variety untainted by capitalist culture), Cuba possessed its 'own vital popular music' (Manuel 1987: 163). Even when concerned with the condemnation of anti-revolutionary music, Cuban state cultural policy has remained essentially flexible and 'responsive to the diversity of tastes and attitudes within Cuba' (Manuel 1987: 163).

North American and British popular music – mostly rock – continues to enjoy popularity. Both Cuban radio and television have given extensive airplay to rock music, most probably out of a realization that to do otherwise would simply drive young Cubans to tune in to commercial Florida stations, the Voice of America, or the Reagan Administration's Radio Marti (Manuel 1987: 163–4).

There has been a good deal of ambiguity in official Cuban attitudes to many types of popular music, and especially imported music. This ambiguity has also characterized Cuban intellectual critical responses. Until the late 1970s jazz was considered highly problematic, despite having strongly influenced Cuban dance music since the 1930s. Associations with drugs, bohemian cultures, and Soviet condemnation of the music for many decades probably influenced Cuban attitudes. *Salsa* was also cause for concern. It not only competed with Cuban dance music (although having strong musical connections with it), but also its outside origins in Cubans and Puerto Ricans living in Puerto Rico and New York City posed political-ideological problems. Calls for pan-Latin solidarity in *salsa* lyrics scarcely amounted to a left commitment since the audience for *salsa* was polarized between extreme right-wing Cuban-Americans living in New York, and radical urban proletarians living in San Juan and Caracas (Manuel 1987: 169). Cuban critics expressed concern that the internationalization of *salsa*, and its development as another type of disco music, served to conceal the uniqueness of its Cuban origins as well as to contribute to United States efforts to isolate Cuba economically, politically, and culturally.

The popularity of rock music in Cuba apparently represents a contradiction since the music is a product of capitalist society and in some way expresses the values of that society (Manuel 1987: 164). Hard-line Cuban critics have condemned the music for its role in cultural colonialism/imperialism, and for its destructive impact on artistic production. This is in line with the commonly held view in Cuba that artistic creation outside the collective nature of capitalist artistic or cultural production is strongly preferable because it is non-alienating. More moderate critics have rejected cultural imperialist claims, arguing first, that Cuba has a long history of importation and adoption of foreign musical styles, and second, that when transplanted to Cuba rock music 'loses its negative features, for the alleged commercialism, hedonism, and excessive individualism of rock are extramusical features dependent upon their cultural milieu and dissemination' (Manuel 1987: 164). Indeed, borrowing from North American music, according to the Cuban author León, can be part of an anti-imperialist struggle by showing that it is possible to select what is worthwhile without importing the whole system. Other Cuban critics have been rather more sceptical, pointing out that it is difficult, if not impossible, to separate any music or art from the 'ideology of the class that sired it' (Manuel 1987: 165). In the thought of some critics nationalist and Marxist elements are combined to produce an opposition to music imported from the United States in particular.

Nueva trova (new song) is clearly the one musical genre in Cuba which is a product of the revolution and not either foreign or pre-revolutionary (Béhague 1986; Manuel 1987: 173). After initial difficulties with *nueva trova*'s problematic linking with North American 'protest' music, and frequent use of traditional *trova* elements and bland mainstream *canción* style which seemed to deny the possibility of revolutionary form as well as content, it became quite compatible with Cuban cultural policy and revolutionary goals (Manuel 1987: 174). *Nueva trova* expressed in important ways the history, struggles, and ideology of the Cuban revolution without having recourse to explicit political rhetoric (Béhague 1986: 46). Rather, the young people associated with the emergence of the *nueva trova* movement 'wanted to express through song their experience and feelings within the Revolution' (Béhague 1986: 46). The music itself had important roots in earlier Cuban musical genres. Stylistically it is an extension of traditional *nova*, especially the Cuban *canción* (Manuel 1987: 173). However, while *nueva trova* is concerned in a self-conscious manner with the revival of folkloric elements, it freely draws upon both North American rock and pop music and occasionally from non-Cuban Latin American folk traditions. The latter, involving instruments and forms, is an attempt, however symbolic, to express fraternal solidarity with others throughout Latin America engaged in struggle.

If not representing a radical departure in basic form, *nueva trova* nevertheless represented a significant shift in its texts and social movement base. While the ideology of *nueva trova* lyrics had some roots in nineteenth-century nationalistic and revolutionary *puntos* and *canciónes*, its socialist content was of much more recent origin. Lyrics drew inspiration from prominent poets such as the Chilean communist Pablo Neruda, as well as North American singers such as Bob Dylan and Joan Baez (Manuel 1987: 173). As with so much popular song, the lyrics of *nueva trova* often dealt with love and personal relationships, but relocated them in the framework of the more humane society which Cuban socialism was concerned with creating. There was a deliberate avoidance in the lyrics of romantic stereotypes and rhetoric, and the machismo cult of the objectification of women. *Nueva trova* was opposed to the banality of commercial song and to the perpetuation of a star syndrome in which barriers were erected between performers and audience (Benmayor 1981: 14).

BRAZILIAN MUSIC

In the case of Brazil it is almost impossible to summarize briefly the diversity and complexity of musical production. Brazil's musical culture, which draws upon European, African, and Amerindian sources, is immensely rich and defies easy categorization. Music ranges from the tribal music which flourishes in the Amazon, to folk/traditional forms in urban and rural areas, to 'cosmopolitan art music', the various forms of the *bossa nova*, and imported rock and popular music mainly from the United States (Perrone 1987: 219). Despite the importance of imported styles, and the role of international record producers in marketing and distributing them,[11] most Brazilian musical production defies any easy media or cultural imperialist explanation.

Contemporary Brazilian popular music basically began with the emergence of *bossa nova*, a movement which became internationally known and popular in the 1960s. *Bossa nova* originated with musicians from upper middle class families who initiated an essentially elitist urban popular music trend. The music, rather than being simply an imitation of jazz or other imported styles, was early in its development thematically derived from a truly popular music, *samba*. For Perrone the music represented a crossing of the traditional *samba* with a cool jazz derived from Miles Davis and others of his generation (Perrone 1987: 219). Jazz influences in early *bossa nova* pieces could be heard in particular harmonic practices (altered chords on acoustic guitar and a heavy reliance on non-harmonic tones), the choice of blending of instruments (small ensembles of piano, double bass, acoustic or electric guitar, saxophone, trumpet, drums), and some performance traits such as the cool, subdued tone of the vocal delivery. However, as Béhague (1980: 440) notes, 'the typical vocalizing on nonsense syllables had precedents in the classic era of the samba' and not in 'scat' singing associated with jazz.

Bossa nova song lyrics were based predominantly on romantic love themes which 'generally appealed to the sentimental and leisure-time concerns of the middle class' (Perrone 1987: 219). Such thematic concerns, however, represented largely a continuation of those of previously popular genres, the *samba-cançâo*[12] especially (Béhague 1980: 441). Where significant innovation occurred was in the poetic substance and treatment of *bossa nova* songs. From the very beginning the substantial involvement in the music of poet-composers ensured unprecedented poetic refinement and creative originality. As a musical form characterized by intimacy, *bossa nova* lyrics relied on a simplicity of language and a preoccupation with the sound effects of words. In this, *bossa nova* was somewhat akin to concrete poetry of the early 1960s (Béhague 1980: 441).

The second generation of *bossa nova* musicians which emerged in the mid-1960s was much more closely identified with politically engagé attitudes and nationalistic concerns and often integrated elements of folk culture in their work (Béhague 1980: 443; Perrone 1987: 219). Most frequently the protest simply took the form of exposing some of the social problems of underdevelopment, hunger, and injustice in the distant hinterland of the Northeast. Chico Buarque de Hollanda, one of the earliest and principal musicians to express social protest through *bossa nova* form, was able clearly and successfully to establish a link with the more traditional *samba* of the 1930s and 1940s and carnival music in general (Béhague 1980: 443). In *Pedro Pedreiro* (1966) Chico Buarque indicated the trend towards greater social engagement and protest by *bossa nova* musicians by taking issue with the urban conditions of migrant workers in the large southern cities of Brazil. The composer used repetition in the song to convey the idea of 'the monotony and limitations of the typical slum life of a Northern immigrant worker' (Béhague 1980: 444).

Although the second generation of *bossa nova* musicians was much more socially aware and committed, it was still marked by its class origins. Nevertheless there was an attempt to portray sympathetically the lives of, and identify with, the urban working classes. Chico Buarque's music has provoked a variety of critical responses including state censorship of many of his songs and plays in the late 1960s and early 1970s (Béhague 1980: 447). Songs such as *Bom Conselho* (Good Advice), *Cotidiano* (Daily Routine), and *Apesar de Vocè* (In Spite of You) seemed to suggest that the only hopeful attitude to contemporary Brazilian problems was a 'certain subtle action of subversion and anarchy' (Béhague 1980: 444). Some 'left' critics interpreted this as a 'conservative fatalism' which dwelled on human misfortune and individual destiny and failed to provide any sign of more advanced consciousness in popular music production. Given the thoroughly repressive nature of state censorship at this time it was perhaps a little unreasonable to expect much more from the lyrics.

Another interesting development in Brazilian popular music occurred at the end of the 1960s in *tropicalismo*. Begun in 1968 by Caetano Veloso and Gilberto Gil, *Tropicália* incorporated concepts of literary modernism into song-writing and helped blur, 'distinctions between committed national music and so-called alienated popular music' (Perrone 1987: 220).

Perhaps inevitably restricted to the intelligentsia, *Tropicália* represented an attempt through music to awaken the consciousness of the Brazilian middle classes to the contemporary reality of poverty, exploitation and oppression. With its musical innovations it was instrumental in bringing about a widening of popular musical production to incorporate and adapt the 'most relevant musical trends of the 1960s, i.e., the rock-Beatles phenomenon, and the experimental, new music of the electronic age' (Béhague 1980: 449).

During the period of severe political repression (1965–9) there was a 'golden age' of festivals of popular music (Perrone 1987: 219). The initials MPB were used to refer to music of national character rather than imported pop and its local variants. This period was marked by the emergence of outstanding poet-songwriters, composers, and singers, and by the incorporation of concepts of literary modernism into songwriting. Increasingly critics recognized song as a major vehicle of national poetry (Perrone 1987: 220). It also became an important instrument of protest and dissent under continuing authoritarian rule and political censorship. Many Brazilian musicians were able to incorporate an abundance of foreign (rock, blues, soul, disco, funk, reggae, even African *highlife*) as well as local regional elements into the structure and repertoire of their music. At the same time local urban musical forms such as the instrumental *choro*, and *samba*, were revitalized.

In the 1980s radio airplay and record sales were dominated by the rock sound (Perrone 1987: 221). Although local imitations of American rock 'n'roll had been in existence since the late 1950s it was not until the mid-1960s, with considerable television promotion, that the movement known as *iê – iê – iê* (yeah, yeah, yeah) took hold to compete with *bossa nova* and derivatives (Perrone 1987: 221). Throughout the 1970s rock continued as a minority manifestation and it was not until 1985 that the Rock in Rio festival signalled the ascendancy of different forms of rock as the major musical fare among urban youth. The nationalistic, engagé music of the 1960s and 1970s, often in traditional musical genres such as *samba*, has been overshadowed by commercial rock music in which there is little explicit socio-political content (Perrone 1988: 167). For some observers the popularity of commercial rock music resides precisely in its lack of concern with issues which force listeners to think.

Nevertheless the themes of Brazilian redemocratization – amnesty, censorship, direct presidential elections, and the re-evaluation of the 1960s – have found expression in popular music, especially in song texts. Songwriters such as Chico Buarque retained a critical distance from the military regime as it embarked on redemocratization measures. Perrone notes that although they

> resisted the didactic stance of much 60s protest song when addressing issues of Brazil's transition . . . (t)hey used song as a platform for careful reflection on the whole period of dictatorship and on social and personal implications of liberalization.
>
> (Perrone 1988: 180)

CONCLUSION

Although it is the case that the music industries and tastes of the advanced capitalist economies have been able to exert a disproportionate, largely non-reciprocated influence, musical production and taste in 'Third World' countries nevertheless show enormous variations. This is partly the result of the size of the countries concerned (Brazil, Nigeria, India), levels of investment in musical production, extent of differentiation of the market, continuation and adaptation of indigenous musical traditions for commercial and oppositional purposes, and state and ruling-party policies with regard to local and imported music. Indigenous musical traditions have been substantially transformed as a result, not simply of the preponderating influence of foreign musical styles and musical technologies, but also of the basic changes in the social relations of production which affect both the production and reception of music. Such indigenous traditions have, however, been drawn upon to create new forms of urban, popular music, some of it with a sharp, critical edge. Many musicians in 'Third World' countries have been concerned to challenge the musical domination of the advanced capitalist world. In most countries musical forms outside the basic capitalist relations of musical production continue to survive and develop, and together with some modern commercial forms, often provide a means for articulating the experiences and aspirations of oppressed groups and classes. The anti-imperialist dimension usually involves the critique of local dominant classes who are identified with imperialist interests.

Chapter 11

Folk and alternative media

In mass communications analysis the recognition of the interaction of informal and inter-personal communications with centralized mass ones is commonplace. Modern, often highly centralized communications institutions in 'Third World' countries, are located in societies where there is the persistence of older communications networks, albeit networks which operate within a greatly changed communications environment and different social relations. Class, ethnic, linguistic, literacy, regional and religious differences, affect not just simply the way people have access to and use the modern mass media, but also the ways in which other, including new forms of communication, operate in relation to them.

Folk and alternative media, including popular theatrical expression such as street theatre, community religious festivals, pavement radio, and music and song, are often linked to popular movements and struggles. In some instances the forms may include an underground or alternative press (for example, pamphlets critical of the Kenyan government and regarded as seditious), and in Latin American countries in particular, alternative video (Sarti 1988),[1] and film production. Such forms develop and operate outside the major media apparatuses, whether state- or privately owned, and usually represent means of expression which are effectively denied through the major media institutions and state-sponsored cultural organizations. Of course media apparatuses may attempt, and indeed succeed, in co-opting and incorporating such alternative and folk media. Some popular forms of expression may have quite explicit anti-imperialist and anti-dominant class orientations, and involve theorization, direction, and participation by intellectuals drawn from quite different class locations and cultural milieus, while others may represent long-established folk practices which have been progressively adapted to basic shifts in production and social relations and the influence of other media.

The application of the term 'folk' to media is highly problematic. In much sociological and other social scientific usage 'folk' has referred to pre-industrial and pre-urban societies in which cultural expression has been primarily oral and essentially localized. Through the development of trade and more extensive transportation networks folk forms became more regional. Folk art or culture was generally concerned with the concrete world intensely familiar to its audience. It dealt with common situations within familiar patterns of life, and was marked by a direct relationship between performer and audience. The threshold of participation was high. Folk culture or art was never isolated from other cultures; it interacted with that of the court, the upper classes, and clergy, and subsequently with the urban, commercial forms of entertainment and communications characteristic of capitalist industrialization and the emergence of more generalized commodity production. It was both the source for 'intellectual' and popular commercial forms, as well as influenced in its general development by them.

While for many writers urbanization and industrialization, combined with literacy and the new mass communications institutions, eventually brought about the disappearance of folk art or culture (Katz and Wedell 1978: 141), for others new folk forms, some with their roots in the older rural culture, emerged out of the experience of both rural and urban people undergoing the dislocation of industrialization and wage labour (Williams 1965; Thompson 1968). In Britain and other European countries a vigorous industrial folk song emerged which expressed in basic and sometimes poignant ways the response of labouring people to the changes which fundamentally affected their lives (Craig 1973). It needs stressing, however, that the social relations in which various expressions of traditional 'folk' culture or art occur have changed fundamentally. The people who produce traditional crafts such as textiles with religious and other motifs and symbolism in West Africa (Opoku-Agyeman 1987), or pottery with strong resistance and oppositional functions in countries such as Colombia, do so within quite different sets of social relations. If there are new types of folk expression, especially in the urban areas of 'Third World' countries, they represent responses to the dominant cultures encapsulated in the major communications and other institutions of society and adaptation to the harsh realities of urban labouring and lumpenproletarian

existence. The diverse forms of expression associated with the
barrios of Latin American cities involve the continuation and
adaptation of older religious, festive, and communal forms, as well
as the selective incorporation and adaptation of mass media products and manufactured commodities.

It is difficult to specify precisely what is meant by alternative
media. Usually they are understood as media which have been
developed and used by groups which are in some way denied access
to and opposed to the dominant mass media apparatus of the press,
broadcasting, and in Latin America especially, the cinema. Such
groups are often, perhaps inevitably, identified with radical, reformist, even revolutionary movements, and use the alternative media
as a way of trying to counteract ideological hegemony, sharpening
political consciousness, and providing outlets for the cultural expression of subordinated, oppressed, and minority groups.

In some instances alternative media are associated with powerful
religious organizations which have been fostering social reform
through 'liberation theology', and which have at times been at
loggerheads with local ruling classes and the controllers of the state
apparatus. In Latin American countries such as Brazil the Roman
Catholic Church has developed an extensive network of radio
stations which are concerned with the propagation of values quite
distinct from those of the highly concentrated commercial mass
media.

Whereas in many advanced capitalist countries the churches have
pressed for the reform of the major media apparatuses, in Latin
America they have tended to press for alternative media forms 'to
serve peasant and urban labouring groups'. There has been a clear
intention to enable such groups – the 'disadvantaged' in general – to
become better organized and to gain access to the media and
'establish their own internal, horizontal communication system'
('Contribution of the Church to National Broadcasting Policy' 1980:
III). A major part of the churches' strategy has been the provision of
local cultural-educational radio services in market towns to serve
lower-class groups. Since the early 1980s the emphasis has shifted to
convert radio stations into instruments in the hands of worker and
peasant groups – as a 'voice of the voiceless'. Another key part of
this strategy has been the promotion of '*communicación popular*'.
This refers to small-scale, folk media – folk theatre, community
newspapers – which people produce for themselves rather than have
produced for them. The churches have also emphasized group

communication and the establishment of popular documentation centres such as CEDI in Sao Paulo which help labour unions, community organizations, and other journalistically inexperienced groups prepare their own newsletters or pamphlets and establish links with other organizations. CEDI, which was an object of suspicion for the Brazilian military regime, investigated and publicized the problems of Indian tribes in the Amazon, and trains non-professionals to communicate effectively.

There is a clear recognition by church representatives that there are limitations to the churches' ability to initiate dominant media institutional reform, as there is social structural reform more generally. Many of the 'minority' groups are only interested in gaining access to the 'system' rather than changing it. Church membership cuts across class lines, which makes it virtually impossible to sustain concerted action on key issues. Many individual Christians consider religion a personal matter which has nothing to do with the formulation of national media policy.

In some instances forms of cultural expression and media normally regarded as part, if only in a peripheral way, of the dominant mass media apparatus function as alternative media. This is the case in Tanzania with 'popular' literature, including comic books and chapbooks, which deviate sharply from that which has been sanctioned and supported by party and state. A combination of a commitment to the implementation of socialism and anti-imperialism, and the continuing influence of a puritanism derived from Islam, led to the denunciation and banning of popular Kenyan literature which was seen as the product of, and pervaded by, the most egregious capitalist and neo-colonial values. The state and party literary emphasis, linked to functional literacy campaigns and socialist transformation, was to produce relatively cheap and simple booklets for the newly literate. In this climate the production of a popular, commercial literature similar to that of Kenya in the 1970s had no place.

It is necessary to draw two further basic distinctions. The first is between folk and alternative media which have been incorporated into governmental 'developmental' strategies and which are used for social control purposes, and those which are basically oppositional in nature and often grounded in substantial bases of social and political dissent. A second distinction is between alternative media associated in their development with an urban-based intelligentsia, and those which at least appear as more spontaneous or traditional expressions of urban and rural life such as folk religious practices in many Latin American countries. In the case of Third Cinema, people's theatre, and alternative video, it is clear that intellectuals, under the influence of a multitude of ideas drawn from Marxist aesthetics in particular, have sought to define an intellectual role, and the nature of different types of communications and cultural practices, in relation to 'oppressed' peoples (rural and urban labourers, the landless, poor peasants, the lumpenproletariat) and a socialist transformation of society. Regardless of how closely and collaboratively intellectuals work with different constituencies in the production of alternative means of communication, their imprint is always present.

THIRD CINEMA

Third cinema and people's theatre represent perhaps the two most significant, heavily theorized examples of efforts to develop systems of communication, geared to particular notions of political and social practice, which challenge the dominant institutional order of communications in 'Third World' societies. Both have strong associations in their development with Latin America, with the latter rather than the former exerting considerable influence in Africa and to a lesser extent Asia.

The notion of a Third Cinema, Willemen (1989: 4) notes, 'was first advanced as a rallying cry in the late 1960s in Latin America'. Strongly influenced in its development by the Cuban Revolution (1959) and Brazil's *cinema nova*, it drew heavily on different strands within Marxist aesthetics, and non-revolutionary currents such as Italian neo-realism and Grierson's notion of the social documentary. The last two provided examples of low-cost, 'artisanal' cinema, which, relying on a mixture of public and private funding, would enable film makers first, to avoid the economic scale of Hollywood production and its national industrial rivals and thus to develop quite different ways of working, and second, to create a cinema which would be able to avoid the homogenizing tendencies associated with the mainstream industrial cinemas (First Cinema).[2] Third Cinema would be able to explore the 'national', as well as the divisions and contradictions, ranging from class and political conflict to the existence of regional language dialects within national social formations.

The early theoretical articulation and integration of Third Cinema was to be found in Solanas and Getino's 'Towards a Third Cinema' (1987) and the Cuban Espinosa's 'For an Imperfect Cinema' (1987 [1969]). The latter argued that it was necessary, first, to distinguish between popular, mass, and cultivated art, and second, to develop an imperfect cinema which would find new audiences, and find its themes in their problems. Such a cinema would essentially shatter the distinction between popular, mass, and cultivated art, in the last case abolishing 'artistic culture as fragmentary human action'. Film would become a genuinely popular medium (as distinct from mass art which is created for the masses and requires them to 'have no taste') in which the distinction between creators and audiences, or intellectuals and people,[3] would be largely collapsed. The distinction between art and life would be abolished, with film allowing for the reintegration of the self.

Solanas and Getino's position rested on a similar view of the role of cinema in 'constructing a liberated personality'. It was located within a dependency perspective in which local ruling classes were subordinate to international capitalism and imperialism. The dominance of the Hollywood industrial model of cinema had destroyed the national characteristics of different national cinemas, and had even affected cinema in socialist societies and author's cinema. The only real alternative to the dominant, as part of decolonization, were films that could not be assimilated by 'the system' and which were foreign to its needs, and films which set out directly and explicitly to fight the system. Central to the concept of Third Cinema is the demystification of the film making process and the overcoming of the limitations of the technology normally employed in industrial cinema. This necessarily involves a changed concept of collective production in which 'vanguard layers and even masses participate collectively in the work when they realize that it is the continuity of their daily struggle'.

Third Cinema films may take any number of militant forms – pamphlet, didactic, report, essay, and witness-bearing films – but should resist the temptation to lay down aesthetic norms. They should counter the cinema of characters, that is, first cinema, with themes, that of individuals with masses, and the author with the operational group. In order to overcome basic problems of censorship and other forms of state suppression and repression they should be distributed through alternative networks which require the establishment of an 'underground base structure'.

Although the concept of Third Cinema is not exclusively associated with 'Third World' countries, its Latin American origins and identification with former European colonies means that this is usually the case. It does tend to be predicated on a certain uniformity of the experience of 'Third World' societies in the face of colonialism and imperialism and as such runs the risk of 'essentialism' (Willemen 1989). This is clear in Teshome Gabriel's re-working of the concept in terms of Frantz Fanon's *The Wretched of the Earth* distinction between different stages in the liberation of 'Third World' societies from colonial oppression. Gabriel uses Fanon's framework as a 'methodological device for a critical inquiry into Third World film' (Gabriel 1989b: 30). Fanon's assimilationist phase in the case of film coincides with an identification with a dominant Hollywood film industry model in which the principal thematic concern is entertainment and profit-making (Gabriel 1989b: 31). Fanon's remembrance phase, where the intellectual almost craves forgiveness by rediscovering the indigenous culture and people, corresponds to the 'indigenization and control of talent, production, exhibition and distribution' (Gabriel 1989b: 32). Thematically, in this phase, film is concerned with the return of the exile and the exploration of the strength of traditional culture and history, often in an uncritical and romanticized way. Stylistically there is some indigenization, although the conventions of the first phase are still dominant. In Fanon's third phase, the combative, film making has shifted to a public service institution which is owned by the 'nation' or government and is 'managed, operated and run for and by the people' (Gabriel 1989: 33). Thematically film in this phase deals with the lives and struggles of 'Third World' peoples. Stylistically film is an ideological tool in which public and film maker share the same ideological position, and in which the dominance of character has been replaced by an ideological point of view (Gabriel 1989b: 34).

Willemen draws attention to what appears to be a contradiction between on the one hand the diversity of the lives, subjects and styles which Third Cinema seeks to portray, and nationally specific forms, and some unifying aesthetic for non-Euro-American cinemas on the other. A unifying aesthetic would run up against not simply the lives portrayed, but also nationally specific forms. The lives of people are governed and circumscribed by histories and institutions made 'nationally specific' by the very existence of geopolitical boundaries, and the legal, educational, and other institutional arrangements within them.

Gabriel's three phases 'are not organic developments' (Gabriel 1989b: 35). Individual film makers may indeed flit from phase to phase, perhaps in a regressive fashion. There are 'grey areas' between the different phases. In many countries it is difficult to speak of anything approximating a Third Cinema phase simply because there is virtually no indigenous film making. With the major exception of Egypt, African film making is sporadic at best. Even where, as in India, there may be a massive commercial film production, it is still difficult to speak of a third phase and Third Cinema, even if state-supported authorial second cinema exists. In most 'Third World' countries the rejection of the assimilationist phase can only occur at the distribution and exhibition level where it is possible to draw film from other countries where a greater diversity of production occurs.

Throughout 'Third World' countries an aesthetically and ideologically diverse cinema opposed to 'commercial cinema's values, theories, and stylistic approaches' has developed (Binford 1987: 148). In some cases, as in the African, this was largely determined by the inability to engage in commercial cinema production. In India, as in other countries, this 'new' cinema has been dependent on funding from governmental sources (the central government-funded Film Finance Corporation in the case of India) and it remains essentially a directorial or author's cinema in which the author tends to 'play an active role in all phases of production'. This is partly the result of financial pressures, but also indicates 'a desire for maximum aesthetic control' (Binford 1987: 151).

PEOPLE'S THEATRE

The emergence of people's theatre is usually associated with a specific set of conditions. The combination of an awakening cultural identity in 'communities' and considerable cultural and political repression is particularly conducive to its development. This is especially the case where, Sylvia Moore notes, there are politically repressive regimes and the 'modern media are owned and controlled by government officials or wealthy landowners and industrialists'. In such conditions live performance provides one of the few channels 'open for political expression, historical consciousness, the assertion of group identity and the source of alternative information' (quoted in Srampickal and White 1988: 3).

If there is a common denominator in the various expressions of people's theatre throughout the world it is a protest against a relentless modernization which obliterates traditions and distinctive sub-cultures and promotes a global consumer culture. It is associated primarily with those, including peasant farmers in India, Latin America and some African countries, and proletarians and lumpenproletarians crowded into the swelling shanty towns of the major commercial and industrial cities, who have been increasingly 'squeezed' by the uneven nature of the transformation.

PEOPLE'S THEATRE IN LATIN AMERICA

At least three principal factors have contributed to the development of people's theatre throughout Latin America. One has been the development of alternative means of communication within popular socio-political movements (Srampickal and White 1988: 17). Throughout the nineteenth and twentieth centuries Latin American development has been characterized by the division between dominant classes of mainly European racial and cultural background who have had privileged access to education, literacy, and mass media (especially print media), and peasantries of quite different racial and cultural backgrounds who have lived their lives in village folk cultures increasingly encroached upon by capitalist social relations. Peasant communications with the wider world usually occurred within patronage relationships dominated by local landowners or through other intermediaries who spoke for them.

Early twentieth century economic and industrial development, which involved substantial foreign investment, brought often great benefits to the dominant classes. However it placed heavier demands on the labour of semi-subsistence peasants, increased landlessness, and drove many off the land. The worsening situation of peasant farmers gave rise to great peasant movements, initially in Mexico (1910–20), and subsequently in other countries. These movements, with their horizontal, internal means of communication, provided the basis of people's communication in Latin America. In Bolivia the miners' labour unions even established their own radio stations. The economic and industrial development from 1940 to the early 1960s greatly accentuated the problem. During this period massive immigration to the major commercial-industrial cities led to the spread of shanty settlements – *favelas* in Brazil – around them. Rising political unrest and political mobilization in the 1960s produced brutally repressive military coups in Brazil in 1964 and Chile in 1973. While the harsh repression eliminated some political parties and leaders, it was instrumental in driving the 'popular' classes back on their own grass roots and underground organizations and communications resources.

A second major factor associated with the rise of popular people's theatre and alternative means of communications was the intellectual reaction against the dominant conception of Latin American modernization. During the 1950s and 1960s this was based on an essentially North American prototype. Earlier in the century – in the 1920s and 1930s – intellectuals were engaged in the search for Latin American cultural roots. Latin American countries had developed their own traditions of local festivals, travelling theatres, popular poetry and literature. In the 1930s in the growing cities popular film genres (the Mexican 'western', for example) and radio melodramas emerged. However, during and after World War II Latin American countries were subject to an aggressive overseas expansion of United States culture and mass communications which was part of the overall expansion of United States investment and economic interest in the region. This cultural expansion ranged from Hollywood film, pop music records, and United States television programming, to advertising, and versions of American popular magazines from *Reader's Digest* to *Cosmopolitan* (Srampickal and White 1988: 17).

As we have already seen, the dominant mass communications models at this time were closely based on American prototypes, with American corporations, media, and advertising agencies pushing strongly for the creation of media structures conducive to their interests. This aggressive cultural expansion was eventually opposed in countries such as Brazil by national capitalist interests, as well as by intellectuals and other cultural leaders who sought to link their reaction to broadly based popular movements.[4] The Catholic Church, which had deep roots in folk culture and was allied to many popular movements, was an important part of the search for indigenous culture. The development of a 'liberation theology' which caused some division within the church was an important manifestation of this.

The overthrow of civilian governments by repressive military regimes in Brazil, Argentina, Chile, and other countries in the 1960s

and 1970s, forced underground many involved in journalism, literature, music, and film and theatre, and into closer contact with 'grass
roots popular culture'. Many intellectuals began work with popular
movements and changed the whole notion of their cultural and
political practice as a result. Paulo Freire developed new methods of
popular education – the 'pedagogy of the oppressed' – which were to
prove influential throughout Africa and Asia as well. Augusto Boal
developed a 'theatre of the oppressed' which has been similarly
influential. In his early theatrical career in Sao Paulo, Boal was
committed to a political theatre (plays by Brecht, Steinbeck) designed to produce innovation for certain sectors of the Brazilian
petty bourgeoisie. After the military coup of 1964 his work was
subject to increasing censorship. In 1971, after imprisonment and
torture, he joined Freire and many other Latin American intellectuals in a wandering exile. It was through his involvement in popular
education programmes in Peru and other countries that he devised
his 'theatre of the oppressed'.

Boal challenged the very basis of western theatre theory, and
especially the Aristotelian view of catharsis. He saw the latter
providing justification for a vicarious emotional release which did
nothing to disturb (indeed, it deflected attention from) the dominant social and political order. It was one of the means whereby
volatile social frustration was denied real political action. In *Theatre
of the Oppressed* Boal asserted that the human body was the
principal medium of theatrical production. His theatre was designed
to make participants aware of their bodies and the deformation
which had been produced by oppressive working conditions. Boal's
large number of exercises for the body were designed to lead to the
analysis of social contradictions and the transformation of ordinary
people from passive observers into active engagement. His theatre
is above all concerned with the incompleteness of the action of the
play. Drama could be seen as a type of rehearsal in which the
participants could work out solutions for real-life problems.

INDIA: IMPORTANCE OF PERFORMANCE ARTS

In India traditions of dramatic ritual and literate theatre stretch back
more than two thousand years to the classical Sanskritic drama
which re-enacted the foundational religio-historical myths of Hindu
culture. Contemporary India is characterized by an immense diversity of performance arts which are still concerned to a considerable

extent with this re-enactment. In the 550,000 or more Indian towns and villages the yearly round of religious, agricultural, and civic festivals centres on performances of religious pageants, hired folk opera troupes, local balladeers, song and dance teams, and political plays. Indian theatrical tradition, unlike that of Western Europe, has never really fragmented into specialized performance areas such as opera, ballet, and drama based on dialogue. Rather, it has remained essentially a composite form which relies on dancing, prose dialogue, singing and verse, interspersed with social criticism.

Badal Sircar's 'Third Theatre' challenged the premises of the commercial theatre and indirectly questioned 'the viability of the revolutionary theatre practiced by Utpal Dutt' (Bharucha 1983: 127). Sircar's theatre followed Grotowski's 'poor theatre' in its emphasis on the stripping from production of all accessories associated with commercial theatre – sets, lights, costumes, sound, and make-up – in order to communicate more effectively using bodily, facial, and emotional expressions of symbolic significance (Bharucha 1983: 128–9). Performance made use of elements drawn from traditional mime, rhythmic movements, and songs and dances. This theatre was also concerned with changing the relationship between audience and performers by moving the performance into the midst of audiences and capturing their involvement imaginatively or with active participation. This necessitated a reduction in the scale of the audience, certainly when compared with the mass ones Dutt sought to sway. Sircar's most important innovation was to institute training workshops which replaced director-dominated rehearsals and allowed the actors to make use of their own experiences, perceptions, and emotions on the problematic of a script.

> The workshop also emphasized learning to project emotions physically with the body and voice. These exercises gradually evolved into the model of a workshop in which the actors first analysed social reality, wrote the script and designed the play themselves.
>
> (Srampickel and White 1988: 7)

The widespread integration of folk media into the nationalist movement, the success of the Indian People's Theatre Association, and use of theatre by other political groups, encouraged the Congress Party-dominated Indian government to use performance as one of the means to promote its five-year development plan campaigns and to carry out political education. In 1954 the Song and Drama

Division of the Ministry of Information and Broadcasting was formed. Under its auspices forms such as puppetry, narrative ballads, folk songs, and operatic folk theatre, have been used in a diversity of campaigns ranging from family planning and health education in the 1970s, to national civic education where there have been major problems with communal and ethnic tensions and regional separatist movements. Folk media have also been used for introducing new agricultural techniques, rural co-operatives, and social welfare provision. The development education programmes associated with the Song and Drama Division have been criticized on several grounds including, first, a failure to encourage local participation in the design of material and critical reflection on local problems, second, a failure to identify and use local folk performers, and third, a too-close relation between the types of performances and supervision by the 'local village elites'. The performance policy and practice of the SDD has largely relied on a top-down, propagandist model of communication which has left little room for local participation.

Throughout the 1950s and 1960s the Indian government introduced a series of extension programmes designed to introduce new health, agricultural and other technologies into the rural areas. Such extension programmes were supported by All India Radio educational broadcasting. It was soon apparent, however, that these programmes – the Green Revolution being a good example – brought great benefit to those who were already better off, but not to poor farmers and landless labourers. Indeed the technological and other changes associated with these extension programmes often greatly intensified class and caste inequalities. In the 1970s and early 1980s substantial numbers of young activists pushed for the organization of landless labourers and poor peasant farmers into social action groups which would press issues of agrarian reform, minimum wages, and constitutional guarantees favouring the *harijans* (untouchables), which the Indian government had been reluctant to implement against the power of dominant castes and classes in the countryside.

Many of the social action groups received assistance from non-governmental aid agencies in the advanced capitalist countries. They experimented with a variety of small media which ranged from audio-visuals and video for group *conscientization* to the preferred means of 'street theatre' strongly indebted to a mixture of ideas drawn from Paulo Freire, Augusto Boal with his notion of the 'theatre of the oppressed', and the IPTA, Badal Sircar and others. A clear distinction emerged, as critics such as Kidd (1981) observed, between the Indian government's use of 'folk' theatre for social control purposes and the type of people's theatre based on independent popular organizations. This is especially the case with *harijan* mobilization and the theatre of the Action for Cultural and Political Change (ACPC) based in Tamilnadu. This theatre, against concerted opposition from the landlord class in the region, has used drama to extend literacy to enhance organizational abilities among the *harijans*, provide training for leadership purposes, and encourage the formation of a more assertive *harijan* culture. Largely segregated from central Hindu religious practice and culture which merely reproduces their debasement in a caste hierarchy, *harijan* organizations have been encouraged to develop a folk theatre which relies on drama, music, and song, and is able to create myths of liberation rather than of continual subjugation and debasement.

This theatre has not been without its critics, some of whom draw attention to the lack of a continuing participation of the poor and the constant recycling of old scripts rather than the development of new ones out of the combined activities of poor peasants and outside activists. Rao (1986) has suggested that such action is capable of making the plight of villagers even worse since middle-class catalysts impose their own ideological positions, create expectations which cannot be met, and depart before the full brunt of the stirred-up oppositional forces is felt.

AFRICAN THEATRE

The 'modern' African literary theatre which initially developed in West Africa in the 1950s and 1960s, as well as popular entertainment, contained strong themes of satirical and moralistic protest against colonial, political and cultural domination. After independence, in a new theatre of social protest, the concern shifted to exposure of the corruption of the new African governments and ruling classes and their flagrant abuses of human rights. Most playwrights, despite often using dramatic forms and language largely inaccessible to all but narrow literate strata, regarded themselves as in some way giving expression to neglected and exploited peasants and industrial workers. Many younger playwrights in Tanzania, Zambia, and more recently Nigeria (Amuta 1989), came under the influence of Brechtian theatre which was linked with socialist transformation.

It is not surprising that the centrality of the performance arts to historical and contemporary African societies has led to various movements to 'take theatre to the people', and to use theatre for developmental purposes. This has been expressed in the growth of government departments, different centres, and university-based projects supporting a diversity of participatory people's theatre. Where participatory people's theatre has been introduced it has usually been 'under the general umbrella of government development agencies' and has been concerned with community problem analysis and has served as a basis for community organization. More rarely, certainly compared with Latin America and India, a people's theatre has provided an important alternative means of communication and political consciousness-raising within popularly based oppositional movements. In Tanzania to some extent, and in Mozambique and Zimbabwe more particularly, forms of people's theatre developed as part of national liberation movements. During the armed struggle in Zimbabwe, for example, all-night *pungwes* were organized by villagers and fighters 'in which the combatants and their supporters put on skits, composed songs, read poetry and adapted traditional dance as a way of strengthening morale' (Srampickel and White 1988: 15). People's theatre is also an important part of the black liberation movement in South Africa.

In Africa there is quite a long history of experiment with popular theatre for development purposes. Colonial governments in Ghana and Uganda in the 1950s, under pressure from nationalist movements and with independence imminent, launched theatre for development experiments, usually in agricultural extension schemes. During the 1960s many African universities began 'travelling theatre' projects which took students and tutors to the rural areas, as well as to urban squatter settlements, where they dramatized the conflict between tradition and modernity and provided a type of cultural democratization. In many countries drama, songs, puppetry and story telling have been used in rural health education and preventative medicine schemes. Drama has been used in literacy campaigns in Tanzania and Botswana, and in Kenya and Guinea-Bissau community theatre has been involved in translating literacy classes into a concern with the relationship of literacy to the understanding of the community's history and the building of a political-economic power base for the poor.

In the 1970s in countries such as Botswana, Malawi, Swaziland, Zambia, and Zimbabwe, a new emphasis developed on a village theatre in which local issues were dramatized after research and identification of central issues had occurred. After presentation of the issues in a way the villagers could comprehend, there was post-performance discussion designed to facilitate community education and action. In an effort to make theatre truly participatory and serve as a 'catalyst for collective community action' the Theatre Collective of Nigeria's Ahmadu Bello University 'involved the villages throughout the process from information/data collection to the follow-up action' (Malamah-Thomas 1987: 82).

Etherton (1982), amongst others, has suggested that the relatively late development of an oppositional, participatory people's theatre in Africa possibly reflects the long-standing preoccupation with problems of colonial dependency and 'inter-tribal' conflicts. In Latin American countries, as well as in India, the much earlier intellectual and political concern with class exploitation, inequality, and contradiction, and the depressed conditions of agricultural and industrial workers, provided conditions much more conducive to an earlier development of popular people's theatre. The example of Ngugi wa Thiong'o's collaborative association with the Kamiriithu Theatre to produce two plays represents a significant attempt to ground participatory theatre in a popularly based movement of opposition and resistance (Thiong'o 1981; 1986; Bjorkman 1989).

Many writers on African media have stressed the importance historically, and contemporarily, of 'oramedia' which have established interesting connections with radio, television, and print media. Ellis draws attention to the importance of 'pavement radio' which he defines as 'the popular and unofficial discussion of current affairs in Africa, particularly in towns' (Ellis 1989: 331). It is to be found on urban pavements, in bars, markets, living rooms and taxi-parks and, 'unlike the press, television or radio . . . is not controlled by any identifiable individual, institution or group of people'. Pavement radio thrives on scandal and malicious stories about prominent politicians and persons involving corruption especially.

The specific features of both the structure and content of pavement radio, as well as its importance, derive from its operation within an essentially oral culture (Ellis 1989: 322). According to Ellis, in Africa great weight is attached to the spoken word as a source of political and other information. Whereas in advanced capitalist or industrial society authority and credence is mainly attached to national political news from written and electronic media sources, in Africa a combination of the persistence of oral tradition and the use of mass media for quite explicit political purposes by ruling regimes gives non-dominant media sources considerable importance. 'The most believable purveyors of information are likely to be those whose jobs give them some access to either top-level gossip, such as government drivers, servants and hairdressers, or people with wide social or geographical contacts, such as market-sellers and long-distance lorry drivers' (Ellis 1989: 322). In many cases pavement radio may provide coverage of events such as demonstrations involving deaths, which receive scant or no coverage in national media, or where national media reports are directly contradicted by eye witness accounts of what happened (Ellis 1989: 323).

Many African regimes have been highly sensitive to rumour mongering, and have made it a serious offence, while others are believed to have employed it as a political weapon to try to discredit opponents, including rivals within government (Ellis 1989: 328). Pavement radio perhaps represents some popular restraint on government, providing the poor and the powerless with some means of self-defence. However,

> At the same time . . . *radio trottoir* often expresses admiration for the enterprise and acquisitiveness of the very politicians whom it lambasts for their corruption. This paradox is also found in village politics.
>
> (Ellis 1989: 329)

CONCLUSION

In 'Third World' societies, just as in the advanced capitalist, there are attempts by urban-based intellectuals to develop alternative and folk forms of media. Such media as street theatre, 'Third Cinema', and alternative video, are frequently linked to popular movements and struggles and represent attempts both to circumvent powerful private and state mass media which are unlikely to be reformed in their interests and to make use of particular cultural forms and practices which are still present in the lives of people in rural and urban areas. To a considerable extent alternative and folk media are built on the recognition that despite the importance of centralized mass media institutions, and radio and television in particular, education, and state-sponsored forms of 'official' culture, people in rural and urban areas develop their own cultural practices outside, and with reference to, the modern mass media. In African and Asian societies, as well as much of Latin America, capitalist and industrial transformation of culture has been uneven and incomplete so that the major residue of rural and urban cultures continue to exercise an important influence on the forms of communication and cultural expression of a great many people. Undoubtedly many states grasp the oppositional nature of alternative and folk forms and respond to them with a combination of repression, including banning and arrests, and attempts to integrate them into official cultural apparatuses.

Notes

PREFACE

1 Industrialization relying on very high levels of international borrowing, and thus of debt servicing, does not allow the substantial transfer of surplus to the Brazilian and Mexican labouring classes.

2 Unfavourable exchange rates, not just with the advanced capitalist economies, but also with neighbouring countries, can have a profound impact on the flow of cultural commodities and ideas. In the early years of the now defunct East African Community, the Kenyan and Tanzanian currencies were equal in value; as a result of successive devaluation, the Tanzanian shilling is now worth approximately one-fourteenth of the Kenyan shilling. As a result, books, newspapers and magazines published in Kenya are prohibitively expensive. One slightly absurd result of the devaluation is that it is possible to buy a monograph published in Tanzania several years ago for less than the cost of the daily newspaper, the *Daily News*.

1 INTRODUCTION

1 Poor exchange rates, worsening terms of trade, often inhibit importation of cultural commodities without promoting import substitution cultural and communications industries. In Tanzania recent American films have not been imported because they have been too expensive. Instead there has been a reliance on Italian spaghetti westerns, Indian films, and cheap-to-import old American films, Westerns especially. The inability to import large quantities of foreign-produced cultural commodities, combined with their limited reach in domestic markets, poses major problems for media and cultural imperialist theories which tend to assume an uninterrupted flow of influence.

2 Highly concentrated transnational cultural producers are either unable to innovate or tap into the sub-cultures where new artistic forms are developing or undergoing transformation, or not prepared to bear the risks of experimentation. The latter can be borne by small, 'independent' companies which can effectively be controlled through a dependence on the distribution networks of the major companies. A country such as

Australia occupies a key position in the musical international division of labour by providing 'artists' for United States and British musical production.

3 Workers from countries such as Egypt, India, Indonesia, Pakistan, the Philippines, South Korea, Taiwan, and Thailand who have been employed in Gulf States have been important in the spread of VCR use. VCRs have been perhaps the most popular gift a worker returning home could bring.

2 DOMINANT PERSPECTIVES

1 Daniel Lerner's book, *The Passing of Traditional Society* (New York: Macmillan, 1958), was influential in communications and modernization analysis. Lerner hypothesized that there was a causal link between exposure to mass media and various indices of modernization and industrialization. Other influential works include David McLelland's *The Achieving Society* (Princeton: Van Nostrand, 1961) and Everett Hagen, *On The Theory of Social Change* (Homewood, Ill.: Dorsey, 1962).

2 Hamelink (1983: 5) prefers to refer to 'cultural synchronization' rather than cultural imperialism, since the former occurs even where imperialist relations are not prevalent.

3 See also Hamelink 1983: 7.

4 This has been a major debate in development literature. It was particularly intense in Kenya during the late 1970s. See Colin Leys, 'Capital accumulation, class formation and dependency – the significance of the Kenyan case', *The Socialist Register*, 1978, pp. 241–66, and Bjorn Beckmann, 'Imperialism and capitalist transformation: critique of a Kenya debate', *Review of African Political Economy*, no. 19, 1980, pp. 48–62.

5 The nature or content of this development is never questioned. Anyone who raises doubts is dismissed as a saboteur, a colonial stooge, an imperialist agent or lackey, or worse still, a Marxist. State suppression of such critics can be justified on the grounds that their questioning is both subversive and anti-national. See Clive Thomas, *The Rise of the Authoritarian State in Peripheral Societies* (New York: Monthly Review Press, 1984), p. 116.

6 In Kenya, for example, the cost of daily consumption of a newspaper for a month is between 120/- and 135/-. This represents more than 10 per cent of the 'official' minimum wage.

7 The buying and reading of newspapers is also governed by factors peculiar to an urban mode of existence. Using newspapers is part of being 'modern' and of an urban existence increasingly dominated by commercial forms of culture.

3 MEDIA IMPERIALISM THESIS

1 Tracey refers to the way the issue of 'national culture' in the advanced or western capitalist societies is usually not addressed in media imperialist analysis, despite the class and other bases of contradiction and diversity.

2 An element of caution is required. It would be important to distinguish between different historical periods. For example, under European colonial rule in Africa and Asia news flow and coverage of the 'Third World' were fundamentally constrained by the colonial power in question.

3 The major suppliers of communications technologies are obviously interested in stressing the advantages of their technologies or systems, and exercise a good deal of pressure to ensure they are adopted. The business communications systems are predicated upon particular management practices and hierarchical authority structures.

4 Haynes finds little support for Galtung's theory of structural imperialism. The supposedly vertical nature of the interaction between centre and periphery, which involves the creation of 'similar cognitive worlds' in the latter, is challenged by high levels of interaction between 'peripheral' states in Latin America, as well as by levels of interaction between peripheral countries and centres which are not their own (Haynes 1984: 214).

4 STATE AND COMMUNICATIONS

1 Singhal and Rogers (1989: 75–80) note that the successful commercialization of Doordarshan has provoked often intense debate about television's role in Indian society, including its role in the promotion of consumerism, competition between consumer goods manufacturers, and in exacerbating inequalities.

2 The conflict over traditional forms, and their content, was expressive of the broader conflict over the nature of socialist culture. Those associated with the Cultural Revolution were pushing for a uni-dimensional art and literature, which, placed at the service of the party, would intensify the struggle against anti-revolutionary and reactionary factions which were prepared to make concessions to western capitalism.

3 In some liberal-democratic systems the existence of well-established, 'relatively autonomous' media institutions meant that changes of government did not necessarily threaten them. Of course, financial and political controls ensured that such broadcasting institutions were sensitive to executive power and served to circumscribe their activities.

5 THE NEW INTERNATIONAL INFORMATION ORDER

1 Those who run the News Agency of Nigeria would clearly like to see much greater capital investment in satellite telecommunications and computerization of services to strengthen existing news services and expand into areas such as financial news. The realization that Nigerian corporate managers are prepared to pay for financial services is a strong incentive to invest in new technologies, but costs remain essentially prohibitive (Musa 1990: 339).

2 Musa (1990: 327) notes that Reuters derives 56 per cent of its revenue from the sale of money market and foreign exchange information, 12 per cent from securities information, and 10 per cent from commodities

information. Thirteen per cent of Reuters' revenue comes from client systems such as hardware and software for dealing rooms, while only 9 per cent of its revenue is derived from media services.

3 This may be useful for the encouragement of private foreign investment and state bilateral foreign aid purposes.

4 Roach (1987) details the way in which the state intervenes in the mass media in the United States despite the constant reiteration of the absence of government control of the media and the 'free flow of information' doctrine.

5 Brazilian policy with regard to telematics and informatics is obviously constrained by a concern both to develop indigenous production and to create a telematics and informatics infrastructure necessary for economic development and political and administrative purposes. The principal users of transnational computer-communication systems are transnational corporations. As such the concern of government policy is to establish some means of control over such systems, while at the same time protecting the interests of national capital. The development of Brazilian telematics and informatics policy is outlined in the United Nations Centre on Transnational Corporations report, *Transborder Data Flows and Brazil* (1984).

6 For conventional economic analysis the major difficulty with transborder data flows is that they overwhelmingly constitute non-market information flows (Jussawalla 1985); they are usually routine intra-organizational activities within the transnational corporation. Conventional economic analysis deals only with the part of the transnational data flow that covers point-to-point transmission of proprietary information between two or more different parties in different locations.

7 Transnational corporations, which in an important sense are only possible as a result of the development of more sophisticated international communications, have incurred long-term investments in 'value-added networks and closed-user group networks' (Jussawalla 1985: 302). Their monitoring of the activities of affiliates, and the implementation of an increasingly integrated global strategy of production and marketing, is based on corporate data flows.

8 The World Administrative Radio Conference on the Use of the Geostationary Satellite Orbit and the Planning of Space Services Utilizing It (Space WARC) held in Geneva, 28 August to 6 October 1988.

9 Mexico and Brazil's commercial television networks have been able to gain almost universal penetration in their national territories as a result of the introduction of domestic satellite systems.

6 DATA: TECHNOLOGICAL 'DEPENDENCE' AND COMMUNICATIONS

1 As part of a new 'liberalization' IBM has recently re-entered the Indian computer industry in conjunction with Tata.

2 Rada (1985: 580) notes that 'the main issue for developing countries in terms of employment/technology lies in the field of agriculture rather than computerization in manufacturing or services'. This is primarily

because even in countries such as Brazil and India, which are amongst the largest users of computers in the developing world, the displacement of employment is minimal. Their applications remain 'traditional' and 'tend to optimize administrative systems that in turn create beneficial effects in the rest of the country's economy'.
3 In 1992, after many years of attempting to develop and manufacture its own technologies (including switching systems) for a modern telecommunications system, the Indian government decided to allow major foreign companies such as AT & T and Ericsson to enter production and supply.
4 The dominance of notions of technocratic efficiency and rationality in the modernization of the Mexican economy has not been extended to the formulation of national policies in which domestic computer production would have a major role.

7 ADVERTISING

1 Vilanilam (1989: 489–90) suggests that the creation of a fantasy world by television and advertising contributes to the rural dweller's hatred of the environment which cannot provide the means of purchasing comsumer goods, and ultimately to a frustration which may lead to migration to the towns. Commercials also 'reinforce feelings of inferiority which are politically advantageous to the already advantaged sectors of society'. In 1981 Indonesian President Suharto banned commercials from the government-owned Televisi Republik Indonesia on the grounds that they raised the expectancy of the public (Lent 1982: 184).

9 FICTIONS

1 The *fotonovela* represents an omnipresent part of the culture of the masses in Latin America, Northern Africa, France and Italy (Flora and Flora 1978: 135). It can also be found in Kenyan magazines such as *True Love*, as well as in *Film Tanzania*. According to Flora (1981: 524) the *fotonovela* is 'a logical marriage of technological advance and traditional stories of romance'. It serves as a powerful means of moulding women in particular into a 'dependent capitalist structure' in which consumption becomes a key to identity, self-esteem, upward mobility, and participation.
2 In the case of Nigerian film making it is clear that production increasingly relies on both new original scripts and adaptation of novels and plays which have already proven popular. For example, Wole Soyinka's play *Kongi's Harvest*, popular Yoruba plays by Hubert Ogunde, and the Kenyan writer Meja Mwangi's novel about Mau Mau, *Carcase for Hounds*, have provided the basis for films.
3 Valicha (1988) identifies four emerging, but not sharp genre divisions in the Hindi film: mythological; social, which focuses on situations relating to the family; sex-violence-crime films which are contemporary and multi-starred; and full-length comedy. There is also a type of hybrid which mixes comedy with sex, violence, and crime.

4 Prime-time soap operas such as *Dallas* represent a significant departure from the depiction of predominantly suburban middle-class settings in which women have been the principal characters. The importance of male characters has increased, and the settings shifted to the glamorous, cut-throat world of Texas oil barons. Higher-production budgets have meant a much greater concern with visualization, including lavish costuming and outdoor location shots. In Britain *Coronation Street* introduced the working-class district; subsequent series such as *Brookside* and *Eastenders* represent the continuation of the 'social realist' type of soap opera.

5 In Tanzania, in contrast to Kenya, until recently there was a strong emphasis on the creation of a non-commercial popular literature in Kiswahili which was geared to functional literacy programmes and the propagation of socialist and production values (Arnold 1984). An interesting small-scale development in the last three years has been the emergence in Dar es Salaam of a commercial, 'popular' Swahili literature – a literature of violence, crime stories, kung-fu action adventures, and comic books, published by small local companies, most of them stationers and printers. Possibly a response to economic liberalization and some ideological 'loosening' under the Mwinyi regime, such publications operate almost as an underworld or undergrowth of literature outside the 'official' state cultural organs; certainly there was no sign of them in the bookshops and on the news stands in central Dar es Salaam.

10 SOUNDS

1 Generalizations of this nature can be quite misleading and dangerous. In the case of the development of Latin American music throughout the twentieth century there has been considerable interaction between the different countries, with Cuba in particular, and Argentina and Brazil, innovating styles which have been highly influential in other Latin American countries (see Béhague, 1986). Zaïrean music has been similarly influential in other African countries such as Kenya and Tanzania, although it has undergone considerable change as it has been relocated in different linguistic conditions and social relations.

2 Often intense political controversy surrounds the choice of the 'traditional' musical forms to be transformed and elevated to the status of national culture, since most have strong regional and 'ethnic' origins and associations. Musical traditions and forms associated with resistance and oppositional forces are generally carefully excluded.

3 *Jatras* are a form of folk drama, including song, which was popular in Bengal and surrounding areas. They are to be distinguished from Sanskrit drama which 'became an ornament of the courts' (Barnouw and Krishnaswamy 1980: 71).

4 Dr Balkrishna Vishwanath Keskar became Minister of Information and Broadcasting in 1952. He was a devotee of Indian classical music and envisaged AIR playing a prominent role in the revival of Indian classical culture, and especially its music. Under Dr Keskar more than 50 per cent of all broadcast music came to be Indian classical music. Indian folk

music in traditional styles was also strongly represented. According to Barnouw and Krishnaswamy (1980: 210) 'All India Radio accumulated a list of over 7,000 approved classical music artists who were to make intermittent appearances and each year the list was increased.'

5 For the Agikuyu the *Ituika* and the *Muthirigu* dances and songs of the 1930s were important forms of cultural expression. The latter, according to Thiong'o (1981), voiced 'people's rejection of forced labour, their disgust with cultural imperialism, their uncompromising opposition to political repression, and their strong condemnation of Kenyan collaborators with colonialist enemy occupation.'

6 The word *ngoma*, common to many East African Bantu languages, captures the combination of music, dance, and drama characteristic of these styles.

7 Films, television programmes, radio broadcasting, and the print media, are generally relatively easy to censor and suppress since they are usually dependent on highly centralized forms of production and distribution. The strategy of alternative video and film makers, as well as some small, politically oppositional publishing houses, is to develop alternative distribution networks which are much more difficult for the state to control.

8 Nigeria has a population of about 115 million and some 400 distinct ethnic groups.

9 *Afro-beat* was a reaction to the slavish relationship which many other Nigerian bandleaders then had with black American music.

10 The Brazilian composer Hector Vila-Lobos (1887–1959) enjoyed considerable success in Europe and North America. His work was inspired by national and nativist themes. In the *Cancôes Brasileiros* Vila-Lobos ambitiously aimed to fuse Brazilian folk music with the technique of Bach.

11 Although information is sketchy it is clear that the transnational record companies prefer imported records to local ones on economic grounds (Mattelart 1983: 50). Locally produced records normally require larger sales to recover costs than imported records. In smaller markets even limited 'volume' local production cannot be sustained with the result that major transnational companies prefer to pull right out of local production and simply become distributors of imported material. The rise of piracy further reduces the incentive to engage in local musical production as opposed to importation.

12 The *samba-cançâo* is a 'highly sentimental, slow-paced samba which first appeared around 1928 and suffered *bolero*, rhythmic influence in the 1950s (hence sometimes referred to as *sambolero*' (Béhague 1980: 441).

11 FOLK AND ALTERNATIVE MEDIA

1 In Latin America especially, many film makers and artists engaged in alternative production saw video technology allowing much greater visual experimentation, permitting the development of a new visual language, and as challenging the ideological position of conventional

television programming and film. Video held out the possibility of the experiences and feelings of ordinary people becoming a key part of media production.

2 Third Cinema theorists, Willemen (1989: 8) observes, fell into the trap of homogenizing 'dominant cinema' by ignoring the diversity within it. A film maker such as Nelson Pereira dos Santos showed in films such as *O Amuleto de Ogum* and *Na Estrada da Vida* that it was possible to retain important components of the 'old' cinema while rejecting an unacceptable cinematic regime.

3 Willemen (1989: 6) notes that the apparent antagonism Espinosa and other theorists have towards 'professional intellectuals is in fact an opposition to colonial and imperialist intellectuals, and this antagonism is never used to devalue the need for the most lucid possible critical intelligence to be deployed as an absolutely necessary part of making films'.

4 Ruy Guerra's film *Kuarup* (1989) almost provides an intellectual history of these shifting concerns in Brazil. The young Jesuit priest Father Nando, who at the beginning of the film engages in repeated self-flagellation as a way of overcoming the temptations of the flesh (he actually succumbs quite often) believes that the Indians in the proposed Xingu National Park should be restored to, or protected in, a pristine, primitive communist state. After leaving the church, his interest in the Indians continues. However, he is caught up in popular urban- and rural-based movements, is detained and tortured, and is eventually present at the killing of his tormentor, a colonel whose harsh, unremitting Catholicism ties in with the pursuit of militarism and violence as the route to national glory and salvation.

Bibliography

Abubakar, Dauda (1987) 'The mass media and ideological apparatuses in post-colonial Africa', in Jerry Domatob, Abubakar Jika and Ikechukwu Nwosu (eds), *Mass Media and the African Society*, Africa Media Monograph Series, no. 4, Nairobi: The African Council on Communication Education, ch. 6.

Abuoga, John B. and Mutere, Absalom A. (1988) *The History of the Press in Kenya*, Nairobi: The African Council on Communication Education.

Adaba, A. Tom, Ajia, Olakon and Nwosu, Ikechukwu (eds) (1988) *Communication Industry in Nigeria. The Crisis of Publications*, Africa Media Monograph Series, no. 6, Nairobi: The African Council on Communication Education.

Adler, Emmanuel (1986) 'Ideological "guerrillas" and the quest for technological autonomy: Brazil's domestic computer industry', *International Organization*, vol. 40, no. 4, pp. 673–705.

—— (1987) *The Power of Ideology: The Quest for Technological Autonomy in Argentina and Brazil*, Berkeley and Los Angeles: University of California Press.

Agovi, Kofi E. (1989) 'The political relevance of Ghanaian high life songs since 1957', *Research in African Literatures*, vol. 20, no. 2, pp. 194–201.

Agrawal, Binad C. (1986) 'Cultural response to communication revolution: many modes of video use in India', *Gazette*, vol. 38, pp. 29–41.

Ainslie, Rosalynde (1966) *The Press in Africa, Communications Past and Present*, London: Victor Gollancz.

Amuta, Chidi (1989) *The Theory of African Literature*, London: Zed Books.

Antola, Livia and Rogers, Everett M. (1984) 'Television flows in Latin America', *Communication Research*, vol. 11, no. 2, pp. 183–202.

Armes, Roy (1987) *Third World Film Making and the West*, Berkeley, Cal.: University of California Press.

Arnold, Stephen (1984) 'Popular literature in Tanzania', *Kiswahili*, vol. 51, nos. 1 and 2, pp. 60–87.

Awasthy, G.C. (1978) 'India', in John A. Lent (ed.), *Broadcasting in Asia and the Pacific, A Continental Survey of Radio and Television*, Philadelphia: Temple University Press, pp. 197–211.

Barnouw, Erik and Krishnaswamy, S. (1980) *Indian Film*, New York: Oxford University Press.

Barthakur, P.B., Patanjali, V. and Parameswaran, P. (eds) (1978) *Mass Media in India 1978*, New Delhi: Publications Division, Ministry of Information and Broadcasting.

Barton, F. (1979) *The Press of Africa*, London: Macmillan.

Bascur, Raquel Salinas (1985) 'Information in the Third World: adjusting technologies or strategies?', *Media, Culture and Society*, vol. 7, pp. 355–68.

Baskaran, S. Theodore (1981) *The Message Bearers, The Nationalist Politics and the Entertainment Media in South India 1880–1945*, Madras: Cre-A.

Bebey, Francis (1975) *African Music. A People's Art*, trans. Josephine Bennett, London: Harrap.

Béhague, Gerard (1980) 'Brazilian musical values of the 1960s and 1970s: popular urban music from Bossa Nova to Tropicália', *Journal of Popular Culture*, vol. 13, no. 3, pp. 437–52.

—— (1985) 'Recent studies on the music of Latin America', *Latin American Research Review*, vol. 20, no. 3, pp. 218–27.

—— (1986) 'Popular music in Latin America', *Studies in Latin American Popular Culture*, vol. 5, pp. 41–67.

Benmayor, Rina (1981) '*La Nueva Trova*: new Cuban song', *Latin American Music Review*, vol. 2, no. 1, pp. 11–44.

Berger, John (1972) *Ways of Seeing*, Harmondsworth: Penguin Books.

Bharucha, Rustom (1983) *Rehearsals of Revolution, The Political Theatre of Bengal*, Calcutta: Seagull Books.

Bhatia, B.S., Jain, G.C., Karnik, Kiran S., Pal, Yash and Seghal, Narendar K. (1984) 'Television broadcasting in India', in Alan Hancock (ed.), *Technology Transfer and Communication*, Paris: UNESCO, pp. 35–71.

Binford, Mira Reyan (1983) 'State patronage of India's new cinema', *Critical Arts* (Grahamstown), vol. 2, no. 4, pp. 33–46.

—— (1987) 'The two cinemas of India', in John D.H. Downing (ed.), *Film and Politics in the Third World*, New York: Autonomedia, ch. 13.

Bjorkman, Ingrid (1989) *Mother, Sing for Me, People's Theatre in Kenya*, London: Zed Books.

Boafo, S.T. Kwame (1987) 'Democratizing media systems in African societies: the case of Ghana', *Africa Media Review*, vol. 2, no. 1, pp. 24–37.

Boal, Augusto (1979) *Theatre of the Oppressed*, London: Pluto Press.

Boran, Anne (1989) 'Popular movements in Brazil: a case study of the movement for the defence of *favelalas* in Sao Paulo', *Bulletin Latin American Research*, vol. 8, no. 1, pp. 83–109.

Boyd, Douglas A. and Straubhaar, Joseph (1985) 'Developmental impact of the home video cassette recorder on Third World countries', *Journal of Broadcasting and Electronic Media*, vol. 29, no. 1, pp. 3–21.

Boyd-Barrett, Oliver (1977a) *Mass Communications in Cross-cultural Contexts: The Case of the Third World*, Milton Keynes: The Open University Press.

—— (1977b) 'Media imperialism: towards an international framework for the analysis of media systems', in James Curran, Michael Gurevitch and

Janet Woolacott (eds), *Mass Communication and Society*, London: Edward Arnold, ch. 5.

—— (1980) *The International News Agencies*, London: Constable.

—— (1981) 'Western news agencies and the "media imperialism" debate: what kind of data-base?', *Journal of International Affairs*, vol. 35, no. 2, pp. 247–60.

—— (1982) 'Cultural dependency and the mass media', in Michael Gurevitch, Tony Bennett, James Curran and Janet Woolacott (eds), *Culture, Society and the Media*, London: Methuen.

Brewer, Anthony (1980) *Marxist Theories of Imperialism, A Critical Survey*, London: Routledge & Kegan Paul.

Brockmann, Magdelena (1978) *Three Days in the Latin American Press*, Mexico: Instituto Latinamericano de Estudios Transnacionales.

Bystrom, John (1977) 'A satellite communication system: global development and cultural imperialism', in Jim Richstad (ed.), *New Perspectives in International Communication*, Honolulu: East–West Communication Institute, East–West Centre, pp. 149–79.

Canclini, Néstor García (1988) 'Culture and power: the state of research', *Media, Culture and Society*, vol. 10, pp. 476–97.

Cham, Mbye Baboucar (1987) 'Film production in West Africa', in John D. H. Downing (ed.), *Film and Politics in the Third World*, New York: Autonomedia, ch. 1.

Chanan, Michael (1985) *The Cuban Image*, London: British Film Institute.

Chatterji, P.C. (1987) *Broadcasting in India*, New Delhi: Sage.

Chu, Godwin C. (1978) 'Popular media: a glimpse of the new Chinese culture', in Godwin C. Chu (ed.), *Popular Media in China, Shaping New Cultural Patterns*, Honolulu: The University Press of Hawaii, ch. 1.

Chu, Godwin C. and Cheng, Philip H. (1978) 'Revolutionary opera: an instrument for cultural change', in Godwin C. Chu (ed.), *Popular Media in China, Shaping New Cultural Patterns*, Honolulu: The University Press of Hawaii, ch. 4.

Chu, James C.Y. (1978) 'People's Republic of China', in John A. Lent (ed.), *Broadcasting in Asia and the Pacific, A Continental Survey of Radio and Television*, Philadelphia: Temple University Press, ch. 2.2.

Chu, Leonard L. (1978) 'Sabers and swords for the Chinese children: revolutionary children's folk songs', in Godwin C. Chu (ed.), *Popular Media in China, Shaping New Cultural Patterns*, Honolulu: The University Press of Hawaii, ch. 2.

Clad, James (1990) 'Paradise abroad', *Far Eastern Economic Review*, 26 April.

Clark, Paul (1987) *Chinese Cinema: Culture and Politics Since 1949*, Cambridge: Cambridge University Press.

Collins, Richard, Garnham, Nicholas and Locksley, Gareth (1988) *The Economics of Television, The UK Case*, London: Sage.

(1980) 'Contribution of the Church to national broadcasting policy', *Research Trends in Religious Communication*, vol. 1, no. 1, 4 pages.

Craig, David (1973) *The Real Foundations. Literature and Social Change*, London: Chatto & Windus.

Curran, James, Gurevitch, Michael and Woolacott, Janet (eds) (1977) *Mass Communication and Society*, London: Edward Arnold.

Dagnino, Evelina (1973) 'Cultural and ideological dependence: building a theoretical framework', in Frank Bonilla and R. Girling (eds), *Structures of Dependency*, Stanford: Stanford University Press, pp. 129–48.

Dassín, Joan (1989) 'Cultural policy and practice in the Nova Republique', *Latin American Research Review*, vol. 24, no. 1, pp. 115–23.

Delapierre, Michel and Zimmerman, Jean-Benoit (1989) 'La nouvelle politique industrielle: le cas d'informatique', *Revue Tiers-Monde*, vol. 30, no. 119, pp. 559–76.

Devadas, David (1990) 'Media autonomy. A fettered freedom', *India Today*, 31 January, pp. 86–8.

Domatob, Jerry (1987) 'Ethical implications of transnational corporation advertising in sub-Saharan Africa', in Jerry Domatob, Abubakar Jika and Ikechukwu Nwosu (eds), *Mass Media and the African Society*, Africa Media Monograph Series, no. 4, Nairobi: The African Council on Communication Education, ch. 25.

Domatob, Jerry, Jika, Abubakar and Nwosu, Ikechukwu (eds) (1987) *Mass Media and the African Society*, Africa Media Monograph Series, no. 4, Nairobi: The African Council on Communication Education.

Downing, John D.H. (ed.) (1987) *Film and Politics in the Third World*, New York: Autonomedia.

D'Silva, Anthony (1989) 'The year that was', *TV and Video World*, 31 December, pp. 40–7.

Egbon, Mike (1988) 'Perspectives on freedom of information in reporting Africa', in A. Tom Adaba, Olakon Ajia and Ikechukwu Nwosu (eds), *Communication Industry in Nigeria. The Crisis of Publications*, Africa Media Monograph Series, no. 6, Nairobi: The African Council on Communication Education, pp. 167–83.

Ellis, Stephen (1989) 'Tuning in to pavement radio', *African Affairs*, vol. 88, no. 352, pp. 321–30.

Espinosa, Julio Garcia (1987) 'For an imperfect cinema (1969)', in Coco Fusco (ed.), *Reviewing Histories: Selections from New Latin American Cinema*, Buffalo, NY: Hallwalls, pp. 166–77.

Etherton, Michael (1982) *The Development of African Drama*, London: Hutchinson.

Fejes, Fred (1980) 'The growth of multinational advertising agencies in Latin America', *Journal of Communication*, vol. 30, no. 1, pp. 36–49.

—— (1981) 'Media imperialism: an assessment', *Media, Culture and Society*, vol. 3, no. 3, pp. 281–9.

Fernandes, Cajetan P. (1989) 'Communication technologies and economic development in India', *Media Development*, vol. 36, no. 1, pp. 29–32.

Flora, Cornelia Butler (1981) 'Fotonovelas: message creation and reception', *Journal of Popular Culture*, vol. 14, no. 3, pp. 524–34.

—— (1984) 'Roasting Donald Duck: alternative comics and photonovels in Latin America', *Journal of Popular Culture*, vol. 18, no. 1, pp. 163–83.

—— (1986) 'Photonovels', in Charles Tatum and Harold Hinds (eds), *Handbook of Latin American Popular Culture*, Westport: Greenwood Press, ch. 6.

Flora, Cornelia Butler and Flora, Jan F. (1978) 'The fotonovela as a tool for class and cultural domination', *Latin American Perspectives*, vol. 5, no. 1, pp. 134–50.

Fox, Elizabeth (1988a) 'Media policies in Latin America: an overview', in Elizabeth Fox (ed.), *Media and Politics in Latin America. The Struggle for Democracy*, London: Sage, pp. 6–35.

—— (1988b) 'Conclusions', in Elizabeth Fox (ed.), *Media and Politics in Latin America. The Struggle for Democracy*, London: Sage, pp. 171–88.

Franco, Jean (1970) *The Modern Culture of Latin America, Society and the Artist*, Harmondsworth: Penguin Books.

Frederick, William H. (1982) 'Rhoma Irama and the Dangdut style: aspects of contemporary Indonesian popular culture', *Indonesia*, no. 32, October, pp. 103–30.

Frey-Vor, Gerlind (1990a) 'More on soaps', *Communication Research Trends*, vol. 10, no. 2, pp. 1–12.

—— (1990b) 'Soap opera', *Communication Research Trends*, vol. 10, no. 1, pp. 1–16.

Frith, Simon (ed.) (1989) *World Music. Political and Social Change*, Manchester: Manchester University Press.

Gabriel, Teshome H. (1989a) 'Third cinema as guardian of popular memory: towards a third aesthetics', in Jim Pines and Paul Willemen (eds), *Questions of Third Cinema*, London: British Film Institute, pp. 53–64.

—— (1989b) 'Towards a critical theory of Third World films', in Jim Pines and Paul Willemen (eds), *Questions of Third Cinema*, London: British Film Institute, pp. 3–52.

Galtung, Johan (1972) 'Structural theory of imperialism', *The African Review*, vol. 1, no. 4, pp. 93–138.

Gardner, P. Dale and Stevenson, Robert L. (1988) 'Communication development in Venezuela and Mexico', *Journalism Monographs*, no. 188.

Gargurevitch, Juan and Fox, Elizabeth (1988) 'Revolution and the Press in Peru', in Elizabeth Fox (ed.), *Media and Politics in Latin America. The Struggle for Democracy*, London: Sage, ch. 4.

Garnham, N. (1979) 'Contribution to a political economy of mass communications', *Media, Culture and Society*, vol. 1. pp. 125–46.

—— (1982) 'Sky's the limit', *New Socialist*, May/June, pp. 30–2.

Gifford, C. Anthony (1984) 'Inter press service: news from the Third World', *Journal of Communication*, vol. 34, no. 4, pp. 41–59.

Golding, Peter (1977) 'Media professionalism in the Third World: the transfer of an ideology', in James Curran, Michael Gurevitch and Janet Woolacott (eds), *Mass Communication and Society*, London: Edward Arnold, ch. 12.

Goodwin, Andrew and Gore, Joe (1990) 'World beat and the cultural imperialism debate', *Socialist Review*, vol. 20, no. 3, pp. 63–80.

Graham, Ronnie (1989) *Stern's Guide to Contemporary African Music*, London: Pluto Press.

Greenberg, Allen (1985) 'Impasse?: The US stake in Third World telecommunications development', *Journal of Communication*, vol. 35, no. 2, pp. 42–9.

Grieco, Joseph M. (1982) 'Between dependency and autonomy: India's experience with the international computer industry', *International Organization*, vol. 36, no. 3, pp. 609–32.

Guimarães, Cesar and Amaral, Roberto (1988) 'Brazilian television: a rapid conversion to the new order', in Elizabeth Fox (ed.), *Media and Politics in Latin America*, London: Sage, ch. 10.

Gutierrez, Felix F. and Reina, Jorge (1984) 'Spanish international network. The flow of television from Mexico to the United States', *Communication Research*, vol. 11, no. 2, pp. 241–58.

Hachten, William H. (1971) *Muffled Drums: The News Media in Africa*, Ames: Iowa State University Press.

—— (1981) *The World News Prism. Changing Media, Clashing Ideologies*, Ames: Iowa State University Press.

Hamelink, Cees (1983) *Cultural Autonomy in Global Communications*, New York: Longman.

Hamilton, Annette (1990) 'Video crackdown, or, the sacrificial pirate, video censorship and cultural consequences in Thailand', Asian Cinema Studies Society Conference, La Trobe University, Vic., 10–13 July, 35pp.

Harris, Nigel (1990) *The End of the Third World*, Harmondsworth: Penguin Books.

Harris, Phil (1985) 'The West African wire service of Reuters', in Frank Okwu Ugboajah (ed.), *Mass Communication, Culture and Society in West Africa*, London: Hans Zell Publishers, pp. 260–76.

Harsono, Andreas (1989) 'A star is banned', *Inside Indonesia*, December, pp. 14–15.

Haynes, R. (1984) 'Test of Galtung's theory of structural imperialism', in Robert L. Stevenson and Donald Shaw (eds), *Foreign News and the New World Information Order*, Ames: Iowa State University Press, pp. 200-16.

Head, Sydney W. (ed.) (1974) *Broadcasting in Africa, A Continental Survey of Radio and Television*, Philadelphia: Temple University Press.

Heath, Carla W. (1988) 'Private sector participation in public service broadcasting: the case of Kenya', *Journal of Communication*, vol. 38, no. 3, pp. 96–107.

Hebdige, Dick (1987) *Cut 'n' Mix, Culture, Identity and Caribbean Music*, London: Comedia.

Heider, Karl (1991) *Indonesian Cinema: National Culture on Screen*, Honolulu: The University Press of Hawaii.

Hinds, Harold E. (1979) 'Kalimán: a Mexican superhero', *Journal of Popular Culture*, vol. 13, no. 2, pp. 229–38.

—— (1980a) '*Chanoc*: adventure and slapstick on Mexico's southeast coast', *Journal of Popular Culture*, vol. 13, no. 3, pp. 424–37.

—— (1980b) 'Latin American popular culture, a new research frontier: achievements, problems and promise', *Journal of Popular Culture*, vol. 14, no. 3, pp. 405–12.

—— (1984) 'Latin American popular culture: recent research trends and a needs assessment', *Journal of Popular Culture*, vol. 18, no. 1, pp. 58–64.

Hinds, Harold E. and Tatum, Charles (1984) 'Images of women in Mexican comic books', *Journal of Popular Culture*, vol. 18, no. 1, pp. 146–62.

Horton, Philip (ed.) (1978) *The Third World and Press Freedom*, New York: Praeger Publishers.

Hoskins, Colin, Mirus, Rolf and Rozeboom, William (1989) 'US television programmes in the international market: unfair pricing', *Journal of Communication*, vol. 39, no. 2, pp. 55–75.
Jalée, Pierre (1968) *The Pillage of the Third World*, New York: Monthly Review Press.
Janus, Noreene Z. (1981a) 'Advertising and the mass media in the era of the global corporation', in Emile G. McAnany, Jorge Schnitman and Noreene Janus (eds), *Communication and Social Structure*, Critical Studies in Mass Media Research, New York: Praeger Publishers, ch. 11.
—— (1981b) 'Advertising and the mass media: transnational link between production and consumption', *Media, Culture and Society*, vol. 3, no. 1, pp. 13–23.
Jika, Abubakar (1987) 'International communication and cultural imperialism: the African experience', in Jerry Domatob, Abubakar Jika and Ikechukwu Nwosu (eds), *Mass Media and the African Society*, Africa Media Monograph Series, no. 4, Nairobi: The African Council on Communication Education, ch. 17.
Jones-Quartey, K.A.B. (1974) *A Summary History of the Ghana Press 1822–1960*, Accra: Ghana Information Services.
Jordao, Fatima (1982) 'TV Globo rules the Brazilian skies', in Richard Peterson (ed.), *Brazilian Television in Context*, London: British Film Institute, pp. 4–11.
Jouet, Josiane (1984) 'Advertising and transnational corporations in Kenya', *Development and Change*, vol. 15, pp. 435–56.
Jussawalla, Meheroo (1985) 'Constraints on economic analysis of transborder data flows', *Media, Culture and Society*, vol. 7, pp. 297–312.
Kaplan, Ruben Sergio Caletti (1988) 'Communication policies in Mexico: an historical paradox of words and actions', in Elizabeth Fox (ed.), *Media and Politics in Latin America*, London: Sage, ch. 5.
Kaplinsky, Raphael (1980) 'Micro-electronics in the Third World', *Radical Science Journal*, no. 10, pp. 37–51.
—— (1982) 'Trade in technology – who, what, where and when?', paper presented at International Workshop on Facilitating Indigenous Technological Capability, University of Edinburgh.
Katz, Elihu and Wedell, George (1978) *Broadcasting in the Third World*, Cambridge, Mass.: Harvard University Press.
Kay, Geoffrey (1975) *Development and Underdevelopment*, London: Macmillan.
Kidd, Ross (1981) 'Domestication theatre and conscientization drama in India', in Ross Kidd and Nat Coletta (eds), *Tradition for Development: Indigenous Structures and Folk Media in Non-Formal Education*, Berlin: German Foundation for International Development and International Council for Adult Education.
Kincaid, Lawrence (ed.) (1987) *Communication Theory: Eastern and Western Perspectives*, New York: Academic Press.
King, John (1990) *Magical Reels, A History of the Cinema in Latin America*, London: Verso.
Kinyatti, Maina wa (1980) *Thunder from the Mountains, Mau Mau Patriotic Songs*, London: Zed Press.

Kottak, Conrad Phillip (1990) *Prime-Time Society, An Anthropological Analysis of Television and Culture*, Belmont, Cal.: Wadsworth.

Laing, Dave (1986) 'The music industry and the 'cultural imperialism' thesis', *Media, Culture and Society*, vol. 8, pp. 331–41.

Langdale, John (1987) 'Transborder data flows and national sovereignty', in Trevor Barr (ed.), *Challenges and Change*, Australia's Information Society, Melbourne: Oxford University Press, ch. 11.

Langdon, S. (1975) 'Multinational corporations, taste transfer and under-development: a case study from Kenya', *Review of African Political Economy*, vol. 2, pp. 12–35.

Langer, Erick D. (1989) 'Generations of scientists and engineers: origins of the computer industry in Brazil', *Latin American Research Review*, vol. 24, no. 2, pp. 95–112.

Leal, Ondira Fachel (1990) 'Popular taste and erudite repertoire: the place and space of television in Brazil', *Cultural Studies*, vol. 4, no. 1, pp. 19–29.

Leal, Ondina Fachel and Oliven, Ruben G. (1988) 'Class interpretations of a soap opera narrative: the case of the Brazilian *novela* "Summer Sun"', *Theory, Culture and Society*, vol. 5, no. 1, pp. 81–100.

Lee, Chin-Chuan (1980) *Media Imperialism Reconsidered, The Homogenizing of Television Culture*, Beverly Hills: Sage.

Lee, Paul Siu-Nam (1988) 'Communication imperialism and dependency: a conceptual clarification', *Gazette*, vol. 41, no. 2, pp. 69–84.

Lent, John A. (ed.) (1971) *The Asian Newspapers' Reluctant Revolution*, Ames: Iowa State University Press.

—— (ed.) (1978) *Broadcasting in Asia and the Pacific. A Continental Survey of Radio and Television*, Philadelphia: Temple University Press.

—— (1982) 'ASEAN mass communications and cultural submission', *Media, Culture and Society*, vol. 4, pp. 171–89.

—— (1984) 'A revolt against a revolution: the fight against illegal video', *Media Asia*, vol. 11, no. 1, pp. 25–30.

—— (1989) 'Mass communications in Asia and the Pacific: recent trends and developments', *Media Asia*, vol. 16, no. 1, pp. 16–25.

—— (1990) *The Asian Film Industry*, London: Christopher Helm.

Litewski, Chaim (1982) 'Globo's telenovelas: a Brazilian melodrama', in Richard Paterson (ed.), *Brazilian Television in Context*, London: British Film Institute, pp. 12–16.

Liu, Alan P.L. (1971) 'Communist China', in John A. Lent (ed.), *The Asian Newspapers' Reluctant Revolution*, Ames: Iowa State University Press, ch. 4.

Lull, James (ed.) (1988) *World Families Watch Television*, London: Sage.

Lycett, Andrew (1990) 'Kenya turns on to music television', *African Business*, July, p. 52.

McAnany, Emile G. (1989) 'Brazil, satellites and debt: who trades what to acquire new technologies?', *Media Development*, vol. 36, no. 1, pp. 6–9.

McAnany, Emile G. and Atwood, Rita (eds) (1986) *Communications in Latin American Society, Critical Communication Trends 1965–1981*, Madison: University of Wisconsin Press.

MacBride, Sean (1980) *Many Voices, One World*, Paris: UNESCO.

Mackay, Ian (1964) *Broadcasting in Nigeria*, Ibadan: Ibadan University Press.

Mahalingam, Sudha (1989) 'Computer industry in India. Strategies for late-comer entry', *Economic and Political Weekly*, 21 October, pp. 2375–84.

Mahan, Elizabeth (1985) 'Mexican broadcasting: reassessing the industry–state relationship', *Journal of Communication*, vol. 35, no. 1, pp. 6–75.

Malamah-Thomas, David (1987) 'Theatre for development in Sierra Leone: a study of CARE's project LEARN', *Africa Media Review*, vol. 1, no. 3, pp. 81–94.

Malik, O.P. (1990) 'Bappi Lahiri', *Sunday Mail* (Magazine), vol. 5, no. 1, pp. 5–9.

Manuel, Peter (1987) 'Marxism, nationalism and popular music in revolutionary Cuba', *Popular Music* (Cambridge), vol. 6, no. 2, pp. 161–78.

—— (1988) *Popular Musics of the Non-Western World, An Introductory Survey*, New York: Oxford University Press.

Martín-Barbero, Jesus (1987) *De los medios a las mediaciones comunicacion,cultura y hegemonia*, Barcelona and Mexico: Ediciones G. Gili.

—— (1988) 'Communication from culture: the crisis of the national and the emergence of the popular', *Media, Culture and Society*, vol. 10, pp. 447–65.

Masmoudi, Moustafa (1979) 'The New World Information Order', *Journal of Communication*, vol. 29, no. 2, pp. 172–85.

Masud, Iqbal (1985) 'Sponsored TV: triumph of the middle class', *Imprint*, September, pp. 53–5.

Matta, Fernando Reyes (1979) 'The Latin American concept of news', *Journal of Communication*, vol. 29, no. 2, pp. 164–71.

Mattelart, Armand (1978) 'The nature of communications practice in a dependent society', *Latin American Perspectives*, vol. 5, no. 1, pp. 13–34.

—— (1979a) 'For a class analysis of communication', in Armand Mattelart and Seth Siegelaub (eds), *Communication and Class Struggle, 1. Capitalism, Imperialism*, New York: International General, pp. 23–70.

—— (1979b) *Multinational Corporations and the Control of Culture, The Ideological Apparatuses of Imperialism*, Sussex: Harvester Press.

—— (1979/80) 'Cultural imperialism, mass media and class struggle: an interview with Armand Mattelart', *Insurgent Sociologist*, vol. 9, pp. 69–79.

—— (1980) *Mass Media, Ideologies and the Revolutionary Movement*, Sussex: Harvester Press.

—— (1983) *Transnationals and the Third World, The Struggle for Culture*, South Hadley, Mass.: Bergin & Garvey.

Mattelart, Armand, Delcourt, Xavier and Mattelart, Michèle (1984) *International Image Markets, In Search of an Alternative Perspective*, London: Comedia.

Mattelart, Michèle and Mattelart, Armand (1987) *Le Carnaval des Images*, La Fiction brésilienne, Paris: La Documentation Française.

Mattelart, Armand and Schmucler, Hector (1985) *Communication and Information Technologies: Freedom of Choice for Latin America?*, Norwood, NJ: Ablex.

Mattos, Sergio (1984) 'Advertising and government influences. The case of Brazilian advertising', *Communication Research*, vol. 11, no. 2, pp. 203–20.

Miège, Bernard (1989) *The Capitalization of Cultural Production*, New York: International General.

Mody, Bella (1989) 'Satellite debt in Mexico's mañana', *Media Development*, vol. 36, no. 1, pp. 14–15.

Monfils, Barbara S. (1985) 'Mass media in West Africa: a bibliographic essay', in Frank Okwu Ugboajah (ed.), *Mass Communication, Culture and Society in West Africa*, London: Hans Zell Publishers, pp. 285–308.

Moore, Barrington (1966) *Social Origins of Dictatorship and Democracy*, Boston, Mass.: Beacon.

Mosier, John (1986) 'Film', in Charles Tatum and Harold Hinds (eds), *Handbook of Latin American Popular Culture*, Westport: Greenwood Press, ch. 7.

Murdock, G. and Golding, P. (1973) 'For a political economy of mass communication', in Ralph Miliband and John Saville (eds), *The Socialist Register*, London: Merlin Press, pp. 205–34.

Murphy, Sharon M. and Scotton, James F. (1987) 'Dependency and journalism in Africa: are there alternative models?', *Africa Media Review*, vol. 1, no. 3, pp. 11–35.

Musa, Mohammed (1990) 'News agencies, transnationalization and the new order', *Media, Culture and Society*, vol. 12, pp. 325–42.

Mytton, Graham (1983) *Mass Communication in Africa*, London: Edward Arnold.

Ng'wanakilala, Nkwabi (1981) *Mass Communication and Development of Socialism in Tanzania*, Dar es Salaam: Tanzania Publishing House.

Nketia, J.H. Kwabena (1966) 'Music in African culture', in *Colloquium on Negro Art*, Society of African Culture, Paris: Editions Présence Africaine, pp. 143–86.

—— (1968) 'Music in African culture', in *Colloquium on Negro Art*, Society of African Culture, Paris: Editions Présence Africaine, pp. 143–86.

Noble, Grant (1989) 'Some comments on video in India', *Australian Journal of Communication*, no. 16, December, pp. 64–73.

Nordenstreng, Kaarle and Ng'wanakilala, Nkwabi (n.d.) *Tanzania and the New Information Order: A Case Study of Africa's Second Struggle*, Dar es Salaam: Printpak Tanzania Ltd.

Nordenstreng, Kaarle and Schiller, Herbert (1979) *National Sovereignty and International Communication*, Norwood, NJ: Ablex.

Nordenstreng, Kaarle and Varis, Tapio (1973) 'The nonhomogeneity of national state and the international flow of communication', in G. Gerbner, L.P. Gross and W.H. Melody (eds), *Communication Technology and Social Policy*, New York: John Wiley pp. 393-412.

Noriega, Luis Antonio de and Leach, Frances (1979) *Broadcasting in Mexico*, London: Routledge & Kegan Paul.

O'Brien, Rita Cruise (1975) 'Domination and dependence in mass communications: implications for the use of broadcasting in developing countries', *IDS Bulletin* (University of Sussex), vol. 6, no. 4, pp. 85–99.

O'Connor, David C. (1985) 'The computer industry in the Third World: policy options and constraints', *World Development*, vol. 13, no. 3, pp. 311–32.

Oduko, Segin (1987) 'From indigenous communication to modern television: a reflection of political development in Nigeria', *Africa Media Review*, vol. 1, no. 3, pp. 1–10.

Ogan, Christine (1988) 'Media imperialism and the videocassette recorder: the case of Turkey', *Journal of Communication*, vol. 38, no. 2, pp. 93–106.

Ogot, Bethwell A. (1977) 'Politics, culture and music in central Kenya: a study of Mau Mau hymns, 1951–1956', *Kenya Historical Review*, vol. 5, no. 2, pp. 275–86.

Okigbo, Charles (1988) 'Bad news in Nigerian newspapers: a case for content analysis textbooks', in A. Tom Adaba, Olakon Ajia and Ikechukwu Nwosu (eds), *Communication Industry in Nigeria. The Crisis of Publications*, Africa Media Monograph Series, no. 6, Nairobi: The African Council on Communication Education, pp. 129–47.

Oliveira, Omar Souki (1989) 'Media and dependency. A view from Latin America', *Media Development*, vol. 36, no. 1, pp. 10–14.

Omu, Fred I.A. (1978) *Press and Politics in Nigeria 1880–1937*, London: Longman.

Omvedt, Gail (1977) 'Revolutionary music of India', *The Journal of Peasant Studies*, vol. 4, no. 3, pp. 244–57.

Opoku-Agyeman, K. (1987) 'Textiles, language and communication in the Gold Coast', in Jerry Domatob, Abubakar Jika and Ikechukwu Nwosu (eds), *Mass Media and the African Society*, Africa Media Monograph Series, no. 4, Nairobi: The African Council on Communication Education, ch. 29.

Osakue, John (1988) 'Domestic financing of communication in developing countries: a preliminary investigation of the Nigerian case', *Africa Media Review*, vol. 2, no. 3, pp. 123–34.

Osundere, Niyi (1980) Review of *Aiye* in *West Africa*, 12 May, pp. 826–8.

Passin, Herbert (1963) 'Writer and journalist in the transitional society', in Lucian W. Pye (ed.), *Communication and Political Development*, Princeton: Princeton University Press, pp. 82-123.

Paterson, Richard (ed.) (1982) *Brazilian Television in Context*, London: British Film Institute.

Penacchioni, Irene (1984) 'The reception of popular television in northeast Brazil', *Media, Culture and Society*, no. 6, pp. 337–41.

Pendakur, Manjunath (1983) 'The new international order after the MacBride Commission report: an international powerplay between the core and the periphery countries', *Media, Culture and Society*, vol. 5, pp. 395–412.

—— (1985) 'Dynamics of cultural policy making: the US film industry in India', *Journal of Communication*, vol. 35, no. 4, pp. 52–72.

Perrone, Charles A. (1987) 'Brazil (Sources and Resources)', *Popular Music* (Cambridge), vol. 6, no. 2, pp. 219–26.

—— (1988) 'Open Mike: Brazilian popular music and redemocratization', *Studies in Latin American Popular Culture*, vol. 7, pp. 167–81.

Poon, David Jim-tat (1978) 'Tatzepao: its history and significance as a communication medium', in Godwin C. Chu (ed.), *Popular Media in China. Shaping New Cultural Patterns*, Honolulu: The University Press of Hawaii.

Pye, Lucian W. (ed.) (1963) *Communication and Political Development*, Princeton: Princeton University Press.

Rada, Juan (1981) 'The microelectronics revolution: implications for the Third World', *Development Dialogue*, vol. 2, pp. 41–67.

—— (1985) 'Information technology and the Third World', in Tom Forester (ed.), *The Information Technology Revolution*, Oxford: Blackwell, pp. 571–89.

Ramachandran, K. (1978) 'Radio', in *Mass Media in India 1978*, Delhi: Publication Division, Ministry of Information and Broadcasting, Government of India, pp. 20–30.

Ramachandran, T.T. and Rukmini, S. (1985) *70 Years of Indian Cinema (1913–1983)*, Bombay: Cinema India-International.

Ramakrishnan, Ganapati (1990) 'The singing sisters (Kalyani and Lakshmi)', *Sunday Mail*, 28 January to 3 February, p. 32.

Rao, P.V. Poornachandra (1986) *To The Rural Masses Through Street Plays*, Secunderabad: National Council of Developmental Communication, Varanasi.

Real, Michael R. (1985) 'Broadcast music in Nigeria and Liberia: a comparative note', in Frank Okwu Ugboajah (ed.), *Mass Communication, Culture and Society in West Africa*, London: Hans Zell Publishers, pp. 95–9.

Reddy, Usha (1989) 'Media and culture in Indian society: conflict or cooperation?', *Media, Culture and Society*, vol. 11, pp. 395–413.

Reeves, Geoffrey W. (1984) *Popular Kenyan Literature and Politics*, AFSAAP Conference, University of Melbourne, 70pp.

Righter, Rosemary (1979) *Whose News? Politics, the Press and the Third World*, London: André Deutsch.

Roach, Colleen (1987) 'The US Position on the New World Information and Communication Order', *Journal of Communication*, vol. 37, no. 4, pp. 36–51.

Roberts, John Stewart (1974) 'Kenya', in Sydney W. Head (ed.), *Broadcasting in Africa, A Continental Survey of Radio and Television*, Philadelphia: Temple University Press, ch. 4.1.

Robinson, Deanna Campbell (1981) 'Changing function of mass media in the People's Republic of China', *Journal of Communication*, vol. 31, no. 4, pp. 58–73.

Robinson, Deanna Campbell, Buck, Elizabeth B. and Cuthbert, Marlene (1991) *Music at the Margins, Popular Music and Global Cultural Diversity*, London: Sage.

Rogers, Everett M. and Antola, Livia (1985) 'Telenovelas: a Latin American success story', *Journal of Communication*, vol. 35, no. 4, pp. 24–35.

Rones, Julie E. (1989) 'Space WARC and planning implications for Third World nations', *Media Development*, vol. 36, no. 1, pp. 26–8.

Salinas, R. and Paldan, L. (1979) 'Culture in the process of dependent development: theoretical perspectives', in K. Nordenstreng and H.I. Schiller (eds), *National Sovereignty and International Communication*, Norwood, NJ: Ablex, pp. 82-98.

Samarajiwa, Rohan (1984) 'Third World entry to the world market in news: problems and possible solutions', *Media, Culture and Society*, vol. 6, pp. 119–36.

Sarkar, Kobita (1982) *You Can't Please Everyone! Film Censorship: The Inside Story*, Bombay: IBH Publishing Company.

Sarkar, R.C.S. (1984) *The Press in India*, New Delhi: S. Chand & Company.

Sarti, Ingrid (1981) 'Communication and cultural dependency: a misconception', in Emile G. McAnany, Jorge Schnitman and Noreene Janus (eds), *Communication and Social Structure*, Critical Studies in Mass Media Research, New York: Praeger Publishers, pp. 317–34.

—— (1988) 'Between memory and illusion: independent video in Brazil', in Elizabeth Fox (ed.), *Media and Politics in Latin America*, London: Sage, ch. 13.

Sauvant, Karl P. (1979) 'Socio-cultural emancipation', in K. Nordenstreng and H.I. Schiller (eds), *National Sovereignty and International Communication*, Norwood, NJ: Ablex, pp. 9-20.

Scandlen, Guy B. (1978) 'Thailand', in John A. Lent (ed.), *Broadcasting in Asia and the Pacific. A Continental Survey of Radio and Television*, Philadelphia: Temple University Press, ch. 3.3.

Schement, Jorge and Rogers, Everett (1984) 'Media flows in Latin America', *Communication Research*, vol. 11, no. 2, pp. 305–20.

Schiller, Herbert (1969) *Mass Communications and American Empire*, New York: Kelly.

—— (1976) *Communication and Cultural Domination*, White Plains, NY: International Arts and Sciences Press.

—— (1979) 'Transnational media and national development', in K. Nordenstreng and H.I. Schiller (eds), *National Sovereignty and International Communication*. Norwood, NJ: Ablex, pp. 21–32.

Schmidt, Nancy J. (1989) 'Recent perspectives on sub-Saharan African film-making', *Africa Today*, vol. 36, no. 2, pp. 17–22.

Schramm, Wilbur (1964) *Mass Media and National Development, The Role of Information in the Developing Countries*, Stanford: Stanford University Press.

Scott, Margaret (1990a) 'Dishing the rules', *Far Eastern Economic Review*, 14 June, pp. 34–5, 38–9.

—— (1990b) 'The sky's the limit', *Far Eastern Economic Review*, 14 June, pp. 39–40.

Seers, Dudley (1970) 'Rich countries and poor', in Dudley Seers and Leonard Joy (eds), *Development in a Divided World*, Harmondsworth: Penguin Books, ch. 1.

Shils, Edward A. (1972) *The Intellectuals and the Powers and Other Essays*, Chicago: University of Chicago Press.

Sinclair, John (1986) 'Development and broadcasting: the Mexican formula', *Media, Culture and Society*, vol. 8, no. 4, pp. 81–101.

—— (1987) *Images Incorporated: Advertising as Industry and Ideology*, London: Croom Helm.

—— (1990) 'Neither West nor Third World: the Mexican television industry within the NWICO debate', *Media, Culture and Society*, vol. 12, pp. 343–60.

Singh, S. Nihal (1990) 'A limited autonomy (media watch)', *India Today*, 31 January, p. 129.

Singhal, Arvind and Rogers, Everett M. (1988) 'Television soap operas for development in India', *Gazette*, vol. 41, no. 2, pp. 109–26.

—— (1989) *India's Information Revolution*, London: Sage.

Smith, Anthony (1980) *The Geopolitics of Information, How Western Culture Dominates the World*, London: Faber & Faber.

Smythe, Dallas W. (1977) 'Communications: blindspot of Western Marxism', *Canadian Journal of Political and Social Theory*, vol. 1, no. 3, pp. 1–28.

Snow, Marcellus S. (1985) 'Arguments for and against competition in international satellite facilities and services: a US perspective', *Journal of Communication*, vol. 35, no. 3, pp. 51–9.

Solanas, Fernando and Getino, Octavio (1987) 'Towards a Third Cinema', in Coco Fusco (ed.), *Selections from New Latin American Cinema*, Buffalo, NY: Hallwalls, pp. 56–82.

Sommerlad, E. Lloyd (1969) *The Press in Developing Countries*, Delhi: Atta Ram & Sons.

Sonaike, S. Adefemi (1988) 'Communication and Third World development: a dead end?', *Gazette*, vol. 41, pp. 85–108.

—— (1989) 'Telecommunications and debt: the Nigerian experience', *Media Development*, vol. 36, no. 1, pp. 2–5.

Srampickal, Jacob and White, Robert A. (eds) (1988) 'Popular theatre', *Communication Research Trends*, vol. 9, nos. 1 and 2, pp. 1–24.

Sreberny-Mohamaadi, Annabelle (1984) 'The "World of the News" study', *Journal of Communication*, vol. 34, no. 1, pp. 121–34.

Stapleton, Chris and May, Chris (1989) *African All-Stars, The Pop Music of a Continent*, London: Paladin/Grafton Books.

Stevenson, Robert L. (1984) 'Pseudo-debate: a review of World of the News', *Journal of Communication*, vol. 34, no. 1, pp. 134–8.

—— (1988) *Communication, Development and the Third World, The Global Politics of Information*, London: Longman.

Stevenson, Robert L. and Cole, Richard R. (1984) 'Issues in foreign news', in Robert L. Stevenson and Donald Shaw (eds) *Foreign News and the New World Information Order*, Ames: Iowa State University Press, pp. 5-20.

Stevenson, Robert L. and Shaw, Donald (eds) (1984) *Foreign News and the New World Information Order*, Ames: Iowa State University Press.

Straubhaar, Joseph D. (1984) 'The development of the telenovela as the pre-eminent form of popular culture in Brazil', *Studies in Latin American Popular Culture*, no. 1, pp. 138–50.

—— (1989) 'Television and video in the transition from military to civilian rule in Brazil', *Latin American Research Review*, vol. 24, no. 1, pp. 140–54.

Sussman, Gerald (1987) 'Banking on telecommunications: the World Bank in the Philippines', *Journal of Communication*, vol. 37, no. , pp. 90–105.

Sussman, Gerald and Lent, John A. (eds) (1991) *Transnational Communications, Wiring the Third World*, London: Sage.

Tatum, Charles (1980) 'Lá grimas, risas y amori: Mexico's most popular romance comic book', *Journal of Popular Culture*, vol. 13, no. 3, pp. 413–23.

Tatum, Charles and Hinds, Harold E. (eds) (1986) *Handbook of Latin American Popular Culture*, Westport: Greenwood Press.

Thiong'o, Ngugi wa (1981) *Detained, A Writer's Prison Diary*, Nairobi: Heinemann Kenya.

—— (1986) *Decolonizing the Mind, The Politics of Language in African Literature*, Nairobi: Heinemann Kenya.

Thompson, E. P. (1968) *the Making of the English Working Class*, Harmondsworth: Penguin Books.

Tracey, Michael (1985) 'The poisoned chalice? International television and the idea of dominance', *Daedalus*, vol. 114, no. 4, pp. 17–55.

Tunstall, Jeremy (1977) *The Media are American: Anglo-American Media in the World*, London: Constable.

Uche, Luke Uka (1986) 'The debate on New World Information and Communication Order: much ado about nothing', *Communication Socialis Yearbook*, vol. 5, pp. 5–19.

—— (1989) *Mass Media and Politics in Nigeria*, New Delhi: Concept Publishing Company.

Ugboajah, Frank Okwu (ed.) (1985) *Mass Communication, Culture and Society in West Africa*, London: Hans Zell Publishers.

United Nations Centre on Transnational Corporations (1984) *Transborder Data Flows and Brazil, The Role of Transnational Corporations, Impact of Transborder Data Flows, and Effects of National Policies (the Brazilian Case Study)*, Amsterdam: Elsevier Science Publications.

Valicha, Kishore (1988) *The Moving Image: A Study of Indian Cinema*, London: Sangam Books.

Van der Geest, Sjaak and Asante-Darko, N.K. (1982) 'The political meaning of highlife songs in Ghana', *African Studies Review*, vol. 25, no. 1, pp. 27–35.

Varis, Tapio (1974) 'Global traffic in television', *Journal of Communication*, vol. 24, no. 1, pp. 102–9.

—— (1984) 'The international flow of television programs', *Journal of Communication*, vol. 34, no. 1, pp. 143–52.

Vasudev, Aruna (1986) *The New Indian Cinema*, New Delhi: Macmillan India.

Vasudev, Aruna and Lenglet, Philippe (eds) (1983) *Indian Cinema Superbazaar*, New Delhi: Vikas Books.

Vilanilam, John (1989) 'Television advertising and the Indian poor', *Media, Culture and Society*, vol. 11, no. 4, pp. 485–97.

Vincent, Theo (1985) 'Television drama in Nigeria: a critical assessment', in Frank Okwu Ugboajah (ed.), *Mass Communication, Culture and Society in West Africa*, London: Hans Zell Publishers, pp. 100–7.

Wachira-Chiuri (1981) 'Popular gramophone music: a survey on Joseph Kamaru', *Mzalendo* (Literature Students Journal, University of Nairobi), vol. 2, August, pp. 43–57.

Wallerstein, Immanuel (1974) *The Modern World System*, New York: Academic Press.

Wallis, Roger and Malm, Krister (1984) *Big Sounds from Small Peoples, The Music Industry in Small Countries*, London: Constable.

Wanjala, Chris (1980) *For Home and Freedom*, Nairobi: Kenya Literature Bureau.

Wells, A.F. (1972) *Picture Tube Imperialism? The Impact of US Television on Latin America*, New York: Orbis.

Wert, Maria C. and Stevenson, Robert L. (1988) 'Global television flows to Latin American countries', *Journalism Quarterly*, vol. 65, no. 1, pp. 182–5.

White, Robert A. and McDonnell, James M. (1983) 'Priorities for national communication policy in the Third World', *The Information Society Journal*, vol. 2, no. 1, pp. 5–33.

Wigand, Rolf T., Shipley, Carrie and Shipley, Dwayne (1984) 'Transborder data flow, informatics, and national policies', *Journal of Communication*, vol. 34, no. 1, pp. 153–75.

Wilcox, Dennis L. (1975) *Mass Media in Black Africa: Philosophy and Control*, New York: Praeger Publishers.

Willemen, Paul (1989) 'The Third Cinema Question: Notes and Reflections', in Jim Pines and Paul Willemen (eds), *Questions of Third Cinema*, London: British Film Institute, pp. 1–29.

Williams, Raymond (1965) *The Long Revolution*, Harmondsworth: Penguin Books.

Windschuttle, Keith (1988) *The Media*, Ringwood, Vic.: Penguin Books.

Worsley, Peter (1990) 'Models of the modern world-system', *Theory, Culture and Society*, vol. 7, nos. 2–3, pp. 83–96.

Yampolsky, Philip (1989) 'Hati Yang Luka, an Indonesian hit', *Indonesia*, no. 47, April, pp. 1–18.

Ya'u, Y.Z. (1987) 'Satellite technology and national development', in Jerry Domatob, Abubakar Jika and Ikechukwu Nwosu (eds), *Mass Media and the African Society*, Africa Media Monograph Series, no. 4, Nairobi: The African Council on Communication Education, ch. 11.

Index